TOTAL CLUBFITTING IN THE 21st CENTURY

A Complete Program For Fitting Golf Equipment

Acknowledgements

Hireko Trading Company, Inc. is proud of its position as the technical leader in the component industry. In business for over 25 years, Hireko has grown to be a major player in the worldwide golf arena. Hireko continues to pride itself with its top-notch customer service and cutting edge product lines. Through the Internet, Hireko continues to offer technical service that is second to none, as well as providing customer service and model offerings unparalleled in the industry.

© Copyright 2007, Hireko Trading Company, Inc.®

Published by
Hireko Trading Company, Inc.
16185 Stephens Street
City of Industry, CA 91745
800-367-8912

Published in the Unites States of America

Distributed by Hireko Golf Products, Inc.

ISBN 0-9619413-6-7

Table of Contents

Preface

Having been in the golf industry for nearly a quarter century, I have seen many changes to not only equipment, but the improvement in the quality of the equipment we play, plus how and why we purchase clubs today. In my opinion, all these changes have been to the benefit of the consumer.

Starting out on the assembly line for a small OEM manufacturer (Pal Joey) I learned clubmaking assembly, which was far more labor intensive than it is today. In those days, metal woods were just emerging and becoming popular, but we had to stain, fill and paint a lot of persimmon and laminated maple heads that we purchased pre-sanded and unfinished. The smell of the finishing room is not as fresh in mind as it used to be, nor is being able whip heads without thinking hard about it first. Ferrules were quite large and not sized to fit the majority of heads and required much more detail and patience to finish them. We even had to take the time to put on leather grips on many occasions, something of which modern clubmakers may never have an opportunity to try.

Pal Joey was one of the few companies that specialized in "custom fitting". The clubs weren't ready made or sitting on a shelf waiting to be purchased. Rather the club pro or retailer would pick between several models of heads, choose between TT Lite or Dynamic steel shafts, pick a flex based on the golfer's strength, choose amongst a dozen grips and specify the length based on the player's height. This is really no different than fitting clubs today, but now we have far more choices in shafts and grips and more importantly better information and tools in which to fit the golfer.

Long gone are the days when all golfers had to choose from were blades and cavity backs. Those blades have been replaced with hybrids, woods are no longer made out of "wood" and steel shafts in woods have been replaced with graphite shafts which weigh almost half of what they used to. All these changes in such a short period of time have made the game a little easier to play.

When I wasn't on the assembly line, I worked part-time in the Dynacraft warehouse packing component orders. Custom clubmaking was just in its infancy as the golf industry just staring increasing in popularity. Because of the new technology to the equipment, golfers were trading in their forged blades for cavity back irons and their persimmon woods to ones made of metal. In those days we didn't particularly care about the consistency of specifications as we do today as the foundries were in a learning curve in producing their goods. I can attest to that by all the lead we went through to swingweight the clubs. Loft and lies were unfortunately not as tight either, yet we didn't have a loft and lie machine to fix the inconsistencies either. Even though the advances in the equipment were better back then, golfers still had to wrestle with these inconsistencies. One thing is for sure, clubheads today are far superior in those regards.

Clubs sold through custom fitters was a novelty as well in the early and mid 1980s. Almost 100% of clubs were sold through pro shops or retailers, but that changed rapidly as golfers found a new outlet to purchase clubs and that was through independent clubmakers/ clubfitters. A few of the predominate component suppliers not only provided numerous heads, shafts, grips and tools for the trade, but also provided technical assistance in the form of much needed information that the custom clubfitter would use and share with their customers. This grassroots approach has spread that custom fitting today is a widely accepted by the public. It has also forced nearly every name brand manufacturer to establish a custom fitting department instead of just offering stock goods.

Clubfitting shops are no longer armed only with a piece of plywood painted green to determine the lie and a ruler to measure the fingertip to floor dimension to establish length. No, we are much more sophisticated with measurement devises to accurately measure a person swing in great detail that we couldn't even imagine a decade ago.

Even though I don't have the opportunity to play as much golf as I once did, I still manage to hit the ball with reasonable consistency because of the improvement in the equipment. More importantly, I'm more educated as to what type of equipment that best suits my game because of all the information available and the ability to measure my swing and match the clubs precisely. Custom fitting has all been part of that process that I wish all golfers had the opportunity to experience. For those who will read this book, be sure to spread the word so that others can enjoy this game and provide a positive experience for years to come.

Sincerely,

Jeff Summitt
Technical Director
Hireko Trading Company, Inc.
jsummitt@hirekogolf.com

Introduction
TOTAL CLUBFITTING IN THE 21st CENTURY

Golf club fitting is not a new concept. While it certainly has been at the forefront of equipment issues during the past decade, it is not a new phenomenon. Back more than a half-century ago, the legendary Bobby Jones had custom fitted clubs. Did he know that *per se*? Not really, but when his coveted clubs were analyzed using modern day equipment, it was found that the shaft in his #8 iron did not match the rest of his set. The club he claimed he had the most difficulty with: the #8 iron. In effect, his set was

matched; perhaps by trial and error, especially considering the shafts were made of hickory - but matched nonetheless. On the mass production side of things, MacGregor's Tommy Armour line of clubs featured a basic custom fitting system way back in 1935. While it was not as concise as the methods we will use to custom fit in the 21st century, it did recognize that not all players required the same club. The concept of custom fitting is not new; the techniques today are much different than they were 65 years ago, but

the goals are the same: a best fit scenario for all level and ability of player.

Golf club technology today is a constantly changing entity. New heads, shafts and grips are developed almost every month. Golf club manufacturers promise lower scores, better feel, and more accurate shots. These same club manufacturers mass-produce their golf equipment in the vast majority of cases. While it is quite possible that "Company X's" latest design might produce better playability for a particular golfer, just which specific golfers will it help? And how do those specific golfers go about getting those clubs? From a retail store? From off the rack at a pro shop? By calling an 800 number from the back of a magazine? By clicking on an internet icon? Better than 70% of the golf equipment sold in the world is sold in some combination of these manners. The unfortunate truth is that, despite paying big money for brand name clubs full of marketing department promises, most players' games do not improve.

Why not? Nearly all of the golf equipment from major manufacturers is built on an assembly line to a standard set of specifications with potentially wide manufacturing tolerances. This simply means that if a golfer is fortunate enough to be a "standard" player, maybe these clubs will match his or her game. If he or she is lucky enough to fit this standard, then the player will have to get lucky again and trust that the clubs' tolerances are very tight. Sadly, after the golfer spends well into the thousands of dollars, he finds out that he is not one of the lucky few who bought a better game, but is a member of the unfortunate masses who just bought nothing more than an expensive, slickly-marketed set of clubs.

Now what? Good question. Can the player return the used clubs that haven't improved their game? Fat chance...no chance in most cases if the transaction

LADY MACGREGOR
Stylized Clubs

The Most Revolutionary step ever taken in designing clubs for women

The Lady MacGregor Stylized Clubs are scientifically designed throughout and offer all women golfers an opportunity to use equipment which is fundamentally sound and correct.

The design of these clubs was developed from careful observations on many golf courses. Two important facts were revealed. First, the majority of women were playing with misfit clubs. Second, all women could be classified in four distinct and entirely different types, as explained in the table below. To think that any two of them could play successfully with clubs of the same specifications was ridiculous. So the Stylized line was made in four models, so constructed from the standpoint of weight, length, lie and loft as to provide every woman golfer with

equipment accurately fitted to her needs.

The Stylized models put an end to the disastrous mental hazard which is caused by the player having lack of confidence in her equipment.

Then—to check and verify the accuracy of the fit of these clubs—MacGregor created the "Club Selector" illustrated below.

What the MacGregor Club Selector Does:
1. Insures clubs of correct *length*.
2. Insures clubs having *correct lie*.
3. Insures correctly *weighted* clubs.
4. Aids in correcting improper stance and improving golf form in general.
5. Gives correct-feeling clubs that induce confidence and mental relaxation, thereby improving the game.

Model TS   Model PM   Model PT   Model SS

STYLIZED WEIGHT AND LENGTH CHART

KIND	Model TS Wt. oz.	Model TS Lgt. in.	Model PM Wt. oz.	Model PM Lgt. in.	Model PT Wt. oz.	Model PT Lgt. in.	Model SS Wt. oz.	Model SS Lgt. in.
Driver	12¼	41½	12	40	12¼	41	12½	42
Brassie	12¼	41½	12	40	12¼	41	12½	42
Spoon	12½	40½	12¼	39	12½	40	12¾	41
No. 2 Mid Iron	14	37	13¾	35½	14	36½	14¼	37½
No. 3 Mid Mashie	14¼	36½	14	35	14¼	36	14½	37
No. 4 Mashie Iron	14½	36	14¼	34½	14½	35½	14¾	36½
No. 5 Mashie	14¾	35½	14½	34	14¾	35	15	36
No. 6 Spade Mashie	14¾	35	14½	33½	14¾	34½	15	35½
No. 7 Mashie Niblick	14¾	35	14½	33½	14¾	34½	15	35½
No. 8 Niblick	15¼	34½	15	33	15¼	34	15½	35
No. 9 Putter	15	32½	15	31	15	32	15¼	33

© 1935 C. McG. & C. Co.

Page 7, 1935 Armour/Professional

was a mail, department store or internet purchase. Maybe, if the clubs came from a pro shop and the golf professional is willing to make some adjustments to the clubs that may help the player, the clubs might work better...but a return for another set - don't count on it. If these couple of examples sound like horror stories, they are. No doubt about that. Golfers try to buy better games all the time - it's easier than practicing and provides a bit of status when the player shows up on the first tee with the same new clubs as were seen on television during last week's PGA Tour event. It is these same golfers who purchase the most expensive equipment they can find or who try all of the latest "fad" clubs, who are the best candidates for something they may never have heard of before - custom fitting.

Custom fitting might take a bit longer than simply putting down some cash, grabbing some new clubs and heading to the first tee, but the dividends it pays in improved performance are evident from day one. The same person who buys clubs without having them custom fitted is often the same person who wouldn't think of buying a suit or a dress without having alterations made before wearing it. It only makes sense that if clothing is going to fit properly, golf clubs should do the same. Considering golfers who establish a handicap, the average male golfer has a handicap of 19; the average female player carries a 26. These numbers haven't changed but a fraction of a stroke over the past few decades. Players are not improving despite all of the millions of dollars of advertising claims that large companies place on television, in magazines, on the internet, on a golf professional's Tour bag, and just about everywhere else they can buy space. But, just think, if every player in the country had clubs that matched their unique swing characteristics as well as their suit or dress matched their body build, handicaps would likely decrease and their enjoyment of the game would be increased immensely.

Total Clubfitting in the 21st Century takes a look at how a custom fitting situation will help to improve a player's game. It does not matter if the player is male or female, a junior or a senior, a beginner, the average 19 or 26 handicap, or is the

U.S. Open Champion. Do realize that just about all touring pros are fitted with custom clubs; such clubs help these players play to their potential; doesn't the average player deserve the same advantage? Properly fitted clubs help all golfers to potentially improve their game. Through a series of specific fitting steps as detailed in this book, each and every equipment parameter will be analyzed individually and then correlated with all of the other steps. This in the quest to provide the player with a set of matched clubs that will help him to perform to the best of his ability each time he ventures out on the course.

During the fitting session, the player will be encouraged to hit balls with a number of test clubs. Each of these clubs measures a specific element of the player's swing. By watching ball flight or a computer screen and by listening to what a player says a club feels like, a best-fit scenario develops. Notice the term "best-fit" is used. If each player swung exactly the same way each time, a perfect fit could be developed. Many equipment companies use golf swing robots to perfect their clubs. This is fine if all golfers swung like the robot, but we don't. Not even Mr. Tiger Woods swings the same way every time...he may be close, but he's not perfect - at least not yet. We use "best-fit" because the golfer doesn't swing the same way all the time. "Best-fit" simply means that the custom-fitted

clubs will match the way the player swings most often. Regrettably, bad swings are bad swings and will produce poor results. There are no clubs that can prevent this. But, by having clubs as closely matched as possible to a player's swing, the potential for the less than ideal shots is substantially reduced.

More and more players are entering the game each year. The National Golf Foundation notes a rise in the number of juniors and women entering the game - and taking it seriously. The number of "serious" male players - those who play more than 8-10 times per year - is increasing as well. Everyone who plays the game wants to play it well; having the proper equipment to do that will certainly help in achieving that goal. Watch a youngster or a beginner as they first begin to hit the golf ball. The look on their faces when the ball becomes airborne is priceless. It is that same look that a senior player may have walking off the 18th green, having just shot a personal best round. It is certainly the look the female player has after winning her club championship. It is maintaining these looks and making them easier to achieve that *Total Clubfitting In The 21st Centruy* is all about!

This Dynacraft publication will guide the fitter and player through the custom fitting procedure, making the fitting session educational to both. In a step-by-step format, *Total Clubfitting in the 21st*

The player and fitter together will determine which clubs work best during a dynamic fitting.

LADY MACGREGOR STYLIZED CLUBS

To have clubs properly suited to your form and stature, you should get Lady MacGregor Stylized Clubs.

They were designed for women's play by women golfers. They are built to fit the four general types of feminine form and weight covered by the following classifications.

Because of the exactness of detail in these custom-built clubs, they are built by Gold Badge Player-Craftsmen. The specifications were determined by MacGregor research engineers through the study and measurement of three hundred average women golfers.

FOR THE TALL AND SLENDER

If you are of this type, your normal position is fairly erect. The proper clubs for you should allow you to take your natural stance comfortably without strain and distortion —so that you can make your swing freely, gracefully, and accurately. The Lady MacGregor Stylized "TS" Clubs are made especially for you.

FOR THE SHORT AND SLENDER

If you are of this type, you also normally play fairly erect; but you must have a shorter club, a shaft with more flex in it, and a grip of less diameter to accommodate your slighter wrists and smaller hands. Your requirements are met by the Lady MacGregor Stylized "PM" (Petite Miss) Clubs.

FOR THE PERFECT THIRTY-SIX

If this is your type, your most comfortable position is somewhat farther away from the ball. You need a club with a slightly heavier head and stronger shaft. Yet you cannot feel at ease with a man's club which has been shortened, for it would not be suitable for you in grip and weight and balance. Lady MacGregor "PT" Clubs are especially built for you.

FOR THE STOCKY

If this is your type, your normal stance is very flat or at a much greater angle than any of the foregoing. Your club should enable you to extend your arms comfortably when you strike the ball. The shaft must be longer and slightly stronger, the head lighter, and the club so balanced that you can swing with grace and precision. Lady MacGregor Stylized "SS" Clubs exactly meet your requirements.

YOU CAN "TRY ON" MACGREGOR CLUBS
The MacGregor dealer has a Club Selector for fitting you with clubs adapted to your personal stance and swing. When you go to the MacGregor dealer for a fitting, take along a friend whose figure is unlike yours. This will show you how the Club Selector automatically indicates the varying requirements for women of different stature.

Century will define each specification and will detail its effect on ball flight. Further, the text will detail how each specification may influence another specification and how to correlate these interrelationships when golf club specifications are finally determined. For each fitting parameter, a number of possible fitting methods, including fitting materials and demo clubs, will be discussed. From a clubfitter's perspective, it is vitally important to know what each specification is and how it effects not only ball flight, but other specifications as well. It is also a key component of clubfitting to relate this same information - while not in highly technical terms perhaps - to the person being fitted. By both the fitter and the player becoming actively involved in the fitting session, the best-fit goal is readily achieved.

Regardless of whether you are new to fitting, have been at it for a number of years, or whether you are a golfer seeking to learn more about how custom fitting works, *Total Clubfitting in the 21st Century* will provide insight into what fitting is, how it works and how it will help a player's game. This book is not meant to be a highly technical manual filled with reams of data based on ball flight, computer modeling or other surreal testing processes. Rather it is meant to be an understandable reference that will ensure that, through its proper use, a player will be properly fit using easy to understand, uncomplicated methods of evaluation,

testing and selection.

Total Clubfitting in the 21st Century is organized into a logical fitting format in which the earlier fitting steps form the building blocks of the later ones. The initial criteria for any fitting is finding information about the player in some type of interview situation. Next, a look at club designs and playability provide feedback on what the player prefers and how certain designs may help their game. Club length is a key parameter to determine early in the fitting as length influences just about all of the other specifications of the golf club. As lie and length are closely related, lie is studied next; having the proper lie will help the player hit more accurate shots, especially with middle and short irons.

The position of the wood club's face is checked next. Matching the correct face angle to a golfer's swing path will help to produce a higher percentage of fairway-splitting drives. How high or low the ball is hit - the specification known as loft - plays a role in consistency and distance. As the grip is the only contact a player has with the club, it is perhaps one of the most important elements (along with the shaft) contributing to how the club feels to the player. Finally, the weight of the club is determined. Having a club of the proper weight will ensure acceptable feel as well as promoting consistently accurate distance. Short game clubs will be discussed in a specific section. *Total Clubfitting in the 21st Century*

further provides an in-depth look at fitting the club used more than any other in a round of golf - the putter. The most complete glossary of golf club fitting, design and specification terminology in the industry is provided for easy reference. Lastly, appendices detailing a number of fitting parameters, industry standards and helpful fitting information completes our presentation.

FITTING PARAMETERS

A fitting session will include each of the following fitting parameters. The text order of these parameters is also the suggested order in which they be determined during fitting. The reasoning behind this specific fitting order involves the principle that early steps are the basis for later steps; this will be explained fully in each fitting specification chapter. Are you incorrect if you do not follow this order? Not at all, as long as it is certain that each specification be analyzed and proper fitting determined. Without making sure each specification is accurately measured, it would be much like getting your custom made clothing without the buttons! A brief look at each of the fitting parameters in the order they will be found in *Total Clubfitting in the 21st Century*!

PERSONAL INTERVIEW: Learning the Player's Requirements For New Clubs

The main purpose of the personal interview is to determine what the player is seeking in a new set of clubs, how he perceives his game, his perceived ability and perhaps how much money he wants to spend on the clubs for which he will be fit. The interview also serves to "break the ice" and establish a rapport between player and fitter. The interview is not a rigid, clipboard-writing type of interview, but rather an interactive exchange between two golfers - both being players; one being a fitter. The interview may actually be an ongoing thing, with discussion taking place throughout the fitting. Part of the interview is also taking a look at the player's current clubs to determine the specifications on a few of them and also to see if he has a favorite club or a least-favorite one. Such information may help the fitter to determine if what the player is telling him about his game is a result of the swing or is a result of the improper fit of his current clubs.

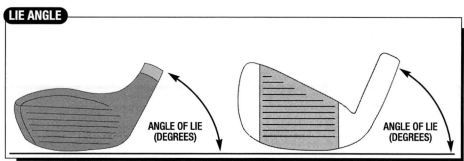

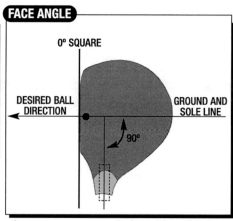

CLUBHEAD DESIGN AND PLAYABILITY: Matching the Clubheads to the Player's Ability

Choosing a clubhead that appeals to a customer's cosmetic preferences in combination with a design that matches his playability requirements is the goal of clubhead selection. This element of the fitting will provide the fitter and player with a myriad of choices. Stainless or titanium woods? Less than 280cc's or 400cc's? 431 steel irons or 1030 carbon steel? It is up to the fitter to explain to the player the potential advantages as well as the possible disadvantages of each design. The player may no doubt have read or heard some of the hype associated with a particular design or material. The clubfitter's duty is to cut through the hype in helping to determine what is best suited for the particular golfer. The actual number of clubs that will be part of the new set purchase must also be determined. Will the set be 9 irons, 8 irons or 7? Will utility woods be recommended? Here again, with the fitter being aware of the playability factors of various designs and combinations and having some idea of what the cost parameters are from the personal interview, set-makeup and head design selection is determined.

LENGTH: A Basis For Accuracy and Consistency

A club's length forms the basis for the fitting of all other specifications. Once length is established, the player is able to maintain consistent posture at address and through impact. The proper length establishes the player's comfortable body and hand positioning during the swing. Matching the longest club to the player that he or she is able to hit consistently will improve both accuracy and distance. Solid feel will result from a club whose length allows the player to repeatedly position the face in the same position

at impact over and over. Proper length fitting is the cornerstone to a successful fitting session.

LIE: A key to Accurate Iron Play

When fitting irons, lie has more effect on ball direction than does any other specification. Lie may be defined as the relationship between the shaft and the ground. If the lie is not matched to a player's swing, the club's face will be tilted either left or right of target. Thus, even when a player makes a "good" swing, if the lie is not correct, accuracy will suffer. This is especially true of middle and short irons...where accuracy counts most. Club lie is a fitting parameter that, when fit correctly, will provide immediate and positive feedback to the player and fitter.

FACE ANGLE: The Most Important Directional Factor For Drives

The position of the clubface relative to the target when hitting woods is the definition of face angle. A face angle that will effectively match a player's swing path (be it square-to-square, inside-to-outside or outside-to-inside) to the clubface position at impact can only help to

improve accuracy. Being able to hit the ball in the fairway is a key confidence builder and score reducer - something properly fitted face angle should accomplish.

LOFT: A Vital Component of Trajectory and Distance

The loft of a club helps to determine how high the ball will travel. Loft also has an effect on accuracy. A shot hit too high may often result in shorter than desired shots; but for slow swingers, added loft may actually allow the ball to stay in the air, yielding increased distance. The fitter will make note of ball trajectory through observation and the use of test clubs, making recommendations for a loft that will provide the player's desired ball height, accuracy and distance.

SHAFT: The Dynamic "Rod" That Drives the Club

The shaft is the only dynamic (shape changing) component of the club during the swing. The shaft will bend, bow and twist in various ways during a swing.

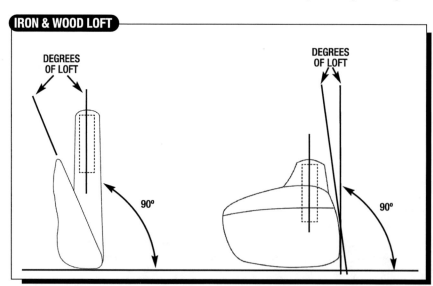

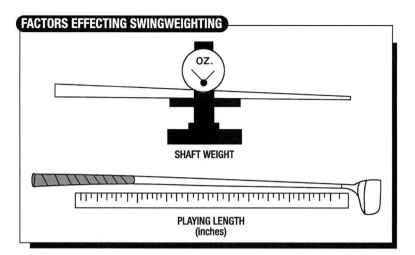

FACTORS EFFECTING SWINGWEIGHTING

OZ.

SHAFT WEIGHT

PLAYING LENGTH
(inches)

The player's swingspeed and tempo, among other things, will dictate which shaft best matches the player. Shaft matching is much like fingerprinting; each player may have very specific individual characteristics. Fortunately with

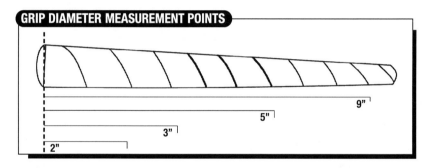

GRIP DIAMETER MEASUREMENT POINTS

9"

5"

3"

2"

the wide selection of shafts available today, there is a shaft that will fit just about every swing path, speed and pattern. While finding this specific shaft may be time-consuming and even baffling at times, the reward of more distance without a loss of accuracy, along with improved feel comes with being matched to the best-fit shaft.

GRIP: The Only Contact a Player Has With The Club

A player only touches the club at one point. This is the grip of the club. Grips come in all types, sizes, colors and price ranges. While grip type and color is a matter of player preference, making sure the grip is sized correctly is more of a factor in playability. A grip that is too large or too small will often cause the player to not feel comfortable with his control of the club during the swing. This correspondingly will cause inconsistent

shot patterns...some to the right, some to the left and some down the middle. The problem is that with improperly sized grips, the player doesn't know which way he may re-grip the club during the swing and which one of the right, left or straight shots will result. Properly sized grips eliminate the tendency of a player to change hand position on the club during the swing, thus promoting a repeatable, pleasant-feeling action.

WEIGHT: Matching For Maximum Playability

Matching a club's weight to a player will have a tremendous influence on how the club feels to him during the swing. Matching the overall weight (the weight of all of the parts of the club after it is assembled) and the swingweight (the relationship between the head and grip ends of the assembled club) to a player's swing will help consistency in addition to feel. Slower swingers may be helped by lighter clubs; faster swingers and stronger golfers may most often prefer heavy clubs. Through a combination of shaft material, grip and head choice and club length, the weight of the club becomes evident. Matching these weight parameters will provide similiar feel throughout the set, while at the same time helping to maintain the ideal tempo for the player.

INTRODUCTION: A Final Look

During any given round a player uses each club in the set a specific number of times. While the exact number of times a club is used will vary from one round to another, there is a definite pattern of club

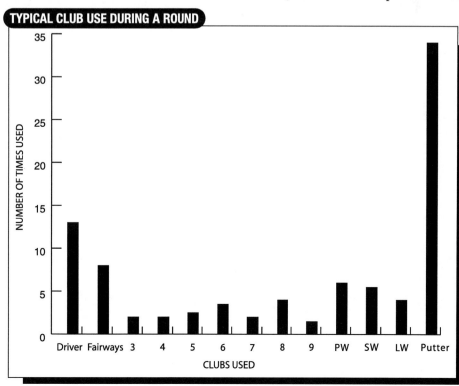

TYPICAL CLUB USE DURING A ROUND

NUMBER OF TIMES USED

Driver Fairways 3 4 5 6 7 8 9 PW SW LW Putter

CLUBS USED

use during a round for most players. The particular course a golfer plays may influence average club usage to some degree; it is important that the fitter be aware that certain courses require more or less specific club usage. Thus the fitter will actually be able to tailor the player's clubs to particular courses further promoting our "best-fit" scenario.

SUGGESTED FITTING STEPS FOR TOTAL CLUBFITTING

CLUBHEADS
• Determine the design that fits a player's game •

LENGTH
• Establishes comfortable address and consistent shotmaking •

LIE
• A key to directional control for irons •

FACE ANGLE
• A critical element in wood shot direction •

LOFT
• A vital component of trajectory and distance •

SHAFTS
• The critical element in feel and performance •

GRIP
• Proper fit promotes feel and consistency •

WEIGHT
• Swingweight and total weight establish overall club feel •

Chapter 1
PERSONAL INTERVIEW

INTRODUCTION

As an initial consideration during a clubfitting, it is important to learn a bit about the player being fitted prior to actually heading to the range or to the swing area. An opening selection of questions intended to find out a bit about the golfer's equipment knowledge, fitting goals and club preferences will help make the fitting situation beneficial to both to both player and fitter. These questions are to be asked as part of a normal conversation; they do not require a clipboard for recording information. (That will come later!) The inquiries you make and the responses which you will consider begin to build a rapport between you and the player. This rapport is crucial when working toward a best-fit set of clubs. There are a several considerations that you should make prior to beginning discussions with a player seeking new clubs. These include, but are not limited to, the following:

Develop a question sequence.

A set of guide questions is provided later in this chapter, but don't utilize these questions only. Use the questions as a guide for starting a conversation or for determining information related to the player's game. By no means memorize the questions, think of them as guides only. Relying too much on a specific format or order of questions does not allow the interaction between the fitter and the player to flow smoothly. When the player asks questions, answer them. If the player wants to discuss an equipment element not on your list of "interview" questions, by all means do so. Never compromise the interaction by not allowing questions to be asked or by changing the subject away from what the player is questioning.

Ask open-ended questions.

An open-ended question is one that cannot be answered simply "yes" or "no."

Open-ended questions offer the player the chance to speak; the fitter will learn much more about the player by asking these types of questions as compared to questions that can simply be answered in a single word. Questions such as, "Describe the ball flight of your normal drive" is a better one to ask as compared to "Do you usually hit the ball straight?" Other obvious questions may include, "How do you expect your new clubs to improve your game?" "What clubs currently on the market have you hit tested? Which did you like best? Why?" The more you are able to get the player to talk about his or her game, the more knowledge you will gain that may be helpful during the fitting session itself.

Be the expert.

The golfer came to you for a reason. Whether the reason was that he thought you were less expensive than another source, that you and he are friends, whether he was recommended by a former customer or whether he had another reason, it really doesn't matter. The fact that the player is in your shop provides you with a captive audience toward which you are able to dispense your golf club knowledge. While you are talking to the player, make sure you speak in a confident tone, use good posture and answer any questions he may pose as fully as possible. You will be able to provide knowledge about certain club models as both of you walk around your shop. You may show him some of your "tools" such as a frequency analyzer, a swing computer or perhaps a loft/lie machine. All of these will enhance your image in the player's eyes - the more he thinks you know, the more confidence he will have in your ability to fit. This is sometimes called the "Wow" effect. When the customer leaves your shop, he thinks (and hopefully tells his playing companions), "Wow, this guy really knows his stuff!"

A specifications gauge measuring an iron's lie.

Use a soft sell.

It is important to let your knowledge, demo clubs and fitting session be your selling tools. Never try to fit a player with a club he doesn't like. Show the player a wide range of options, discussing the pros and cons of each head, shaft, grip or fitting parameter. The player is an integral part of the fitting; feedback from him or her is the key to accurate fitting. The use of statements such as, "Have you seen the latest..., Are you familiar with..., Let me show you..." will help you gain the trust and confidence of the player. The fitter should sell himself and his abilities and the clubs will sell themselves.

Always be positive.

Whether it is in a ball-hitting situation when a player hits a shot poorly or whether you are offering your opinion on a certain club that you do not like, be certain to put a positive "spin" on your comments. For example, if the player mentions a rival company, do not say things to disparage that company. Offer comments such as, "Their philosophy differs from ours. We prefer our philosophy because...". Try not to make sales at the expense of the integrity of the competition, no matter how much you may dislike them. Remember, as the saying

The fitter and golfer should establish a rapport early in the fitting session.

states, "What goes around, comes around." By being positive, there is less chance that what you may say will come back to haunt you in the future.

Be flexible with your time.

Club fitting is a business that performs a service; hence it is considered a service business. If a golfer works from 9:00 to 5:00, schedule a fitting after his working hours. It might be a wise idea to establish evening hours at least once a week, if not more, depending on the location of the shop. Weekend hours will offer golfers a chance to stop by at their leisure, before or after a round. Scheduling fittings may be helpful as well, especially for those with very busy schedules. Fitting players at the time they normally play is a good idea as well. For example, many retired golfers play early in the morning. Why not fit them at that time rather than later in the day? Their bodies will be more "in tune" with the way they will play if you fit them at that same time.

Follow up is important.

After the sale is complete and the money is spent, the fitting is over, right? Well, it really shouldn't be. Offering a follow-up session or a fine-tuning session at no cost within a specified time period (60 days for example) will ensure the clubs are performing as they were intended. Plus, the golfer will again be impressed with the fitter's dedication to custom fitting. A thank you note is a nice gesture, as is perhaps a phone call shortly

A thank you card is a professional touch upon completion of a fitting.

Offer a warranty.

A clubfitter must stand behind his or her work. Some type of warranty should be offered. Is it 30 days, 60 days, a year or lifetime? In all reality, it is up to the fitter, but a lifetime warranty, even if just implied, is reasonable to offer. If the clubs are properly matched to the player, there should be no reason for problems. If you offer the follow-up evaluation after a month or so, any problems should be resolved at that time. Regarding clubs that break during the normal course of play, nearly all reputable component suppliers will replace defective heads or shafts. Thus, in the case of breakage, liability is effectively removed from the clubfitter. If there is a drawback to replacing clubs or components more than a couple of years old, it is that the exact product may be out of production. Golf club product life cycles are closer to three years than to ten...beware of this when offering exact replacements or fill-ins to a player.

after the sale to make certain the player is happy with the clubs. Just as in many other businesses, service after the sale makes for satisfied customers and will potentially add repeat business.

PERSONAL INTERVIEW

In developing a set of questions that may help a fitter guide a player toward the proper set of clubs, certain information should be sought. The following set of guide questions will provide the fitter with a good deal of background information about the player, while at the same time allowing the player to analyze his or her game. These questions are suggestions only; they do not all have to be asked, nor do they have to be asked in any specific order. It is recommended that these become a standard part of the fitter's initial conversation with the player, rather than a written checklist of inquiries.

Current Set Makeup

Even before you check the player's actual club specifications, ask him or her what clubs they currently use. This will give you an immediate idea of how cognizant they are of equipment and will give you a definite indication of their current equipment knowledge.

Right or Left Handed

This is important to know early in the discussion. As there are not as many choices for left-handers, knowing the answer to this prevents the embarrassment of having to tell a player the club he likes very much (after you have just told him all of the good points of the club) is only available in right-hand. This may also be a hint toward having a specific section for left-handed players at a certain location in your shop.

Frequency of Play and/or Practice

Determining how often the golfer plays will give you some indication of his commitment to the game and also to game improvement. If the player hits range balls regularly, that may tell you his game should improve; if on the other hand the player tells you he is strictly a weekend warrior, a full complement that favors game-improvement clubs might be an initial recommendation.

Physical Limitations

Certain physical conditions such as arthritis, tendonitis, effects of past surgeries, etc., may influence a player's ability to swing the club. By knowing these up front, it may help in initial shaft recommendations.

Handicap or Scoring Average

A player expects a fitter to ask this question. Often the response is exaggerated on the low side by the player. However, knowing what a player shoots - or at least believes he shoots - may help in future head and shaft selection.

A USGA handicap card is a true indication of a player's scoring ability.

Driving Distance

This question is asked in an effort to get an idea of the player's swingspeed. Most players really do not know how far they drive the ball, so exaggerations are common to this one. As just about all fitting forms that the player may see ask this question, the fitter should ask it as well, but take the response at times with a grin or chuckle (to yourself of course!)

Putts Per Round

While a golfer may not know his exact average number of putts for 18 holes, he will be able to let you know if he is a "good" or "bad" putter. The number of putts per round will give you an idea of the player's ball-striking ability. For instance if the player claims to shoot 90 but says he is a great putter, that will show his ability from tee-to-green needs improvement. But if the 90-shooter tells you he is a terrible putter and three putts often, this shows his ball-striking ability is probably better than average, but that a change in putter specifications is in order.

Errant Shot Tendencies

Ask the player if he feels that he misses more shots to the right or to the left. Many players, regardless of their ability will state that they hit the ball fair-

ly straight. But, if the player admits to being a slicer (as most are), this will clue the fitter in to looking toward perhaps hook-face woods or offset irons - at least initially.

Goals in a New Set of Clubs

Ask what the player expects the new clubs to do for him or her. This will give you an idea of not only what the player may be looking for, but also probably a very honest clue as to what the biggest problem is with the player's game.

Favorite/Least Favorite Clubs

By knowing what club the player likes best and likes least, when it comes time to measuring the specifications of the player's current clubs, these two should be measured. This will give you a quantifiable picture of why the player hits a club well or poorly.

Likes, Dislikes of On-the-Market Clubs.

Ask what club designs or styles the player likes. Ask if the player has hit any particular club well recently. If the player tells you he likes very large drivers, it will save you the time in showing him the latest in shallow faced heads. This will also provide the perfect opportunity for the fitter to expound on his or her knowledge of clubhead design and playability, further cementing the image of "expert" in the golfer's mind.

Again, these questions serve as a suggested list only and may be modified to fit specific needs. Keep in mind that these questions provide background only; when the player actually hits balls during the fitting session, any discrepancies between the player's perception of his game and his actual game will be evidenced. For example, the golfer may think he hits his drives 280 yards fairly straight, but during hit testing, he actually hits the drives well to the right due to his outside-in swing path and the drives travel closer to 220 yards due to his 90 mile per hour swingspeed. Remember, the personal interview provides you some information about the player; the dynamic fitting supplies the remaining information that will lead to a best-fit scenario.

EQUIPMENT EVALUATION

A second important component of the fitting situation prior to actual hit testing, is the examination of the clubs the player is currently using. While it is not imperative to measure each and every club, certainly the club(s) that the player says he likes best or least should be checked for a number of specifications. Additionally, the driver, #6 iron and putter should be analyzed as these are the clubs that will be commonly used during the hit testing phase of the session. A check of the following specifications will provide the fitter with a definitive concept of the player's current clubs: clubhead type & design, length, lie, face angle, loft, shaft type & flex, grip type & size and the club's weight parameters. These specifications should be recorded and used for reference during and/or after the fitting. Through listening to the player's responses during the interview and combining them with the specifications measurements, the fitter will be able to correlate the player's current playing characteristics with what should be successful when fitting the new set.

A look at a player's current clubs will help later fitting steps.

WOODS

Examining the specs of the driver will be a key to understanding why the player hits it as he does. Each measurement may provide a hint as to why the player hits a certain club a certain way. The measurement, when combined with the player's comments about how he hits that specific club, may provide clues as to how to make the fitted clubs play better than the current ones. Here are some examples:

Clubhead

The golfer makes the comment that he hits his driver "on top" too often. A look at the ball marks on the top of his

CURRENT SET MAKEUP

CUSTOMER: *Robert Slocum* DATE: *11/5/00*

WOODS

SPECIFICATION	①	③	5	7	X
Manufacturer	CALL.	OLLIN			
Model	6BB 9.5°	TRI METAL			
Length	45	425			
Loft	11	13			
Lie	57	57			
Face angle	3°C	5°			
Swingweight	D-0	D-3			
Total Weight	319	329			
Shaft Type	6BB UL	ULTRA LIGHT			
Shaft Flex	R 233	R 258			
Grip Type	CALL STOCK	CALL STOCK			
Grip Size	STD	STD			

IRONS

1	2	③	④	⑤	⑥	⑦	⑧	⑨
		COBRA						
		OVERSIZE						
		39	38¾	38¼	37¾	37¼	36¾	36¼
		21	25	28	31	36	40	44
		58	59	61	61	63	65	64
		X	X	X	X	X	X	X
		D-1	D-1	D-1	D-1	D-0	D-1	D-0
		386	391	397	402	406	413	418
		AUTOCLAVE R						
		280	286	286	288	293	294	298
		COBRA STOCK						
		+1/64 ————————→						

WEDGES

	PW	SW	UW	AW
Manufacturer	TITLEIST			
Model	VOKEY 200			
Length	35½	35¼		
Loft	52	56		
Lie	64	65		
Swingweight	D-3	D-4		
Total Weight	466	475		
Shaft Type	Dynamic Gold			
Shaft Flex	331	328		
Grip Type	TITLEIST			
Grip Size	STD	STD		

PUTTER   OTHER

	PUTTER
Manufacturer	Odyssey
Model	Rossie II
Length	35"
Loft	4
Lie	74

A specification's measurement form (see Appendix II) provides both player and fitter with an accurate picture of the player's current clubs.

shallow-faced club bears evidence to this. Look to a deeper faced driver.

Length

The driver is measured and its length is found to be 42"; the player complains about hitting drives shorter than his playing companions. This shorter length most likely is a contributing factor. Look to possibly a longer length driver.

Lie

As the lie of a wood cannot be changed, along with the fact that lie does not play a substantial part in ball direction related to woods, measure lie for reference only.

Face Angle

A measured face angle of 2 degrees open will confirm the player's comments related to the inability to hit the ball straight. Look to a more closed face club.

Loft:

A player complains about hitting the ball too high, his comments may be verified by checking the loft and determining it to be 13 degrees. Look to a lower lofted driver or one with a deeper face.

A specs gauge shows a face angle of 1.5 degrees open on this driver.

Shaft

The player tells the fitter that the club feels "like a board." The 300 cpm reading of the shaft indicates a very stiff shaft, making the player's comments quite logical. Look to a softer shaft in the club.

Grip

The golfer says he often "loses" the grip during the swing. A check of the grips show them to be worn and undersized. Look to new grips of a larger size than presently.

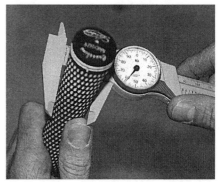

Calipers are the most accurate means of determining a grip's size.

Weight

The player states that he "can't feel the head." Upon weighing the club, the swingweight is found to be C-3. Look toward a heavier wood, especially in swingweight.

IRONS

Irons are the clubs in the set that are designed with accuracy in mind. This is especially true with middle and shorter irons. Analyzing a few irons in the set shows the following trends and possible solutions.

Clubhead

The player tells the fitter he slices most of the time and that shots often sting his hands. It is determined the clubs are non-offset, blade models. Look to more off-

One method of measuring the length of a club prior to assembly.

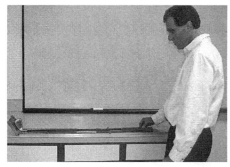

A True Measure is the most accurate way to measure the length of a gripped club.

set, perimeter-weighted designs.

Length

The golfer complains of accuracy problems, except when he hits a shot on center, when the shots go too far. Measurement of the shafts show them to be 2" longer than standard. Look to shorter clubs for more control and consistency.

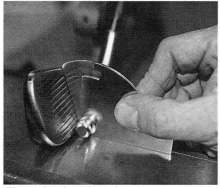

The loft of an iron is accurately measured on a specifications gauge.

Loft

Ball trajectory is much higher than that of the other members of the player's foursome. A loft gauge shows all of the lofts to be 2 degrees weak of modern standard. Look to lower lofted irons.

Lie

The golfer contends that most of his middle and short irons tend to end up right of the target, even though his playing partners tell him that his alignment is correct. A lie measurement shows the lie of all of the player's irons is 2 degrees flat of what is standard for this set. Look to irons more upright than the player is currently using.

Shaft

The player makes the comment that the shafts feel like "noodles." The frequency machine shows the #6 iron frequency to be 275. Look to stiffer-shafted irons.

Grip

The golfer says he often "re-grips" the grip during the swing. A check of the grips find then to be almost jumbo-sized. Look to new grips of a smaller size than at present.

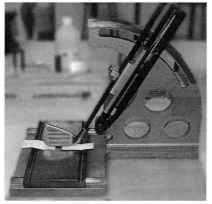

The proper position of an iron when determining its lie.

Weight

The player complains that the clubs feel like he has to really kill the ball in order to make contact, plus at the end of the round he is tired. A swingweight scale shows most of the clubs weigh D-8. Look toward lighter clubs.

Fairway Wedges

Skulled or thin shots are a constant enemy when the player tries to hit a wedge. A look at the bounce angle of the pitching and gap wedges shows them to be 12 degrees. Look for fairway wedges with bounces in the more standard range of 3-5 degrees.

Sand Wedge

Playing a course that has loose, fluffy sand most often, the golfer comments that he has difficulty in even getting the ball out of most sand bunkers. The specification check shows the sand wedge to have a bounce of 7

A frequency machine provides the most accurate means of measuring a club's flex.

degrees. Look to a sand wedge with a bounce exceeding 10-12 degrees for the soft sand conditions.

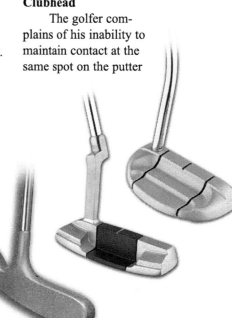

The total weight of a club may be expressed in ounces (as shown) or grams.

PUTTERS

The single most used club during a round is the putter. Often it is overlooked during fitting. A look at these putter specifications may provide a reason that the player may be a successful or a less than successful putter:

Clubhead

The golfer complains of his inability to maintain contact at the same spot on the putter

The three most common putter designs: Bullseye, heel-and-toe weighted and mallet

face. The head design is a "Bullseye type" of design. Look to a heel-toe balanced model, perhaps an oversized type to better allow the club to stay on path during the stroke.

Length

The player's eyes are outside the line of the ball, leading to alignment difficulties. The length of the putter is measured at a short 33". Look to a longer model to re-position the eyes directly over the ball.

Lie

The toe of the putter is slightly off the ground as the player putts. It is measured to be 77 degrees, a bit more upright than typical. Don't do anything if the player is putting well, as lie has little effect on putting. If the player is putting poorly, look to a putter with a flatter lie.

Loft

The player claims that the ball bounces as it comes off the putter face. The loft of the putter is measured at 6 degrees. Look to a more standard putter loft, in the 3-degree range. Note: Too little loft may also be the cause of a ball not rolling smoothly immediately off the putter face as well.

Shaft

The player comments that there is no feel or feedback on almost any putt. The shaft is tested and found to be in the X-flex range. Look to a softer shaft to provide more feedback to the player.

Grip

The player, upon observation, has a very "handsy" stroke. The grip is a small paddle size. Look to a grip that is larger than the one at present to help eliminate excess hand action.

Weight

The player cannot maintain a consistent stroke, neither straight-back & straight-through or inside-square-inside. The total weight of the putter is 440

A swingweight scale is used to determine the relationship of weight in woods, irons or putters.

grams. Look toward a heavier putter, one at least that weighs 500+ grams.

This basic equipment evaluation will serve as a basis for later player testing while hitting balls. Full details of how to measure each specification are found in the specific chapter that describes each fitting parameter. By measuring specifications as part of a fitting, both the player and fitter will learn how the new, best-fit equipment differs from what is being played now and how the specifications of the new clubs will directly influence and improve ball flight.

A typical fitting form will be seen on the next few pages. While this form may vary from fitting to fitting, it does provide valuable qualified information for the fitter to use when recommending clubs. This form should become part of the permanent record in the fitter's files.

DEMO CLUBS: AN INTRODUCTION

At this point in our fitting discussion, demo clubs deserve some mention. While in each chapter of this text, a full explanation of what demos are suggested will be undertaken in detail, some basis parameters for all demo clubs will be discussed at this juncture. Demo clubs are required in order to allow the fitter to provide the golfer with a number of club head, shaft and grip choices that will influence both performance and feel. Each demo club should be chosen for a specific purpose, whether it be to test what loft is best for the player, what grip feels best or what shaft performs most accurately.

All demo clubs should be built to similar specifications - that is, except for the specification of which they are being used to determine, all specifications should be the same. The clubheads that will be selected as demo heads should all be the same - if this is not possible, they should at least be very similar. For example, if #6 irons are going to be the clubs used to test lie and length, use #6's for all of the other fitting parameters as well. The same model heads should be used if at all possible; this eliminates the possibility of the player looking at the head design of a club rather than the actual specification that club is being used to determine. Each demo club should test

A wooden rack is a great way to organize demo clubs.

for one fitting specification only. Thus, the length #6 irons should test length only; they should not have different heads so that the heads do not influence length selection.

The shafts in all of the clubs should be the same, with the exception of the shaft testing clubs, the grips on all clubs should be the same, except for the grip sizing demo clubs, and so on. The best selection for a shaft would be something in the lightweight steel category, most likely in regular flex. While not all players will be best fitted with a lightweight, regular flex steel shaft, this shaft will fit more of a broad spectrum of player than will any other. The weight of all demos (other than those used to test weight) should be the same. All demos, with the exception of the length demos, should be the same length. What length each fitter chooses for standard is up to him, but make certain that once a standard is chosen, it is adhered to in all of the demo clubs. The length standard may be 37" or 37 1/2" for the #6 iron - the choice is up to the fitter. What is important is that all other #6 irons used in the demo are made to this stan-

All demo clubs should be labeled specifically.

dard as well. While the player might never hit the "exact" club he or she will be fit with, by using specific demo clubs, the fitting becomes much like writing a prescription for the player. Length will be determined, lie will be next, face angle is set, and so on through the complete fitting session.

Labeling the demo clubs is a key to organization and understanding during the fitting. Storing the demo clubs in some type of rack or organized bag will make the fitting session flow smoothly. Having demo clubs with no labels will make the fitter look very unorganized as he tries to examine each club and figure out what specification it is supposed to measure. Knowing what the clubs are to measure and where each club is located will make the fitting seem much more professional. The demo club labels should include the club model information, what specification the club is being used to test and what specific parameter the club measures. For example, the label should read, "Model PC3I, #6 iron, Lie Test Club, Standard Lie 61 degrees". This complete label, which may also be color-coded for easier identification, will ensure accuracy in choosing the correct demo club during the actual fitting.

Shaft demo labels do not specifically allow a player to know the shaft type.

These identification labels should be the only labels affixed to the clubs. Do not use the shaft manufacturer's shaft bands. Seeing the fact that the clubs are lightweight steel in regular flex may bias some players who may think they need a heavier of stiffer shaft. To some degree, "what the player doesn't know won't hurt him"; removing any labels helps to eliminate any potential biases that the player may have. While this cannot be done with many graphite shaft offerings as their logos are silkscreened onto the shaft, encourage the player not to be concerned with what the specific shaft is, but more with how it feels and performs. Very often shafts that are softer than the player may believe he should have will be the best

fit. Do not be worried about specific shaft labels, but do be concerned with shaft performance.

Shaft demo labels are required, but they will not be done in the same manner as will the labels for all of the other parameters. Shaft demo labels will be done in a manner that the fitter knows what type of shaft is being tested, but the player cannot determine the same information. This may be known as "blind labeling". For example, a good method of labeling a shaft for testing is, "MI1". This "MI1" (Men's Iron, Test Club #1) related to a listing of shafts that only the fitter knows. Such a system eliminates the problem of having a male player, for instance, who thinks he needs a stiff shaft, looking at the label that may indicate "L" flex and not being willing to hit the club . Actual blind hit testing may prove the "L" flex is the best shaft for the player. With the blind labeling, the fitter is able to say, this steel shaft, "MI1" is the best-fit shaft for you as evidenced by your comments and through both of us watching ball flight.

As part of the head demo selection, there should be a wide variety of choices. Included should be at least one large headed driver, a shallow faced model, a deep-faced model, etc. Having a wide selection of head demos will permit a player to make a decision based on a large choice of head design and playability. While the fitter will steer the player toward heads that he feels will be better choices, at least the player will be able to realize there are a number of possible head selections available. Iron head demos follow the same thought pattern; oversize irons, smaller irons, offset and non-offset designs, etc., are part of a complete demo selection. Obviously a number of putter styles will complete the head section of the demo package. Again, specific demo recommendations will be detailed in upcoming chapters.

A consideration as part of your demo selection includes a study of the player demographics in your particular area. If most of the players in the surrounding area of your shop are senior golfers, your demos should probably include a wider selection of softer shafts and heads with higher lofts. If there is a high percentage of left-handers in your area, then a complete left-handed demo package will be a

wise choice. The same theory would apply if there is a high concentration of female golfers in your region. The initial demo selections mentioned previously provided for right-handed males only; adding demo clubs for lefties and females will only enhance your image and sales. While adding these demo clubs may be costly at first glance, the returns by having complete demo clubs available for all who come into the shop will pay dividends quickly.

Demo clubs will require updating on a constant basis. While the clubs being used to test lie, length, face angle, loft, weight and grips can be used year after year as these specifications will not change, shaft designs and head designs change often. The fitter must remain "current" related to popular designs in the industry. The fitter must be aware of new product offering from suppliers; additionally consider what models are seen on television and in print media as a guide to what players will be looking for. Being among the first to have a test sample of the latest head or shaft design will enhance credibility tremendously. It is also important to remove heads and shafts from your demo selection as they go out of stock from suppliers. The best time to check for what is being discontinued is toward the fall of each year. Reputable manufacturers will be more than happy to let you know which of their models will be no longer available in the near future. Such information is just a phone call away.

Demo clubs are an important part of any fitting situation. By having an up-to-date complete selection of clearly labeled clubs, the fitter is a step ahead of his competition. Maintaining the demos by keeping them clean and organized and by adding or removing clubs as supply or designs dictate will further enhance the ability to offer a player the clubs to provide a best-fit scenario. Each subsequent chapter will provide specific details concerning wise demo choices. Keep in mind though, that proper labeling, updating and organizing are the keys to a good demo program.

STATIC FITTING: A NOTE

In each future section of this text, static fitting methods will be discussed for each fitting specification. While there is no substitute for dynamic fitting, there will be times when the player will not be able to hit balls. Such situations include telephone or internet fittings. A sample static fitting form (Appendix V) will assist in the types of fittings.

Personal Interview
Summary: Do's and Don'ts in a Personal Interview

DO: Listen attnetively to what the golfer is saying.

DO: Be positive with your comments toward the golfer and his equipment questions.

DO: Maintain an up-to-date knowledge of all areas of equipment.

DO: Treat the golfer as you would want to be treated.

DO: Ask relevant, open ended questions.

DO: Answer all questions completely and honestly.

DO: Do not pressure the player into any purchase.

DO: Have an organized demo club area.

DO: Update your demo clubs one regular basis.

DO: Follow up after the sale of custom fitted clubs.

DON'T: Treat the interview as a rigid "clipboard" type of situation.

DON'T: Hesitate to make suggestions related to equipment that you think will help the player.

DON'T: Forget to look at the player's putter during the fitting.

DON'T: Try to "fix" a player's swing during the fitting.

DON'T: Make disparaging remarks about other fitters or equipment companies.

DON'T: Dominate the fitting - it is to be an interactive exchange between player and fitter.

DON'T: Force a player to select a club with which he or she is not comfortable.

DON'T: Limit yourself to fitting only male players; women and juniors deserve equal time.

DON'T: Keep obsolete demo clubs as part of your demo program.

DON'T: Forget to say thank you after the fitting is complete.

Personal Interview Form

Player Information

Name _____

Address _____

_____

Phone (H) _____ (W) _____

Player Profile

Height _____ Weight _____ Age _____ RH/LH _____

Frequency of play _____ Handicap/Average Score _____

Number of times per week of practice _____

Average Putts Per Round _____ Are you getting better, worse or the same? _____

Physical Considerations _____

Rank the following, excellent, good, fair or poor:

Driver _____	Fairway Woods _____	Long Irons _____
Mid Irons _____	Short Irons _____	Full Wedge _____
Chipping _____	Bunker Play _____	Putter _____
Favorite Club _____	Least Favorite Club _____	

Where do your mishits tend to go? (slice, push, hook, pull, high, low, short or long?)

Driver _____	Fairway Woods _____	Long Irons _____
Mid Irons _____	Short Irons _____	Full Wedge _____
Chipping _____	Bunker Play _____	Putter _____

PUSH

FADE

SLICE

PULL

DRAW

HOOK

Custom Golf Club Fitting Form

Player Information

Name _____

Address _____

_____

Phone (H) _____ (W) _____

Player Profile

Height _____ Weight _____ Age _____ RH/LH _____

Number of rounds played per week _____

Number of times per week of practice _____

Handicap/Average Score _____

Average Putts Per Round _____

Physical Considerations _____

Player Goals

To Hit Ball:

_____ Higher

_____ Lower

_____ Longer

_____ Straighter

_____ More Solidly

_____ With Better Feel

_____ More Consistency

To Stop:

_____ Slicing

_____ Hooking

_____ Skying

_____ Topping

_____ Pulling

_____ Pushing

Fitting Procedures

1. Set Makeup
A. Player preferences - IRONS

Blade Configuration	Hosel Type	Head Size
_____ Muscleback	_____ Offset	_____ Standard
_____ Cavity Back	_____ Non-Offset	_____ Oversize
_____ No Preference	_____ No Preference	_____ No Preference

Current Irons _____

Recommendations _____

©Copyright 2001 Dynacraft Golf Products, Inc.

B. Player Preferences - WOODS

Hosel Type	Head Size	Face Angle
_____ Offset	_____ Standard	_____ Open
_____ Non-Offset	_____ Midsize	_____ Closed
_____ No Preference	_____ Jumbo	_____ Square

Current Type of Woods _____

Recommendations _____

_____

2. Loft

Current Driver Ball Flight	Current 5 Iron Ball Flight
_____ Very High	_____ Offset
_____ High	_____ Non-Offset
_____ Acceptable	_____ No Preference
_____ Low	_____ Low
_____ Very Low	_____ Very Low
Recommended Driver Loft _____	Recommended 5 Iron Loft _____

3. Shaft

Player Preference

_____ Steel	Average Driver Distance _____
_____ Graphite	Average Driver Distance _____
_____ No Preference	Clubhead Speed: Driver _____ 5 Iron _____

Shaft Recommendations: Driver _____   5 Iron _____

4. Length

_____ Height   _____ Finger Tip To Floor Measurement

<u>IMPACT FEEL CONSISTENCY TEST RESULTS</u>

5 Iron		Driver	
36 1/2"	_____	43"	_____
37"	_____	43 1/2"	_____
37 1/2"	_____	44"	_____
38"	_____	44 1/2"	_____

Recommended Driver Length _____   Recommended 5 Iron Length _____

5. Lie

Finger Tip To Floor Measurement _____

Sole Impact Test 5 Iron _____

Recommended Lie _____   Driver _____   5 Iron _____

6. Grip

Players Glove Size _____

Players Hand Measurement   A. _____   B. _____

<u>PLAYER FEEL PREFERENCES</u>

- 1/64" _____
Standard _____
+ 1/64" _____
+ 1/32" _____
+ 1/64" _____
Jumbo _____

Recommended Grip Size _____

<u>GRIP TYPE PREFERENCES</u>

_____ Rubber
_____ Cord
_____ Synthetic
_____ Other (specify)
_____ No Preferences

Grip Type Selection _____

7. Weight

Recommended Swingweights: Driver _____   5 Iron _____

8. Miscellaneous Notes

_____

_____

_____

_____

_____

_____

_____

_____

_____

_____

_____

STATIC FITTING FORM

First Name _____

Last Name _____

Address _____

City _____

State/Province _____

Postal Code _____

Country _____

Email Address _____

Phone _____

I play golf: _____ RH _____ LH

I am _____ Male _____ Female

I am _____ feet, _____ inches tall

I weigh _____ pounds

I am _____ years old.

I've played golf for _____ years.

My handicap is _____ (Enter a "?" if you don't know)

My average score is _____.

Do you take golf lessons? _____ Yes _____ No

Woods I play now _____

Irons I play now _____

Shaft type (woods) _____

Shaft type (irons) _____

Shaft flex (woods) _____

Shaft flex (irons) _____

Swingweight driver _____

Swingweight 5 iron _____

Driver length _____

5 iron length _____

STATIC FITTING FORM (continued)

Grip type _____   Grip size _____

What's your glove size? _____

Distance from knuckles to the ground _____ inches

Distance from top of shoulder to fingertips _____ inches

Distance from grip cap to the ground _____ inches

How man yards is your average tee shot? _____

I push _____ % of the time   — **PUSH**

I fade _____ % of the time   — **FADE**

I slice _____ % of the time   — **SLICE**

I pull _____ % of the time   — **PULL**

I draw _____ % of the time   — **DRAW**

I hook _____ % of the time   — **HOOK**

I hit straight _____ % of the time — **STRAIGHT**

I hit my driver _____ yards

I hit my irons _____ yards

Chapter 2
Head Design

In the opinion of most players, the head of the club may be the most important factor in how that club performs. While the head is definitely important, other factors, especially the shaft, meld to determine the specific playability of any golf club. The club head is what most players first look at when they are choosing a club. The name on the head equates with the "kind" of club the player selects. For example, a player choosing a Dynacraft head, will say he plays Dynacraft clubs; he will not often say he plays a Dynacraft head, a Royal Precision shaft and a Golf Pride grip. This despite the fact that all of the components of a club combine to yield its playability.

Golf club heads are available in a variety of materials, shapes and sizes. There are woods that are 400 cubic centimeters in volume; others are less than 200cc's. Titanium woods are popular as are stainless steel heads. Wooden woods and graphite headed woods have had such decreased popularity in the past 20 years that few are seen in player's bags. Iron heads, either cast or forged may be oversized, standard sized or low profile. They may have materials such as copper or brass inserted somewhere in the head to change their centers of gravity. Putter designs run the gamut from traditional blade shapes, to heel-toe weighted models, to mallet styles and beyond. Before examining the intricacies of club head design and playability, a look at how heads are manufactured will provide insight into how they may be fitted to best match a player's swing characteristics.

INVESTMENT CASTING

The vast majority of golf clubs made today - woods, irons and putters - are made through a process known as "lost wax investment casting." Basically this involves pouring (or investing) metal into a mold in order to produce a large quantity of heads that will have the same characteristics and specifications. Investment casting is used to make many other products in addition to golf clubs, some of which include auto and marine parts,

medical equipment and other precision instruments. Most foundries that produce golf heads do exclusively that; their expertise is in the design, form and function of a golf club head.

Golf clubs start out as ideas in a club designer's head. The initial sketches might be done on a drawing table, paper napkin or on a cad-cam computer. From these first ideas, modifications are generally made and a model made of epoxy is produced. This model may be produced by hand or by computer, but is nearly always "tweaked" by the designer filing, sanding or grinding the model until it is exactly as desired. Once a sample model is produced, it, along with the drawings detailing the specifications (loft, lie,

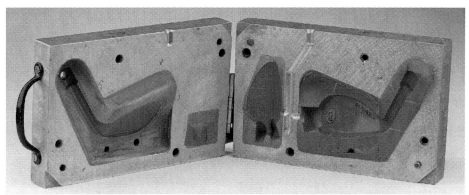

An aluminum mold forms the cavity into which wax will be injected as an early step in the casting process.

weight, face angle, bounce, etc.) are sent to the foundry.

The foundry may be located here in the US, or it may be in Taiwan, China or Thailand. More and more companies, be they major OEM golf companies or component companies have their heads produced overseas. The main reason is a cost versus technology issue. The overseas technology is as good as it is here in the U.S., but the cost of producing a club in the Far East is less than half the cost of producing it here in the US. While there is a decided advantage in shipping time from domestic foundries, not to mention a language advantage, the lower costs of producing a head overseas outweigh these disadvantages. At least 90% of golf club

heads made today are manufactured offshore.

Once the golf company chooses a foundry, the actual manufacturing process begins. From the drawings and/or models, the foundry creates a piece called a "brass master". Each golf club head in the set requires its own master. That is, there will be a master for the #1 iron, #2 iron, etc. (Keep in mind that woods, irons and putters will be made in the same manner.) This master will be an exact duplicate of the final club head, right down to the name, number, specifications and scorelines. It is made by a combination of lathe, electro-etching machine, hand filing, sanding and grinding. Once the club head shape is correct, the name is engraved in the cavity and on the sole, the club number is etched on the sole and the scorelines are engraved in the face following specific template patterns. The master goes through countless quality control checks prior to final approval; even the smallest flaw, in either grinding or specifications in the master, will mean that every club head that is manufactured will have that exact same flaw. Creating a correct master is the key to successful investment casting.

Upon completion and approval by both the foundry and golf club company, the brass master is used to create an aluminum mold of the club head. The master is placed inside a cavity in between two pieces of aluminum or steel that form an enclosed shell. Liquid aluminum is then injected into the cavity, creating a negative image of the club head. When the aluminum cools and hardens, the brass master is removed. A perfect duplicate of the club head is now in the aluminum mold. The master is placed in storage at this point. The only time it will be used again is to create a new mold should the current one become somehow lost or damaged.

The next step in the casting process is wax injection. In this step, the closed aluminum mold is placed in a special machine that melts wax and injects it into the cavity of the mold. This wax is similar to paraffin wax. This creates another exact duplicate of the head, this time in wax. The waxes are carefully examined for any defects, and, once inspected, are affixed to a holder known as a "tree". This tree allows up to a dozen clubs to be cast at the same time. The wax tree is then coated with a ceramic slurry mix. Several layers of this mix are applied, with each layer being force dried at least overnight. The slurry hardens, forming what looks like a plaster cast when it dries. These dried slurry mixes are called "shells." When complete, the shells will be nearly 1/4" thick, providing much protection for the wax inside.

Next the ceramic shells are heated, melting the wax from inside. The wax will be recycled for use in future mold injection. This initial heating and wax removal is the basis for the term "lost wax" casting. These resulting shells, which are now hollow, will be heated and will have molten metal, typically 431 or 17-4 stainless steel, poured into them to form actual cast club heads.

Before moving on in the casting process, a discussion of the various metals used in club heads deserves a mention. There are many types of steel that may be

Wax molds are duplicates of the finished product.

used in casting, 431 and 17-4 being the most common. 431 is a bit softer than 17-4; a higher nickel content makes the latter harder (stronger). 431 is used exclusively in irons and putters; it is not strong enough to make thin-walled metal heads. 17-4 is used in woods, irons and putters. There are few, if any, golfers who can actually tell the differences in metal hardness in golf clubs; differences are more psychological than in actual feel. The past couple of years have seen the evolution of other metals used to make metal wood heads. Among these are 15-5 stainless, which is harder and lighter than 17-4, and maraging steel, a mixture of any number of heat treated alloys that are stronger and lighter yet. Titanium has its place in casting as well, but it must be cast in a vacuum environment due to the nature of its molecular makeup. Its hardness is very similar to 17-4 stainless; the reason many jumbo titanium woods are on the market is due to titanium's lighter weight and higher strength to weight ratio

Next comes the procedure that defines investment casting. The now-empty shells are heated to temperatures approaching 1,000 degrees Celsius. The foundry term for this is obviously enough, "heat." The shells are turned upside down and molten steel (at 1,500-1,800 degrees) is poured inside. This process somewhat resembles a satanic ritual, complete with fire, smoke, and workers donning masks and goggles! The amount of heat generated by the casting process is tremendous; it is this high heat that permits the molten metal to penetrate to all areas inside of the ceramic shells. Immediately after metal pouring (investing), the ceramic shells, now containing actual metal club heads are set aside to cool for at least 24 hours.

Once cooled, the ceramic must be removed from around the club heads. A sledge hammer is hit against the trees, effectively breaking most of the ceramic away. It doesn't take much to break away the ceramic as it has been subjected to such high heat only a day or two before. The heads are now cut away from the tree with chop saws. They are next placed in large tumbling machines in order to remove any remaining ceramic from the scorelines and engravings. If these machines should fail to remove all of the ceramic material, a worker with a dental

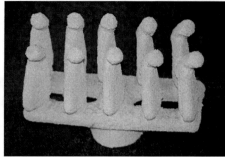

Ceramic material covers waxes prior to investment casting, creating a "tree".

pick must pick away any remaining ceramic - a decidedly slow, tedious process. The clubs are then taken to a grinding machine, where the piece that held the club onto the tree is ground from the head to match the contour of the club head. This step is the only place where the club actually touches any type of grinding or sanding machine; the fact that all of the clubs are made from one mold eliminates virtually all hand shaping of the heads, adding to product consistency and decreased labor and machine costs.

The heads are now the proper shape, but two key steps are yet to be performed. The hosels of the clubs are precision drilled utilizing a holding vise designed specifically for each head. This ensures accuracy of hosel size and depth. A club drilled on a standard drill press could have substantial hosel bore differences, effectively making the finished clubs play quite differently than designed. The final step prior to a finish being applied to the head is that of a check/adjustment of any loft or lie variances of each head as compared to the desired specification. When working with metal wood heads, the soleplate, which is cast as one piece, and the top part of the metal wood, known as the "topshell", are welded together. If a wood was cast in one piece like an iron, it would weigh too much as the inside of it would be solid steel. Minimal specification alterations are usually necessary for any cast club head due to the consistent nature of casting, but as quality control is important in making a top-notch product, all heads go through this check/adjustment step.

At this point in the casting process, we have a club head in which all specifications are correct, but the club is most likely a dark gray-blackish color. The cast iron heads will be either polished on a series of belts or will be placed in a

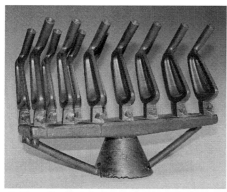

A "tree" of stainless clubheads is ready for removal and finishing.

large tumbler for finishing. It is here that woods may undergo another step that differentiates them from irons. Some woods are foam-filled. That is, they are injected with an "insulation type" foam that is designed to help the club achieve a desired weight or to help the club dampen vibration and sound. Larger heads are not foamed as this would most likely add excessive weight to the heads. Regardless of foam-filled or foamless, the wood heads will either be painted or tumbled.

Many times a urethane finish will be applied as a protective coating, adding a gloss finish to the head. If the heads are irons or woods that require a tumble finish, the heads will be placed in an open tumbler amidst various types of tumbling stones, or "media." A solution is often mixed with the media to create one certain type of tumble finish as compared with another. The amount of time in the tumbler also has an influence on the final finish as well. A head that is finished in this manner is labeled as a "tumble finished" head.

If an iron is not tumbled, it is either satin finished or high polished. Skilled technicians use a series of belts on machines similar to belt sanders to create these finishes. Depending upon the grit and speed of the belts a satin finish, which looks much like brushed aluminum, or a high polish finish, which looks shiny like chrome, is imparted to the head. Satin and high polish are not used on the top of metal wood heads as it is very difficult to use belts on the curving

surface without creating visual waves in the finish; thus satin and polish are used on the soles of metal woods only. A metal wood may receive a painted finish. Painted finishes are applied in the same manner as a finish is applied to your car. Such finishes are not used on irons due to the fact that they are not as wear resistant. Putters may be finished in any of the three manners, tumble, satin or high polish.

The iron heads now need to be masked, as typically the cavities of the heads and the faces are either painted or sandblasted. In any event, the surfaces not to be further finished are masked with strong vinyl tape and the cavities and faces receive their required finishes. All heads, be they woods or irons, are given a close cosmetic inspection; any heads not meeting requirements are rejected and will not be sold. Paintfill is the final step in the making of a head. The engravings are filled with the appropriate color paint, either though the use of a hypodermic needle filled with the paint or by applying paint with a brush and wiping away the excess with a towel. The heads are now inspected one more time for cosmetics, a spot check of head specifications is completed and the heads are packaged for shipment to the golf club manufacturer for whom they were produced.

The investment casting process is complete. From drawing to model, from master to mold, from wax to metal, from unfinished to brand new heads, the lost wax investment casting process is used to produce over 90% of the golf club heads in play today - that's several million heads each year. The entire process takes close to six months, not counting any research and development or hit testing that may take place between first head samples and final production. That means that next year's hottest new design may very well have been someone's club head design doodle on a napkin at last year's New Year's Eve party... In other words, what may be the 21st Century's hottest design may already be in progress; only time and investment casting will tell.

FORGING

In addition to casting, club heads - be they irons, putters or woods made from titanium - may be made through a forging process as well. While casting utilizes

ROCKWELL HARDNESS SCALE

MATERIAL	HARDNESS	PRIMARY USE
Aluminum	B50-60 **Softest**	Woods, Putters
Carbon Steel	B60-70	Irons, Putters
304 Stainless	B75	Irons only
Beryllium Copper	B70-80	Irons, Putters
431 Stainless	C18-25	Irons, Putters
100% Titanium	C24-28	Woods
6-4 Titanium	C32-36	Woods, Faces
17-4 Stainless	C34-38	Woods, Irons, Putters
450 Steel (Supersteel)	C36-40	Woods, Irons
15-5 Stainless	C36-44	Woods
Beta Titanium	C40+	Woods
Maraging Steel	C45-55 **Hardest**	Woods, Faces

Rockwell hardness is a common measurement used to identify metals such as those used for golf club head materials.

molten metal poured into a mold to produce club heads, forging uses a softer metal, applies heat to it and forms it, either by machine or by hand, into the final golf club shape. While casting is more recent development, having been started related to golf club manufacture in the 1970's, forging has been around since golf clubs were first produced by "blacksmith-type" hand forging prior to the 1800's. Forging is more costly than casting due to the higher cost of raw material, plating and the greater amount of hand operations required to make a finished head. A look at the forging process shows the differences and similarities between forging and casting.

Forged heads are typically softer than cast heads. Whether this hardness/softness can be detected by a player hitting a ball is debatable, but the differences is certainly measurable on a Rockwell Hardness Scale. This scale is based upon a letter-number relationship of hardness. Higher letter-number designations show harder metals. Carbon steels, such as those used in forgings, rate a Rockwell Hardness in the B65 range, while cast stainless is in the C20-C35 range. Cast titanium rates at C35, with forged titanium approximately 10 points lower. Despite these hardness differences, most players cannot tell the difference between cast and forged clubs. If two identical heads are produced, one being cast, the other being forged, even the best players in the world will have difficulty determining which is which.

The initial step in iron forging, known as rough forging, involves taking a solid tubular piece of carbon steel, 2" X 5", and heating it to 1200 degrees Celsius. The heated billets are then pressed into rough shape by huge mechanical presses exerting several tons of force on the carbon steel. The presses utilize forging dies to "stamp" the heads into shape. A specific forging die is used for each club in the set. The forging dies are actually a bit larger (approximately 20%) than the finished club head size to allow final shaping of the clubs in the later steps of forging. There are a number of forging die steps, taking the head from a rough shape into one that is much more recognizable as a finished golf club. These heads are known as raw forgings.

A billet of carbon steel (left) and a raw forged wedge head without any hosel.

These raw forgings go through a check for weight and are typically as much as 70 grams overweight at this point. This excess weight will be removed as the head takes final shape. The hosels of the heads are now lathed to ensure correct sizing and consistent diam-

Hosel boring is done at this time as well. Certain forging foundries form the hosel as one step and the head as another; the hosels in such operations are welded to the body of the head at this point. The next several steps involve many hand operations to form the final head shapes. Faces of the heads are pressed flat, stampings are pressed in, and the weights are reduced through grinding and sanding operations. The heads, as a result of these hand operations, now appear to be very much like the finished product, with the exception that no finish has yet been applied to the head.

Titanium wood heads are forged in a several step process. Typically the crown and the sole of forged titanium woods are pressed from 100%, or pure, titanium. The hosel and face are cast from stronger 6-4 or beta titanium. These 3 or 4 pieces are then welded together to create a forged titanium wood head. The cost of such a head is substantially less than for a cast titanium wood head; even though the playability and durability is virtually the same as its cast counterpart. Most titanium woods produced as the century dawns are produced as a result of forging.

Finishing of a forged head involves the use of tumblers - much like those used in casting - to eliminate any irregularities on the surface of the heads. This tumbling process can take more than a day, ensuring a smooth surface finish on the unplated heads. The heads are next polished with linen, fiber or paper belts to bring the heads close to a smooth finish. Assuming the forging is an iron or putter, chrome is now applied to the heads in a two or three part process. 10-15 microns of nickel is first applied; 5 microns of chrome is applied over the nickel. Many companies also use a layer of copper as part of the process. The chrome, nickel and /or copper is electrostatically applied to the heads in a chemical bath. This process is known as electroplating.

The heads are now finished in much the same manner as are cast clubs. They are masked and their faces and cavities (if applicable) are sandblasted or painted. Forged Ti Woods are painted much in the same manner as are stainless heads. The stampings are then paint filled as a final step. From start to finish, each forged club is stamped by a forging die at least four times, is ground over a dozen times

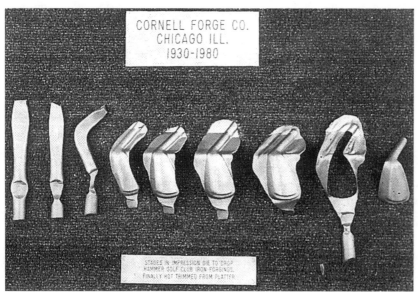

CORNELL FORGE CO.
CHICAGO ILL.
1930-1980

STAGES IN IMPRESSION DIE TO DROP
HAMMER GOLF CLUB IRON FORGINGS.
FINALLY HOT TRIMMED FROM PLATTER

From raw carbon steel to final product, the forging process includes a number of die-stamping steps under high temparature and force.   eter.

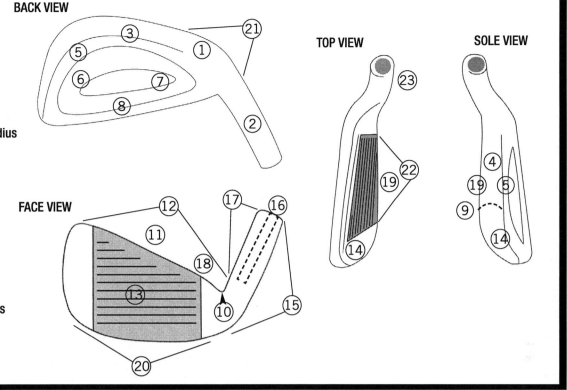

IRONHEAD ANATOMY

1. Heel
2. Hosel
3. Trailing Edge
4. Sole
5. Back Pad
6. Primary Cavity
7. Secondary Cavity
8. Backline
9. Front/Back Sole Radius
10. Crotch
11. Topline
12. Topline Profile
13. Face
14. Toe
15. Hosel Length
16. Bore
17. Bore/Depth
18. Spur
19. Leading Edge
20. Toe/heel/Sole Radius
21. Heel Radius
22. Scoreline Area
23. Neck

BACK VIEW

TOP VIEW

SOLE VIEW

FACE VIEW

by hand and is inspected for accuracy countless times. The forging process is accomplished by two-dozen workers using more than a dozen machines, dies and patterns. Forging is a labor-intensive, time-consuming process that is used to produce irons, putters and, most recently titanium woods. While forged irons comprise less than 10% of the iron market due to their higher costs, it is actually less expensive to forge titanium woods than it is to cast them. As a result, as designers create new titanium wood head offerings, look toward most of them being forged.

IRON HEAD DESIGN AND PLAYABILITY

Any discussion of irons heads should begin with definitions and descriptions of the anatomy of a typical iron head. These specific parts of a head will combine to form its playability characteristics. A thorough knowledge of terminology related to the construction and appearance of an iron will assist the fitter in communicating the properties of an iron head to his customer during a fitting or equipment discussion.

Blade: The general term given to a design that has a relatively smooth back.

A typical mid-oversize perimeter-weighted iron head.

Blade is also the generic term given to the head of an iron.

Bore: The hole into which the shaft is inserted; also the size of the hole.

Bore Depth: The distance from the top of the hosel to the bottom of the bore.

Cavity: The recess(es) in the back of an iron head.

Crotch: The part of the club where the topline and hosel meet.

Face: The striking area of the head.

Face Insert: Any material, other than the primary material of the head, that is installed into the head to be used as a

striking surface.

Heel: The lowest part of the head, closest to the ground nearest the tip of the shaft after installation.

Hosel: The part of the club into which the shaft is inserted.

Hosel Length: The measure from the top of the hosel to the bottom of the heel of the iron head.

Leading Edge: The part of the head nearest to the target when the iron is in its soled position.

Profile: The term given to the shape of the club as determined by its overall shape.

Scoreline: The lines found on the striking face of the iron head.

Sole: The entire bottom portion of the head. The sole is the part of the club that comes in contact with the ground at address or impact.

Sole Radius: The curvature of the sole as measured from heel to toe and/or from leading edge to trailing edge.

HEEL/TOE & FACE HEIGHT MEASUREMENTS

SHALLOW
43-mm

FACE HEIGHT

TRADITIONAL BLADE LENGTH
@ 75mm

OVERSIZE
46+mm

FACE HEIGHT

LONGER BLADE LENGTH
@ 80+mm

FIGURE 1

Toe: The upper area of the club head farthest from the hosel.

Topline: The uppermost part of the head running from toe to heel.

Trailing Edge: The part of the sole that is farthest from the face.

In addition to this terminology, there are a number of common iron head designs that are given specific design terminology. Each of these designs has certain features that make the head a good choice for certain types of players. Cosmetics aside, the design, size and weight distribution of an iron head combine to form its playability characteristics. Regardless of specific design type, an iron may be classed as standard size, midsize or oversize. While these terms are somewhat generic and may change from year to year related to specific dimensions, generally an iron that is labeled as standard size will have a toe to heel measurement in the 75 millimeter range, with a face height of approximately

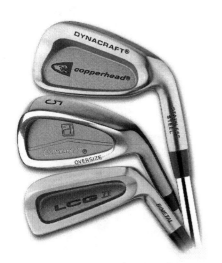

Midsize, oversize and low profile irons show head size differences in three models.

46 millimeters (see Figure 1). An oversize head will have a toe to heel measure of at least 80 millimeters and a face height in the area of 48 millimeters or more. A midsize head is loosely classified as anything in between standard and oversize. It is important to realize that what one company may label as oversize, another may stamp as midsize or vice-versa. The actual sizing versus the nomenclature unfortunately varies across the industry.

IRON HEAD TYPES

Cavity Back Irons

These heads are distinguished by their visible weight distribution. The majority of their weight is distributed around the perimeter of the head, hence the possible terminology of "perimeter weighted" when discussing these heads. Cavity backs are easily identified by their appearance of having a recessed area, or cavity, in the back of the head. Weight is effectively removed from this central area and is redistributed to the sole, heel, toe and topline areas of the club, yielding perimeter weighting. This perimeter weighting helps to maintain the club's stability on any off-center hits.

If a club is struck on-center, the resulting ball flight is generally accurate. But, if a shot is struck on the toe or on the heel, the club will have a tendency to twist as a result. Shots struck toward the toe will cause the iron to rotate to an open position, where shots struck toward the heel have the opposite effect. In either case, accuracy, distance and feel are compromised as energy is lost through the less-than-desired impact. A cavity-backed head in which the weight is distributed toward its perimeters, will have a tendency to twist less on off-center hits, most likely offering some improvement in per-

formance. This tendency to twist less is known as moment of inertia. The less the club twists, the higher its moment of inertia. Typically the larger and more perimeter weighted the iron head, the higher its moment of inertia.

Perimeter weighted irons are the most popular type of iron head in the industry. The first cavity-backed heads were designed by Karsten Solheim in the 1960's. Karsten actually took blade type clubs and milled cavities in them in an effort to raise their moments of inertia. Not long after his initial experiments, cavity backs burst on the scene, offering game improvement to a majority of golfers. Today over 90% of all irons on the market have some type of cavity back perimeter weighting. These clubs are well-suited to most average golfers, as most players do not hit the face center as often as they may like. Plus, as even Tour pros can gain some benefit from cavity-backed clubs, a high percentage of them regularly use cavity backs in competition.

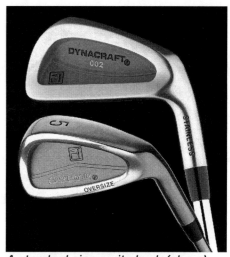

A standard size cavity back (above) and an oversize model show size variation related to irons.

Cavity backs are available in a variety of sizes, the larger heads being better matched to the less consistent golfer, the smaller heads being a better choice for those who hit the face center often. Cavity backs, which may be either cast of forged, are often said to have an "expanded sweet spot." While there is only one best place on the face to hit the ball, which is, in essence the sweet spot, it really cannot be expanded. What the term "expended sweet spot" indicates related to cavity backs is that, due to their higher moments of inertia, they will offer improved accuracy on off-center hits, especially related to toe shots. Thus players using cavity backs will see improved overall accuracy, reinforcing their perceptions of the sweet spot being larger.

If there are any possible drawbacks to cavity backs, some players will state a lack of "feel" or "feedback" from these heads. This may well be true for the best ball strikers as they seem to prefer to tell where on the face they strike the ball. Cavity backs, as they tend to not twist a great deal on slight off-center impacts, will not transmit this feel back to the player. But, as most golfers do not hit the ball on-center most of the time, they will actually benefit from this "feel" situation. Their off-center hits will not cause harsh feedback to the player, making the clubs feel better on most of their shots. Thus, cavity backs are best recommended for average golfers for sure, but are also the club of choice for better players; provided the proper shafts and other specifications are met, cavity backed irons are a wise choice for nearly all golfers.

Muscleback Irons

Muscleback irons, also known as blades or player's clubs, are easily identified by their relatively flat backs. There are no cavities in these clubs. Musclebacks may be either cast or forged, but are most commonly forged. These clubs are preferred by those players who consistently hit the ball on-center most of the time. They offer little in the way of game improvement; most of their weight is centered toward the middle of the club. Shots hit on either the heel or the toe will

produce harsh feel and noticeably shorter, less accurate shots. Less than 10% of the clubs in play today are blade style clubs for the simple reason that they do not offer the same resistance to twisting that cavity back irons offer. Plus, as they are more often than not forged, they are generally more expensive than cavity backed models. Muscleback irons, while they may be aesthetically pleasing due to their clean lines and chrome plating, should be relegated as a club of choice to better players only.

Hybrid Irons

The popularity of hybrids, also known as "iron/woods" or "wood/irons" has increased dramatically in the past two years. These designs (two-piece, cast stainless) may be hollow or may be foam-filled, but in any event, offer some type of internal cavity. Generally sized close to a #7 or #9 wood, but outfitted with an iron shaft, these hybrids offer a measure of control as compared to standard long irons. Most hybrids offer loft options as low as 13 degrees to as high as 26° or more; they are designed to replace a player's longer irons. Many hybrids feature sole rails or specialized sole weighting to help a player get the ball in the air. Their deeper CG's also add to this feature. For a player who struggles with long irons, hybrids offer the possibility of distance with no compromise in accuracy.

Low Profile Irons

Low profile irons are recognizable by their lower face height dimension, often as low as 40 millimeters. The design theory behind the shallow face heights in low profile irons is to lower the center of gravity of the head. The lower the center of gravity, the greater the potential for higher ball flight. Just about all low profile irons are cast stainless steel. Low profile irons are best suited to those players who need assistance in getting the ball airborne. Beginners and those with slower swings will be helped by the lower center of gravities of low profile irons. While such heads may look a bit strange at first due to their reduced face heights, the ease of getting the ball in the air soon surpasses any cosmetic "problems" associated with these club designs. Very few lower handicap players will use low profile irons as they do not require additional design assistance in getting the ball in the air.

Low profile irons feature face heights in the 40 millimeter range.

Sole Weighted Irons

Irons that have a high percentage of weight on or in their soles are considered to be sole weighted. Such irons are identified by a wide sole, thicker lower cavity area or by the addition of some type of weighting in the sole of the club. This weighting may be in the form of copper, brass or tungsten most often and is placed in the sole to lower the club's center of gravity. Most sole weighted irons are not oversized due to the size and or weight of their soles - if the heads were oversized, they would weigh more than is acceptable. Most sole weighted irons are cavity backed; nearly all are stainless steel, investment cast models. For a player who could benefit from a higher trajectory,

Blade style irons do not typically offer perimeter weighting and are a choice for better players.

A hybrid club, fitted with an iron shaft, is a blend of iron and wood playing characteristics.

Irons achieve lower CG's through the addition of sole weighting, such as seen with the copper sole weights on this iron.

sole weighted models present a viable option. Those models that have added weight may be a bit more costly than a standard head, but the game improvement results seem to be worth it to most players. Sole weighted irons, especially those with added material in the sole, have become popular in the last five years. Not popular among better players, these are a good choice for any player who has trouble getting the ball airborne.

Hollow Irons

Irons that are hollow offer a mix of performance features seen in both woods and irons. Hollow irons offer centers of gravity deeper in the head, making it easier for most players to get the ball airborne. Most hollow irons are oversized, adding to their perimeter-weighting and higher moments of inertia. Hollow irons are investment cast in two pieces from either 431 or 17-4 stainless steel. Such irons made their debut in the late 1980's, but did not gain widespread acceptance at first due to their bulbous shapes. Early hollow irons consisted of full sets, from long irons to the wedges. But, in the late 1990's, a resurgence in the popularity of certain hol-

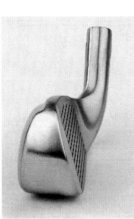

Hollow designs are identified by their bulbous shape and wide sole.

low models occurred. Many players opted for hollow designs, also called hybrids, to replace their longer irons. The added size of these hollow designs, combined with their deep centers of gravity have made them popular not only with average golfer, but with better players as well. These clubs are a good recommendation for any player who may have trouble with the long irons, particularly for those who need assistance getting the ball airborne.

Face Insert Irons

Face insert irons are identified by their having a different material as their striking face when compared to their head material. Face insert irons are cast, usually from stainless steel. The insert material will be a lighter weight material such as titanium, graphite or maraging steel. The benefit from the lighter weight insert will be to enhance the moment of inertia of the club. The insert effectively removes weight from the center of the club, redistributing it to the perimeters;

Titanium inserts take the place of heavier stainless steel in a club's face.

face insert irons generally offer more perimeter weighting than do non-insert models. Most face insert irons are at least midsize; many are oversize, further adding to their potential for game improvement.

Graphite face insert irons have seen limited popularity as a result of durability factors.

The popularity of face insert irons was at its highest in the mid-late 1990's. Despite the higher moments of inertia most insert irons offered, their higher costs may have contributed to the decreased popularity as the 21st century began. Durability was a factor as well; inserts made of graphite had the potential for breakage (and could not be replaced), while face inserts of other materials could come loose as well. Face insert irons offer some playability benefit, albeit at a higher cost. Whether such irons will be a viable alternative for head selection remains to be seen.

IRON HEAD SPECIFICATIONS AND BALL FLIGHT

Each and every iron head has certain specifications which have noticeable effects on ball flight. Some specifications have much more effect than others, but all irons have certain specifications in common. These include loft, lie, offset, sole angle, sole radius and width, weight distribution and center of gravity. While certain of the specifications will be discussed in greater detail in later sections of this

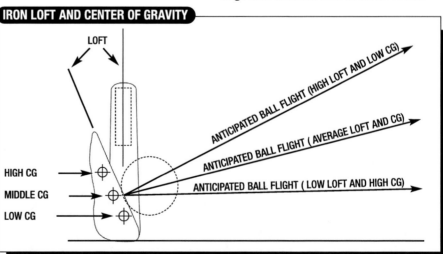

IRON LOFT AND CENTER OF GRAVITY

LOFT

ANTICIPATED BALL FLIGHT (HIGH LOFT AND LOW CG)

ANTICIPATED BALL FLIGHT (AVERAGE LOFT AND CG)

ANTICIPATED BALL FLIGHT (LOW LOFT AND HIGH CG)

HIGH CG

MIDDLE CG

LOW CG

Figure 2

LOFTS THROUGH THE YEARS		
Club	Pre 1980	1980's +
WOODS		
#1	12°	11°
#3	17°	16°
#5	23°	22°
#7	29°	28°
IRONS		
#1	17°	16°
#2	20°	18°
#3	24°	21°
#4	28°	24°
#5	32°	28°
#6	36°	32°
#7	40°	36°
#8	44°	40°
#9	48°	44°
PW	52°	48°
SW	56°	54°
UW	60°	60°

Traditional lofts are more commonly found on irons made prior to 1980; stronger lofts are found on more "modern" irons.

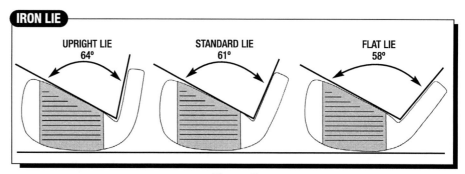

Figure 3

book, the key elements of each specification are noted as follows:

LOFT

The key determinant of ball trajectory in an iron is its loft (Figure 2, page 34). Loft is defined as the angle between the club face and the ground, with the club in playing position. The higher the loft, the higher the resulting ball flight; conversely a club with lower loft will launch the ball on a lower trajectory. Regardless of other design features of an iron, its loft will have the most significant influence on trajectory. Lofts may vary by as much as 4 degrees or more from one iron of the same number to another. That is, one type of #5 iron may have 25 degrees of loft, while another may have more than 29 degrees. The ball flight difference between these two clubs will be significant. It is very important that a club fitter be aware of the lofts of the irons that he or she will be using to fit a given player. Obviously there may be very different ball flight characteristics due to the loft of an iron.

Keep in mind that the lower the loft of an iron, the less backspin it will have. A club with a higher loft will actually cause the ball to slide up the face, creating backspin. The more loft an iron has, the longer the ball stays on the face and the greater the amount of backspin. This is one reason that a wedge will roll less upon landing than will a #9 iron. Also important to consider is the loft of the shorter irons in a set. If most of the irons have stronger than normal lofts, it will follow that wedges will do the same. For example a pitching wedge in a strong-lofted set may have 45 degree of loft, while the sand wedge typically will have 55 degrees of loft. A 10-degree gap exists between these two scoring clubs. Another wedge with 50 degrees will be a good recommendation in order to allow a player more consistent accuracy on approach shots to the green. The lofts of irons generally average between 3-5 degrees between clubs; being aware of the specific progression in a set is a key element in proper fitting.

LIE

The lie of a golf club has a decided effect on its accuracy, particularly related to mid and short irons. Lie is the angle formed between the ground and the shaft as it exits the hosel of the club (Figure 3). If the lie of a give club is matched to a player, it will cause the face plane of the club to be aligned directly at the target. But, if the lie of a club is not well matched to a player, the face plane may be angled to the left or right of the intended target, effectively causing errant shots even though the player aligned to the target and swung at the ball properly. A lie that is too flat for a player will yield shots that will be pushed from the intended target; lies too upright will cause shots to be pulled. Lie is a key determinant of ball direction related to mid and short irons.

OFFSET

Offset is defined as the distance from the leading edge of the club to the leading edge of the hosel (Figure 4). It is generally expressed in millimeters or factions of an inch. A club that has more offset will appear to have its face farther behind the hosel when viewed in playing position. Offset is typically greater on longer irons and less on shorter irons. Offset plays a role in helping to square the club face at impact. Longer irons are generally more difficult to return to impact squarely, thus more offset is desirable in these longer clubs. Many sets have what is known as progressive offset (Figure 5, page 36). This means that there is more offset in the longer irons than in the shorter irons. For

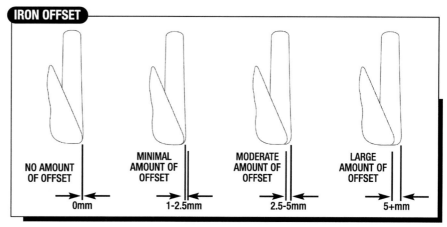

Figure 4

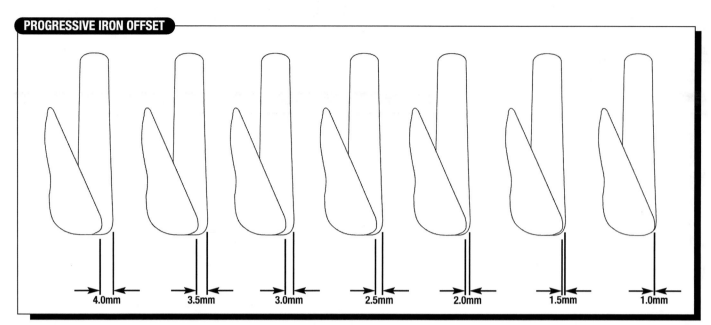

PROGRESSIVE IRON OFFSET

| 4.0mm | 3.5mm | 3.0mm | 2.5mm | 2.0mm | 1.5mm | 1.0mm |

Figure 5

example, the #3 iron may have 6 millimeters (mm) of offset, the #4 may have 5.5mm, the #5, 5.0mm, and so on.

Offset will tend to help a player who has trouble with a slice more than one

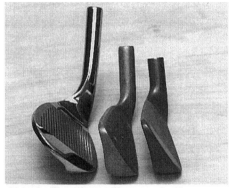

Hosel offset is easily seen in these three irons.

who has difficulty with a hook. As offset tends to position the player's hands ahead of the ball, this will help to reduce the tendency to slice as now the player's hands will also tend to be ahead of the ball at impact. This, in effect, will help to position the club face in a more square position at impact. But, if the player's hands are already ahead of the ball at impact - a situation common in better players or in players who draw the ball - an offset club may quickly turn the draw into a hook. Also, many better ball strikers seem to prefer the appearance of a club with lesser offset, further making offset clubs less desirable for this type of player.

An iron's offset may also have a minor influence on its trajectory. The more a club is offset the lower the resulting ball flight (as well as backspin) from that club. If two clubs, identical in every respect but offset, were tested, the ball flight from the one with more offset would be slightly lower and may tend to run more upon landing. But, as most offset irons are designed with thicker soles and lower centers of gravity, in all reality, offset will not play a great role in how high or low the ball flies.

SOLE ANGLE

The sole angle of an iron is defined as the relationship between the sole of the club and the ground at address or impact. A club that rests flat on the ground is said to have a neutral or flat sole angle. A club in which the leading edge is off the ground at address is said to have a "bounce" sole angle. (Bounce is defined as the distance from the leading edge of the club to the ground line in address position.) One whose trailing edge is off the ground (and whose leading edge is angled into the ground) is termed to have a "scoop" or "dig" sole. A bounce sole may be helpful on wedges or clubs used from high grass or sand, but is not often desired on other irons in the set. A club with a high degree of bounce will appear to have its leading edge off the ground when it is soled. This may cause some visual concerns for the player. Further, if the club is returned to impact in the same

position, the club's sole will tend to hit the ground first, causing the club to bounce into the ball, most likely sending it on a low trajectory, often called a "thinned" or "skulled" shot. While high degrees of bounce may not be helpful on most irons, it is desirable on wedges, particularly those used from the sand. Added bounce helps to prevent the sand club from digging in to the sand; it actually helps it move more easily through the sand.

If a club has a "dig" sole, it will have the tendency to lead to shots in which the club is stuck into the ground at impact, or just before impact. Such shots are known as "fat" shots. Should a player complain of hitting many thin or fat shots, a look at the sole angles of the clubs is in order. The majority of long and middle irons have relatively flat sole angles and little bounce. Shorter irons, such as the #9 iron may have a couple of degrees of bounce; pitching wedges may often have 4 or

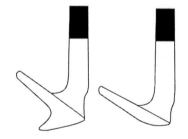

A high bounce wedge (left) has it's leading edge well off the ground; a lower bounce wedge's sole rests more squarely on the ground.

FACE PROFILES

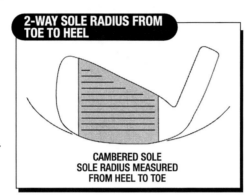

@ 43 mm | @ 48 mm | @ 40 mm

AVERAGE PROFILE | DEEPER FACE | LOW PROFILE

Figure 6

more degrees of bounce and sand wedges may have well over a dozen degrees of bounce. Generally a club with a wider sole will tend to have more bounce than will a thin-soled iron. Also, more clubs will be on the market with bounce types of soles than dig types of soles; bounce soles do have some advantages in certain conditions; there are no playability advantages to a dig sole regardless of conditions.

SOLE RADIUS

An iron's sole radius is the curvature of its sole, either from heel to toe or from leading edge to trailing edge or both. A club's sole curvature will influence the manner in which it cuts through grass as it is swung. A club with more sole radius (a more curved sole) will tend to have less drag, especially in high grass. This could be an advantage for a player who plays in thicker, heavier grasses, commonly called "Bermuda" grasses. Another possible advantage of a radiused soled iron is that it will help some players to properly sole the club on sidehill lies as the sole will tend to conform more with the angle of the hill as compared to a flatter soled model. The majority of irons available today have some degree of sole radius, both from front to back and from heel to toe. This is known as "four-way

2-WAY SOLE RADIUS FROM LEADING EDGE TO TRAILING EDGE

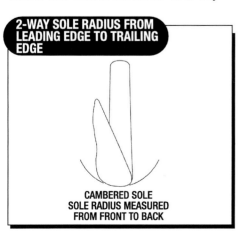

CAMBERED SOLE
SOLE RADIUS MEASURED
FROM FRONT TO BACK

2-WAY SOLE RADIUS FROM TOE TO HEEL

CAMBERED SOLE
SOLE RADIUS MEASURED
FROM HEEL TO TOE

sole radius." As an iron's sole becomes wider, it will almost certainly have this four-way radius; if it did not, a dig sole angle will result.

Clubs with flatter soles are best used from tightly mown fairways that have finer grasses. Such grasses are often given the name "bent grasses". It also seems that many better players will prefer a sole that is flatter from a cosmetics perspective. The direct effect of sole radius on trajectory, distance or accuracy is debatable. But, the radius of an iron's sole may assist certain players from specific types of lies, making sole radius a component of iron head selection that should not be overlooked during a fitting.

WEIGHT DISTRIBUTION AND CENTER OF GRAVITY

The weight distribution in an iron head will have some effect on the resulting ball trajectory from that iron. The lower the weight in an iron head, the higher the resulting ball flight. In order for a ball to become airborne, the center of gravity must be below the equator of the ball at impact. As more weight is moved lower in the head, the center of gravity becomes lower, making the trajectory higher. Locating the center of gravity of an iron may be done through a visual examination of the head. Irons with wide soles or those with more mass toward the bottom of the cavity will tend

to have lower CG's. Weights installed in the soles of the clubs are put in place to help lower a club's center of gravity as well. As a club's profile is reduced, it's CG is lowered also. Simple observation can often indicate whether the center of gravity of an iron is low or not.

Higher center of gravity irons are identified by their higher profiles as well as by a possibly steeper topline (Figure 6). Here again, by observing where most of the mass of the head is located, high CG irons can be identified. Balancing a club head on a pin punch may more accurately determine both the vertical center of gravity (as just discussed) as well as the horizontal CG. Horizontal CG involves measurement of the center of gravity from heel to toe. There are two schools of thought related to the length of an iron's blade and its center of gravity. One concept states that moving the center of gravity toward the heel of the club will tend to cause the club to rotate less on

By balancing an iron head on a punch, its center of gravity can be determined.

off-center hits, leading to straighter shots. The other idea states that as a blade is made longer, the CG moves more away from the hosel. As most players contact the club toward its toe, a longer blade length may help to balance the club by effectively adding more mass behind where the player is most likely to hit the ball. Typically either of these concepts is best related to a player who slices the ball. By testing both types of clubs, a heel weighted iron and a longer blade iron - it can be determined which offers the best performance for any given player.

GROOVE TYPE

Irons may have any number of face markings - lines, dots or milling, among others. The effect each of these play on ball flight is minimal. In the mid-1980's, a controversy arose between Ping and the USGA related to grooves. Many thought the controversy centered around the new square grooves in Ping's Eye 2 irons. In reality, the problem involved the distance between the grooves and not the groove type itself. Ever since though, grooves have become a topic related to irons and particularly to wedges. Grooves typically may be either "V"-shaped or "U"-shaped (also called "box" or "square".) Many players believe that square grooves will impart more spin on the ball then will

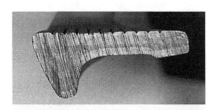

The two types of grooves found in iron heads. "V" grooves are shown above; "U" grooves are below.

"V" grooves. The USGA did extensive tests and agreed that under certain moist conditions, square grooves may impart more spin, but they did not feel it constituted any advantage to a player. A player may notice that square grooves may create a slightly higher and shorter ball flight due to the added spin - again this may or may not be perceived by the player to be advantage, but it something to be aware of when fitting irons to a player. Related to irons, groove type plays a small role in ball flight.

COSMETICS

Cosmetics plays a large part in a player's perception of his or her clubs. If the player likes the way a club looks at address, the chances for success with that club are improved. It is always a wise choice for the fitter to consider the individual likes and dislikes of a given player prior to making a final club head recom-

mendation. If the player doesn't like the looks of a club, all too often the performance will suffer as result. In most cases, cosmetics will not directly influence playability, but will be a considerable factor in player preference. Cosmetics include, among other things, the topline of the club. A club's topline is the part of the club that is seen at impact. It can be thick (4 millimeters or more) or as thin as 2 millimeters. It may be flat or it may be "rolled", radiused from front to back, back to front or both (see Figure 7). The radius and width of the topline play a role in player preference, but not directly in iron performance.

The size of the head is an obvious cosmetic feature of an iron. The effect of head size on playability has been previously discussed, but keep in mind certain players prefer a more compact head size

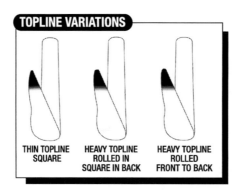

TOPLINE VARIATIONS

THIN TOPLINE SQUARE | HEAVY TOPLINE ROLLED IN SQUARE IN BACK | HEAVY TOPLINE ROLLED FRONT TO BACK

Figure 7

as compared to oversize. As a general rule, golfers who are inconsistent benefit most from larger heads; consistent players tend to favor smaller models. The top of the hosel is another cosmetic factor in head selection, albeit a minor one. Hosels may be flat and be fitted with a ferrule or may be rounded or barrel-shaped. Neither the round nor barrel shaped hosels will be fitted with a ferrule. Hosel type, along with ferrule use and/or type, is strictly a cosmetic feature and has no effect whatsoever on the playability of the iron.

Scoreline configuration is another cosmetic feature of all iron heads. Most iron heads will simply have scorelines on the face that are parallel to the ground at address. There are irons that have a specific alignment mark, such as a ball-shaped scoring area in the center of the face. Other irons may have lines running vertically along the scoring lines to help "frame" the ball at address. Some clubs

Head size and shape are obvious cosmetic features of iron heads.

may have a combination of dots and lines on the face. Any and all of these face configurations are cosmetic only and have no effect on playability. Head finish is also a cosmetic feature to consider. Irons are typically either tumble, satin or high polished in finish. Tumble finishes are non-reflective in appearance and are the most durable iron finish. Satin finishes are a non-glare, brushed looking finish, while a high polish or chrome plated finish is shiny. Again, finish has no effect on playability, but on the appearance of the club only.

Bore through irons eliminate mass in the lower heel area, supposedly adding to player feel.

IRON DEMO CLUBS

Demo clubs for irons should include at least one example of each design feature previously discussed. That is, the demo section should offer a standard, mid and oversize model related to head size; there should be a high center of gravity iron and a low profile one; a long blade length and shorter blade iron are good

The scoreline area of irons is typically sandblasted.

options as are offset and non-offset choices; a flat soled and radiused sole iron are recommended; a wide and thin sole model; a blade and muscleback selection and perhaps a face insert model should be included as well. In addition, a selection of the latest models will keep the demo selection up to date. A hybrid club with an iron shaft deserves inclusion. All of the demo irons should be fitted with lightweight steel shafts in regular flex at a standard length along with a standard sized grip. Keep in mind that not all models will be available in left hand. It is wise to have a separate selection of demos for lefties and have this selection clearly marked. While left handed players realize they will not have as many choices as right handers, specifically identifying their options creates a positive fitting situation. The same philosophy applies to lady golfers. While most clubs can be fitted to a lady's' specifications, having a model or two especially designed for ladies will result in a better experience for the lady player.

SUGGESTED IRON HEAD DEMO CLUBS
Standard size iron
Midsize iron
Oversize iron
Low profile iron
Blade iron
Hybrid iron
Wide sole iron
Flat & radius sole irons
Bi-metal club with sole weighting
Face insert club (optional)
Any current (popular) irons

FITTING IRON HEADS

To determine proper iron fit, whether indoors or out, allow the player to hit a number of iron choices. Things such as cosmetics and feel will play a role only the player can determine. Consider the design features of the heads being tested.

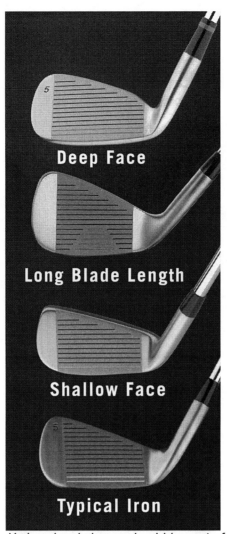

Deep Face

Long Blade Length

Shallow Face

Typical Iron

Various head shapes should be part of a complete demo club program.

That is, do not offer a 20+ handicap player a blade style head. Just the same, do not offer a single digit handicapper a low profile, sole weighted model. Consider what effect design features such as loft, offset, etc. have on ball flight and make recommendations from that point. There really is no good substitute for having the player hit test irons. Simply looking at photos in a catalog will not provide a true picture of what the club looks like at address or feels like at impact. Even having sample heads to look at will not tell anything about the feel of a club. While it is better than a catalog photo, it can provide no feedback about how it looks at address or feels at impact.

Common sense applies when fitting irons. If a player hits the ball too high, look to a lower lofted or a higher center of gravity model. If the player needs help getting the ball in the air, look to lower profiles, wider soles or higher lofts. For

slicers, look to more offset heads or heads with CG's closer to the heel. For the best players, perhaps look to blade irons; for beginners, look to oversize models with much perimeter weighting. For players who play a hilly course or play mostly Bermuda grass layouts, consider radiused soles. For players who struggle with long irons, consider some type of hybrid club. Knowing what design types are likely to produce what type of ball flights, the fitter can easily recommend irons that will best match a player's swing and will often lead to game-improvement.

WOOD HEAD DESIGN AND PLAYABILITY

Our discussion of wood heads begins with a study of the anatomy and definition of the parts of a wood head. Nearly 100% of the wood clubs on the market today are actually made of metal - either titanium or stainless steel in most cases. Wooden woods, which until the 1970's comprised 100% of the market, now make up less than 1% of all new wood sales in the world.

Back: The part of the wood farthest from the face; the curving rear of the wood head

Backweight: A metallic attachment on the back part of certain woods. The weight is a material heavier than the metal in the wood itself and is typically made from brass or copper.

Bulge: The horizontal curvature of the face of a wood, as measured in inches of radius, from heel to toe.

Crown: The top part of a wood head; the part of the top of the club viewed at address.

Face Insert: A feature of certain woods in which a material other than is used in the body of the wood is used as the striking face. Possible wood face insert materials are titanium (in stainless steel woods) and maraging steel.

Face Progression: The distance from the leading edge of the face of a wood to the centerline of the hosel

WOODHEAD ANATOMY

1. Neck
2. Crotch
3. Crown
4. Topline
5. Toe
6. Heel
7. Horizontal Bulge
8. Vertical Roll
9. Leading Edge
10. Sole
11. Trailing Edge
12. Hosel
13. Back
14. Weight Port
15. Sole Radius
16. Face Progression
17. Face

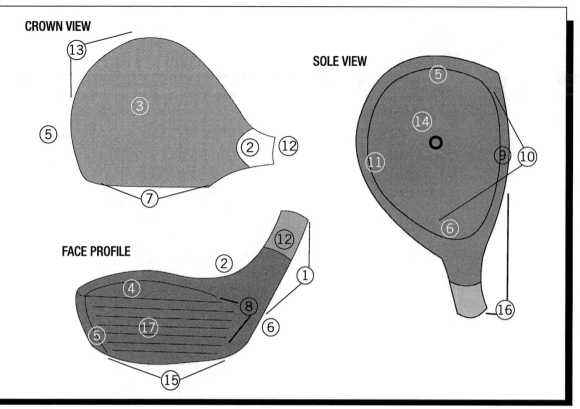

CROWN VIEW

SOLE VIEW

FACE PROFILE

Heel: The part of the metal wood closest to the shaft bore; the portion of the club where the sole joins the hosel area.

Hosel: The place of shaft attachment to the wood head. The part of the head into which the shaft is inserted.

Leading Edge: The lowest part of the wood's striking face that is closest to the target when the wood is in normal playing position.

Offset: The measurement from the leading edge of a wood to the leading edge of the hosel. Most woods are actually "onset" as even woods labeled as "offset" have their leading edges forward of the hosel.

Roll: The vertical curvature of a wood face from top to sole, as measured in inches of radius.

Sole: The lower portion (i.e., bottom) of a wood. The sole is the part of the wood that rests on the ground at address.

Sole Radius: The curvature of the sole of a wood from heel to toe or from leading edge to trailing edge, or both.

Toe: The part of a wood farthest from the hosel.

Topline: The place on a wood head where the face meets the crown.

Trailing Edge: The part of a wood head farthest from the target when the club is placed in the address position.

Weight Port: A feature of certain woods that allows the addition of weight into an enclosed cavity in the head.

Further to these terms, there exist a number of common terms given to metal wood design characteristics. Each design

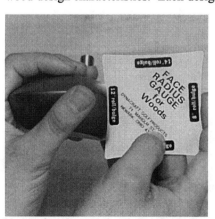

Measuring face roll using a radius gauge.

characteristic will allow the wood to be suited to a specific type of player. A driver may be as small as 150 cubic centimeters in volume or as large as 400cc's; each volume has certain playability benefits. A wood may have a shallow face or a deep face, influencing ball flight. The club may be composed of one metal or several, it may have a railed sole or it may be a hybrid of a wood and an iron. Woods may have face inserts or their faces may actually be designed to flex at impact, creating a "trampoline effect." A look at these features, along with their potential impact on playability follows.

Bi-Metal Woods

During the past 5-10 years, many woods have been constructed of two (or more) metals. The design concept behind bi-metal heads involves some type of weight distribution factor(s). In most cases, a heavier material is placed in the sole of the wood to change (lower) its center of gravity. These materials are typically tungsten, brass or copper. The weight may be recessed into the sole or may be located in sole rails. The trend related to bi-metals is quite common in fairway clubs. A club could also be considered to be bi-metal if it had a metallic face insert. Face insert clubs will be discussed later.

Deep & Shallow Faced Woods

The depth of a wood's face is measured from the groundline to the topline. Face depth will vary related to drivers from approximately 40 millimeters to 55 millimeters of more. The deeper a club's face, the higher its center of gravity.

Copper sole weights lower the center of gravity in this bi-metal driver.

Deeper faced clubs (44mm or more) will tend to launch the ball lower than will those with shallower faces, assuming all other specifications of the clubs are identical. Deep face clubs might be a good choice for a player who has a tendency to hit the ball with a very descending blow, often actually hitting the ball on the crown of the club; the sheer size of the face will help to alleviate this problem. On the other hand, shallow faced clubs are better suited to players needing assistance in getting the ball airborne. Clubs with face depths in the low 40 millimeter range are known as either shallow face clubs or low profile clubs.

Deeper faced clubs, as they tend to hit the ball on a lower trajectory, will result in shots that roll a great deal when they hit the ground. The shots from a deep faced club may carry as far, but added roll will effectively yield more distance. Deep faced clubs might be a good selection if a player plays only courses that are not very well-watered as added roll will equate to more distance. But, if the player's "home" course is lush, featur-

ing softer fairways, the lower flight from a deep faced driver may actually rob the player of distance due to its potentially reduced carry. Such courses may be better suited to a shallower faced driver that can carry the ball longer. Since the ball will not run very far under such conditions, the added carry will result in longer drives. In any event, keep in mind that, while face depth will have some effect on ball trajectory, loft is the primary determinant of how high a ball will carry.

When it comes to fairway woods, deeper faces may not be the best choices for most players. As fairway woods are hit from a variety of conditions, including from the rough, the increased face height of deeper faced clubs may tend to cause them not to travel through the grass consistently. In effect, the larger surface area of deeper faces allows heavy grass to twist them or to slow them down, equaling a loss distance and accuracy. The deeper faced club has a higher center of gravity which makes getting the ball airborne more difficult from certain lies.

Face Insert Woods

As discussed related to bi-metal woods, face inserts in woods tend to allow weight to be distributed to the perimeters of the club head. Any perimeter weighting will help to stabilize the club on off-center hits. Face inserts will definitely provide a club with a different feel, but will most often not provide any added distance on shots hit on-center. If, though, the face insert material flexes somewhat at impact, the potential for

added distance may exist. On less than perfect impacts, face inserts may allow longer and straighter shots due to the higher moment of inertia such inserts provide to the club's design.

In many cases, the different materials are utilized in the faces of woods in order to create a lighter or stronger impact area. For example, early in face insert technology, graphite was utilized as a face material for woods. Graphite is lighter than stainless steel; the idea was that a lighter weight face area would allow a higher percentage of weight to be positioned toward the wood's perimeter to create a higher moment of inertia. While this concept may sound as if it would be effective, there were two drawbacks leading to graphite's demise as a viable insert material. One, graphite was not strong enough

Woods with graphite face inserts have gone out of favor in the past few years, primarily due to durability factors.

to create an insert with no steel backing, limiting its viable use as a material to redistribute weight. Secondly, the durability of graphite face inserts was not as good as expected; the inserts cracked and

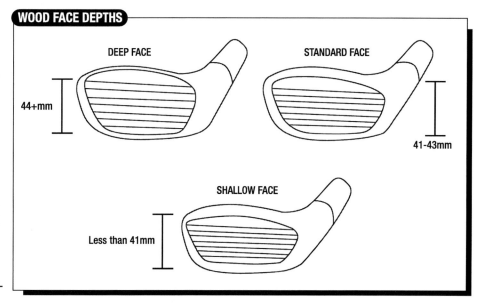

WOOD FACE DEPTHS

DEEP FACE

44+mm

STANDARD FACE

41-43mm

SHALLOW FACE

Less than 41mm

chipped at a much higher rate than expected and in most cases, could not be repaired.

Enter titanium as an insert material for woods. Titanium is stronger and lighter than stainless steel, making it a good insert material. It is also more durable than graphite, further enhancing its potential as an insert material. But, as prices for titanium wood heads have decreased, the costs for stainless heads with titanium inserts are nearly the same price. Thus, titanium insert woods are not as common as they once were. The next popular face insert materials are maraging metals. Maraging metals are alloys that are very strong and very light. These harder metals have been used as face inserts by a number of manufacturers in recent years. But, again, the cost of maraging-faced woods is often as much or more than full titanium wood heads, making them less desirable as a result.

What type of player could benefit from a face insert golf club? In all reality, just about all players may see some accuracy improvement as a result of the redistribution of weight that a lighter insert allows. Any time weight is moved to the perimeters of the club, its balance, especially on off-center hits improves. Just as in irons, twisting is reduced, yielding a higher moment of inertia. Depending upon the availability of face insert clubs in the future, they do offer a possible alternative for those seeking improved accuracy when hitting woods.

Flexible Face Woods

Flexible face technology has become a buzzword as the new century begins. Specifically concerning drivers, the past couple of years has seen a move to create heads with thin faces. Thinner faces maximize what is known as "rebound" or "trampoline" effect. The more a face rebounds upon impact, the more energy that may be imparted to the ball, increasing distance. The United States Golf Association has recently set standards for how much a face can rebound and still conform to the Rules of Golf. A specific test has been established. Any driver that exhibits a rebound coefficient greater than 0.830 is deemed to be non-conforming. Several companies have produced drivers that exhibit a greater rebound effect than this benchmark. As a rule of thumb, the

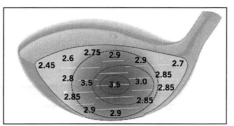

Variable Face Technology allows the thickest location of the face in the center and thinnest around the perimeter. (Numbers represent face thickness in millimeters.)

larger the driver, probably the thinner the face will be; 400 cc drivers, among the largest on the market will most likely have among the thinnest faces as well. Certain models of drivers are designed with the perimeters of their faces to be very thin, thus enhancing this rebound effect.

The question becomes a twofold issue. Initially, will flexible faces add distance to a player's shots, and if so, how much? As this technology is still very new in the year 2001, time will tell. But, if a player strikes a club with a flexible face on-center, there is added potential for increased distance. The faster the swingspeed, the more distance potential; an average increase of less than six yards seems to be typical. Now, consider that is a flexible face may indeed add distance to a shot. If the shot is not struck on-center, the potential for it to now go longer off-line may be increased as well. (Do keep in mind that most flexible face woods are large in volume, adding a measure of forgiveness to an off-center shot.) Added distance always poses a risk-reward dilemma. A second and perhaps more difficult problem to monitor - involves the Rules and flexible face drivers. Drivers that exceed the USGA's parameters cannot be played in USGA sanctioned competitions, nor may they be used in rounds that establish a player's handicap. This may be difficult for a player who just spent several hundred dollars on a brand new club to understand. It will also create a potential problem for golf professionals and tournament committees at clubs that abide by USGA Rules when it comes to any events held at the club or course. A fitter must let a player know if the driver (or other wood) he is testing does or does not conform to USGA Rules. If a model is in question, it is best to call

the manufacturer to learn if the club is conforming or not; the USGA's website (www.usga.com) also maintains an up-to-date list of non-conforming drivers.

Suffice it to say the technology that allows for thinner faces may potentially add a few yards to a player's drives, but at the possible expense of "longer misses" as well as possible Rules problems. It will be up to the player and fitter to weigh the flexible face club options when it comes time to selecting a new driver.

Trampoline Effect

The trampoline effect (also known as rebound effect) is the term given to the face performance of a club that has a flexible face. The flexible face of a club compresses upon impact with a golf ball; that same face will rebound milliseconds after impact. The more it flexes and rebounds, the more potential there is for added distance. The face acts much like a trampoline; when a ball hits it, it "gives"; immediately upon impact it send the ball off the club face at a higher velocity. For a more detailed discussion of the pros and cons of such faces, refer to the previous section.

Wood Head Size

The size of a wood head, particularly a driver, is often the first characteristic noted about the club. Head size is measured in volumetric units of cubic centimeters or cc's. To determine the volume of a head, it is immersed in a known quantity of liquid. The amount the liquid is displaced by the head is its cubic centimeter volume. Generally, the larger the volume of a head, the more forgiving it will be on off-center hits. The larger the head, the deeper the center of gravity is from the face of the club, potentially causing a marginally higher trajectory. Large size heads, however, do not often weigh more than standard sized models. There are specific weights to which most drivers are produced. Thus, as most drivers weigh in the 200-gram range, a 300cc driver and 400cc driver may both weigh exactly the same amount. The same follows for fairway woods; regardless of size or shape, most #3 woods will weigh approximately 208 grams, #5 woods, 218 grams and so on.

Larger volumes are generally seen on drivers only. As previously noted, large

Water displacement is used to determine volume (in cubic centimeters) of a wood head.

fairway woods lose a measure of their effectiveness in longer grass or hardpan lies. It is not at all uncommon for a player to use a 300+ cc driver and complement it with a #3 wood half that size. It is also commonplace to see drivers and fairways of different models in the same set. During custom fitting, the individual's set makeup can be determined and may be a various combination of certain sizes, shapes and designs of woods. The trend in fitting, regardless of ability, seems to be toward larger volume drivers. These larger volumes help even the best players hit more accurate drives. They allow players to potentially swing faster as there is not as much chance for a mishit shot thanks to the large face on a higher volume driver. Driver sizes and the type of player they may best fit are as follows.

Standard Size

A driver whose volume is between 185 and 200 cubic centimeters is classed as "standard" size. These standard size drivers generally have shallower profiles than do larger drivers. Most are cast from 17-4 stainless steel. They may have a face insert of some type. Their centers of gravity are low due to their small size, making them easier to get airborne for a given loft. They are not as forgiving as are larger drivers. Standard size drivers may be recommend as a choice for those who may benefit from help in getting the ball airborne or by those who simply prefer a smaller head shape. These players though, should be aware of the reduction in forgiveness of smaller headed drivers.

Midsize

Drivers whose volume ranges from the low 200 cc's to 250 cc's may be grouped as "midsize". These heads offer improved perimeter weighting due to their size when compared to standard sized heads. There is a wider choice of models in this category as well. Most midsize drivers will be made from stainless steel, but a few titanium heads will be found as well. Titanium allows a head to be produced at a substantially larger volume than steel as it lighter and stronger. Titanium has what is known as a "high strength to weight ratio", making it suitable for the casting or forging of 250+ cubic centimeter driver heads. The upper limit of size for a stainless steel driver is approximately 250 cc's. Anything larger will either weigh too much as stainless is a heavier material or will have walls too thin (leading to breakage) as a result of meeting the driver's weight requirement.

Related to fairway woods and their materials, nearly all fairways are cast from stainless steel. This is due to their smaller volumes as compared to drivers. Titanium is not generally used for fairways; the advantage it provides is for producing larger volume heads. As noted, larger volume fairway woods do not offer the playability benefits that a larger volume driver offers. The cost of a titanium head is far higher than a stainless one; when it comes to fairway woods, it simply does not make sense to make a high cost, smaller size titanium #3, #5 or #7

wood.

Oversize

Larger volume woods are said to be "oversize." The majority of drivers fitted within the past five years fall into this range. Drivers whose volumes are between 250 and 300 cubic centimeters are either cast or forged from titanium. There are a number of options related to specifications in the oversize driver market. Players of all levels may benefit from oversize drivers. Beginners or less experienced players will be helped with both accuracy and distance on off-center hits due to the higher moment of inertia of an oversize driver. In effect, they will have a larger hitting area. Better players and professionals are favoring oversize titanium drivers due to this forgiveness as well. These players are using oversize clubs with longer and lighter shafts. These overlength clubs may be a bit more difficult to control than shorter ones. But, the oversize head helps compensate for slightly off-center impacts by providing an element of correction. The best drives of these players are longer due to the longer shafts; their mis-hits are still playable due to less rotation of the head on heel or toe impacts.

Jumbo

Drivers whose volume exceeds 300 cc's are considered to be jumbo models. Produced mainly from forged titanium,

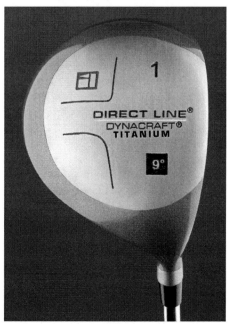

Any driver over 250cc is most commonly made from some form of titanium.

Wood head volume is the common method of identifying head size. Volumes respectively: 400cc, 325cc, 275cc, 205cc.

At 325cc's the PC3 Driver is considered to be an jumbo driver.

these clubs offer the maximum forgiveness available in a driver. Why then, aren't all players using these very large drivers? It may be a matter of personal preference. As a head exceeds 300 cc's and approaches 400cc's (or more), it simply "looks" too big for many players. Cosmetics play just as large of a role related to woods as do related to irons. Very high volume woods appear to be heavier than they actually are; many players believe they have to "heft" the large driver in order to swing it. Jumbo heads are good choices for less consistent players due to the sheer size of the hitting area, again providing the player can accept the look of the larger club. As a head this size is very much perimeter weighted, it is designed solely with straight shots in mind. Many better players who may like to "work" the ball from left to right or from right to left will not prefer larger clubs as the very high moment of inertia actually works against curving shots.

Hybrid Woods

These types of clubs are a cross between a wood and an iron; certain golfers refer to them as irons, some call them woods, but in any case, they are designed to give a measure of control as compared to long irons or traditional woods. There are hybrids outfitted with

iron shafts and made to iron lengths as previously discussed, and there are hybrids outfitted with wood shaft and made to longer lengths. Most hybrids offer loft options as low as 13 degrees to as high as 26 degree or more; they are designed to replace a player's longer irons or standard fairway woods. Most hybrids, even those assembled with wood shafts are shorter than most woods and heavier as well - this in an attempt to gain accuracy without a noticeable sacrifice in distance. The vast majority of hybrids are smaller than most typical fairway woods. Many hybrids feature sole rails or specialized sole weights to help a player get the ball in the air. For a player who struggles with long irons or standard fairway woods, hybrids offer the possibility of distance with no compromise in accuracy.

This hybrid club with a wood shaft features a shallow face and radiused sole.

Sole Design

The shape of a wood's sole, particularly a fairway wood sole, has a noticeable influence related to the playability of the club. Most fairway wood soles have some radius (Figure 8). Typically there will be more radius from heel to toe than from front to back. Heel/toe radius allows the fairway wood to rest on its sole center when positioned in a variety of lies. Radiused sole woods are substantially easier to control from sidehill lies as a result, especially when compared to flat soled fairways. There usually is not much radius from leading edge to trailing edge of a fairway wood; having a large radius would actually create bounce on the wood, making it ineffective from fairway lies.

Many fairway woods feature weight inserts of some type in the sole. These inserts may be made from tungsten, brass or copper. These weights help to lower the center of gravity of the wood, making it easier to get the ball airborne. Such clubs will certainly be a help to most average or below-average players. Many models of fairway woods, especially those intended for use from the rough, include sole rails as part of their design. These rails serve two functions. One, they help reduce drag trough high grass be reducing the surface area of the club that comes in contact with the grass. Two, they lower the center of gravity of the club as they effectively add weight lower in the head. Certain manufacturers place weight in the rails, further assisting their effectiveness from difficult rough conditions. Rail soled woods are generally available in a number of loft choices, making them smart selections for players who often find themselves in the rough or for those looking for a specific type of club to

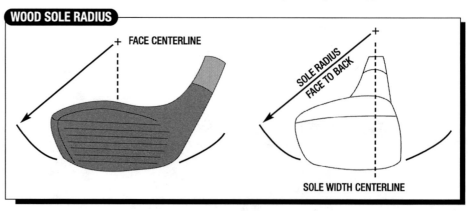

FIGURE 8

Many clubs include rails and/or weights in the sole to alter the center of gravity of the head.

match the rough conditions of the course they play most often.

Fairway wood choices have increased substantially during the past decade. As recently as the 1980's, the highest lofted fairway woods available were #7 woods. Most players carried only a driver, #3 and #5 wood, all with relatively standard lofts (10, 15 and 20 degrees respectively.) Currently, most fairway woods are offered by loft number than by club number. That is, a club may be offered as a 13 or 15-degree model as compared to calling that same club a #3 wood. More and more players are opting for higher-lofted fairway woods in place of longer irons. The wide variety of loft options combined with the lower profiles and lower CG's of these high-lofted woods, makes them eas-

ier for most players to hit consistently, especially from the rough. Many players now carry the equivalent of #9, #11 or even #13 woods, but labeled with the specific loft rather than with a 9, 11 or 13.

WOOD HEAD SPECIFICATIONS AND BALL FLIGHT

LOFT

The loft of a wood is measured in much the same manner as the loft of an iron. There is a slight difference though. The faces of all woods exhibit a degree of radius from the sole to the topline. This radius is known as face roll. In order to accurately measure the loft of a wood, it must be measured in the center of the face. Drivers are available in lofts ranging from less than 6 degrees to more than 13 degrees. Loft is the key determinant of ball trajectory when hitting a driver, or any wood for that matter. Lower lofted woods will tend to fly on a lower trajectory and not carry as far, but roll more than will higher lofted models. In general, it is a good fitting recommendation to match a

WOOD & IRON LOFT EQUIVALENTS			
Wood	**Loft**	**Iron**	**Loft**
#3	15°	#1	15°
#4	18°	#2	18°
#5	21°	#3	21°
#6	23.5°	#4	24°
#7	26°	#5	28°
#8	29°	#5	28°
#9	31°	#6	32°
#11	35°	#7	36°
#13	39°	#8	40°
#15	43°	#9	44°

NOTE: All lofts based upon modern standards.

player with the lowest loft that he or she can hit accurately with the greatest distance. For most faster swinging players, these will be lower lofts of 10 degrees or less. Slower swinging players, seniors and most women will benefit most from the added carry that a higher lofted wood will provide. Further, the higher the loft of any wood, the more backspin it will produce and, in the process, this backspin

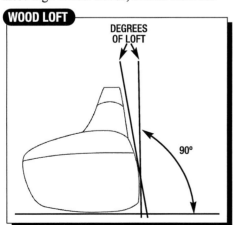

A wood's loft is measured as the angle of the face as compared to a 90° ground line.

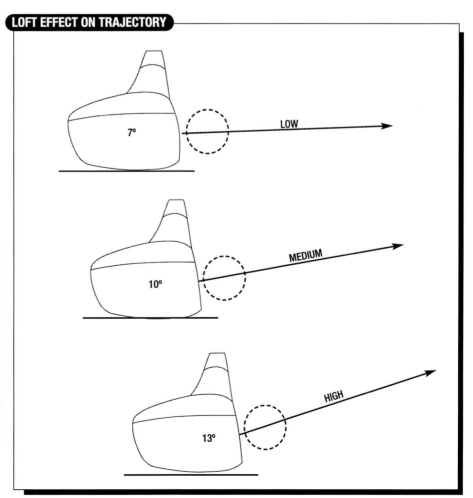

will help to negate any reduce sidespin that may be produced by an inside-out or outside-in swing path.

LIE

The lie of a wood is measured in the same manner as the lie if an iron (Figure 9). But, any effects of an improper lie club are not nearly as great with a wood as with an iron. Woods have less loft than most irons; this is especially true of drivers and longer fairway woods. As loft decreases, any effects on ball flight from the club's lie decreases. Further, most woods have radiused soles allowing them to be positioned at address and impact effectively with a lie that matches a player's stature and swing. As a result, lie does not have a great effect on ball flight related to woods. The trend from manufacturers though is toward more upright lies in woods. This is in an attempt to position the wood's face plane slightly to the left, helping to eliminate a slice. While this may not necessarily be a "good" feature for players who hook the ball, again, the actual amount these upright lies have on a wood's ball direction is not nearly so much as when fitting for the lie of a middle or short iron.

FACE ANGLE

Face angle is the position of the wood's face in relation to the target. If the face is position directly at the target, the club is said to be square. A face that aims to the left of target (for a right handed player), is labeled as closed or hooked, while a face angle aligning to the right

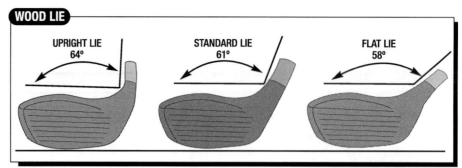

Figure 9

(for the right hander) is most often termed to be "open." A fitter needs to be aware of the face angle of the club being tested as well as the ball flight characteristics of the player using the club. A player who slices or pushes most shots may be helped with a closed face angle, while one who tends to hook or pull may be best assisted with an open face club. Obviously if a player hits the ball straight and desires to continue to do so, a square face club is a wise choice. Do keep in mind that these examples are correct only if the player makes an on-plane swing. Variations from an on-plane swing are discussed in detail in Chapter 5, "Face Angle."

OFFSET

The distance from the leading edge of the wood to the leading edge of the wood's hosel is defined as the offset. Offset serves the same purpose in woods as it does in irons; it is present to help a player keep his hands ahead of the ball, thus helping to square the face at impact. Players who tend to slice the ball will benefit most from offset clubs. Those players who hit the ball relatively straight or who hook the ball will not generally fare well with offset clubs as they may accentuate those hooks or may turn straight shots into pulls. When measuring the offset of a wood, one finds that there really is not an "offset" wood, only woods with less onset. A wood's hosel does not allow it to become a truly offset club; the hosel simply will not be strong enough to create actual offset. An offset wood is easily identifiable by its curved hosel despite the fact that the curvature will not actually bring the leading edge behind the hosel as occurs in an offset iron. Offset woods are available in drivers and fairway woods and make viable fitting options for slicers and those who struggle from the tee.

An oversize offset driver is a good driver for a golfer who slices.

The more a wood is offset, the higher its trajectory due to the CG being farther behind the shaft. While the amount of offset on a wood has only a small effect on how high it will hit the ball, one reason that most offset drivers do not have very low lofts is that added backspin from the higher lofts help counteract sidespin that causes slices. One more specification to be aware of when fitting offset drivers, most of them have faces that are a degree or two closed. This adds to their ability to counteract a slice. Offset drivers may, at first, look a bit unusual to a player at address, but if the player, especially if he or she fits into the 90% of players who slice the ball, is able to accept the look of an offset driver, look for an improvement in the player's accuracy.

Measuring face angle accurately using a specifications gauge.

EFFECTS OF BULGE

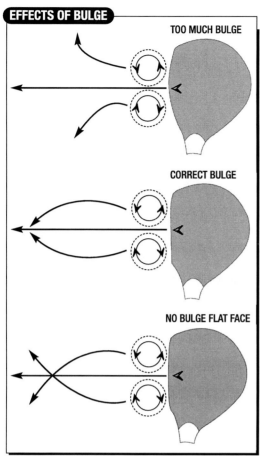

TOO MUCH BULGE

CORRECT BULGE

NO BULGE FLAT FACE

FACE BULGE

Face bulge is the measure, in inches of radius, from the heel to the toe of a wood. The bulge of a wood plays a role in the accuracy of a shot hit towards the heel or toe of the club. While the bulge of a club is engineered into the design of the head, many times a player may inquire as to why the club face is not "flat." Most oversize drivers have face bulge measures of 14-16" of radius, smaller drivers may have more radius - perhaps as low as 10". Larger clubs require less bulge than do smaller ones as they possess higher moments of inertia (less twisting) on off center hits.

If a square-faced club is delivered to the ball on-plane, the ball will tend to go straight if it is hit in the center of the face. But, if the ball is hit on the heel or the toe, the tendency is for the ball to travel somewhat off-line. Face bulge is in place to reduce the amount of directional error on heel or toe impacts. Looking at the following examples for a right handed golfer, we find that a ball struck on the toe begins its flight to the right of the target. This is due to two factors. Initially, the toe impact cause the face to turn to an

open position. Further, the face bulge will send the ball to the right as well since the curvature is toward the right. But, because of this curvature, counterclockwise spin is imparted to the ball. As the ball begins its flight to the right of the intended target, the spin will tend to help it curve back to the left, potentially turning a very poor shot to the right to one that may actually be in the fairway.

The opposite scenario applies to shots struck on the heel side of face center. The ball will begin its flight to the left of target, but due to the clockwise spin imparted by the face's bulge, will tend to curve back toward its intended target. The larger the head, the less it will twist on either heel or toe impacts; thus such heads require less bulge to cause the ball to turn toward its intended target. Smaller heads twist more on heel or toe shots as they do not have as much perimeter weighting. As a result, more bulge is required to help the ball spin back in the direction of its intended target.

Think of the head and ball as gears. As the ball (Gear #1) strikes the head (Gear #2) on the toe, Gear #2 turns to the right. As Gear #2 turns to the right, Gear #1 turns to the left. Gear #2 is aligned to the right, starting the ball flight in that direction, but since Gear #1 is turning to the left, it will spin to the left. The ball (Gear #1) will have begun its flight to the target's right, but will spin back toward the target as it flies through the air. This analogy, used as an advertising tool by a number of manufacturers, is best known as the "gear effect."

FACE ROLL

Face roll is defined as the curvature of the club's face from the sole of the club to the topline. It is also measured in inches of radius. Drivers commonly have 12-14" of roll, while fairways have 14" or more. (The higher the inches of radius measure, the flatter the face. A 14" radius is not as curved as an 8" radius.) The effect of face roll on the actual playability of a wood is negligible. Roll allows a player to see more of the face of a club, instilling confidence at address. If a wood's face were perfectly flat from top to sole, the player would see very little of

GEAR EFFECT

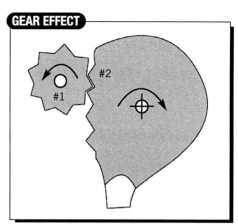

#1   #2

A golf ball hit on the heel or toe will tend to spin back toward the target as a result of gear effect.

it, especially on a lower lofted driver. The more of a face that a player is able to see at address, the more confidence he will have with it and the easier it will be to hit. It may be argued that as face roll adds a degree or two of loft to the very top of the club face, shots struck there will fly higher than desired or that shots struck low on the face will fly lower due

Face roll is a factor in the appearance of a wood; it does not have a great effect on playability.

to the effect of face roll. As shots struck high enough or low enough on the face to cause roll to have an influence on their trajectory are already very poor shots, any effect roll causes is considered to be negligible. Related to fitting, face roll is a specification that is engineered into the club head; there is no need for a fitter to be overly concerned with it.

WEIGHT DISTRIBUTION/CENTER OF GRAVITY

Weight distribution in a wood may be a bit more difficult to determine than it is related to an iron. This is due to the fact that the inside of most metal woods is hollow. Inside the head, the walls may be engineered to be thicker or thinner in certain places. Until a head is cut open - not a viable option in most cases - the actual weight distribution may not be able to be determined. That said, a wood that has a greater percentage of its weight toward the sole will tend to hit the ball higher. One whose weight is higher in the head will raise the center of gravity and assist in hitting the ball lower. Weight more prominent at the heel of the club will tend to reduce twisting on off-center hits, helping to reduce slices. A wood that has a greater percentage of its weight toward the toe (these heads would be very unusual) will help keep the face open through impact, promoting pushes or slices. Fortunately, if there is a unique internal weight distribution inside a wood head, most manufacturers will publish this fact. As the weight distribution is designed to influence playability in some manner, it is only logical that the head manufacturer will make that information readily available to the public.

There are instances in which the weight distribution of a wood is obvious. These instances include the previously discussed sole rails or weights added in the sole. If a wood has a backweight, this is equally as obvious. There have been woods produced that have added weight to the hosel. This weight can be seen in the form of a protrusion or "wing" that is part of the hosel design. Weight added in

300+cc

225cc

Low Profile

Clubs with taller face heights (top) will have higher CG's than with low profile clubs.

this manner is designed to keep the wood head square at impact. It does this by reducing the club's tendency to rotate about its center of gravity, resulting in less open face. A look at the face height of the club is also a tipoff to its center of gravity. The deeper the face, the higher the CG. A wood that is broad from front to back will have a deeper CG than will one that is narrow from front to back, aiding a player in getting the ball airborne. It is a key fact related to weight distribution and center of gravity in a wood: Loft and face angle will have much greater effects on ball trajectory and direction than will changes in the head's center of gravity. CG changes are secondary to loft and face angle as determinants of ball flight.

COSMETICS

While cosmetics are not necessarily a specification of woods, they do deserve a mention since, if a player likes the way a club looks, there is a higher chance of success with that club. Cosmetics, in addition to club specifications, combine to form a player's perception of a given club. A few cosmetic factors that play a part in wood selection include head size and face angle, paint finish and alignment marks. Head size and face angle are the first cosmetic that a player notices when he or she picks up a club. Size and face angle, although previously discussed, form key elements of cosmetics to be aware of when fitting woods. The color of a club head may be very important to some players. Matching a color preference to a playability requirement can sometimes be very difficult as manufacturers only make heads one color. Color should be a minor factor in head selection for most players. Also a minor factor is whether the wood head has an alignment dot, line or arrow on its crown. While these marks are personal preference to most players, they do serve as an aid in positioning the face properly at address. Thus, perhaps selecting heads with alignment marks are a wise choice for all players, but especially related to less-skilled players as they may have more difficulty in aligning a club when compared to an experienced golfer.

An alignment arrow on a wood's crown helps most players position the club accurately at address.

WOOD DEMO CLUBS

In order to best determine the head preference as well as to best match playability to a golfer, a player should have various designs of heads to hit test. All of these test clubs should be fitted with the same shafts and grips so the player is only testing the head's playability and not the shaft's or grips. Lightweight steel or graphite shafts in regular flex and standard length fitted with a popular standard size grip should be basis for the head demo selection. (A exception may be made when choosing demos of 300+cc titanium drivers; such models may be best fit with ultralight graphite shafts as these shafts are the shafts most likely to be matched to these heads.) Heads utilized include a standard size, midsize and oversize model. A jumbo model is also a wise selection. A deep face and shallow face driver will help a player to determine which he or she hits more consistently. As head design popularity comes and goes, be certain to update the demo selection as necessary. Sample fairway woods, at least one each with rails, sole weight added, a flat sole and a radius sole will help a player who is shopping for fairway woods to determine which club best fits his or her needs. A hybrid club fitted with a wood shaft should be part of the demo selection as well.

Keep in mind that not all woods will be available in left hand. It is wise to have a separate selection of demos for lefties and have this selection clearly marked. While left handed players realize they will not have as many choices as right handers, specifically identifying their options creates a positive fitting situation. The same philosophy applies to lady golfers. While most clubs can be fitted to a lady's' specifications, having a model or two especially designed for ladies will result in a better fitting experience for the lady player.

FITTING WOOD HEADS

Whether indoors or out, allow the player to hit a number of both driver and fairway wood choices. Things such as the cosmetic look and feel will play a role only the player can determine. Consider the design features of the heads being tested. That is, do not offer a player who slices an open-faced driver; choose something closed instead. Consider what effect design features such as loft, face angle, offset, etc. have on ball flight and make recommendations from that point. There really is no good substitute for having the player hits test various models and designs of woods. Simply looking at catalog photos will most often not provide an accurate representation of what the wood looks like at address or feels like at impact. Even having sample wood heads to look at will not tell anything about the feel of the wood. While it is better than a catalog photo, it unfortunately can provide no feedback about how the wood actually looks at address or feels at impact.

Just as when fitting irons, common sense applies when fitting woods. If a player hits the ball too high, look to a lower lofted or higher center of gravity model. If the player needs help getting the ball in the air, look to lower profiles, sole weighting or rails or higher lofts. For those who slice, look to closed face angles, more offset heads or heads with centers of gravity closer to the heel. For just about all players oversize heads will provide some margin of potential game improvement. For players who struggle with typical fairway woods or long irons, consider some type of hybrid club. Knowing what design types are likely to produce what type of ball flights, the fitter can easily recommend drivers and fairway woods that will best match a player's swing and playing ability.

HEAD DESIGN
Summary: Do's and Don'ts of Clubhead Fitting

DO	DON'T
DO: Match the head design characteristics with the player's ability.	**DON'T:** Force a player to select a head(s) with which he or she is not comfortable.
DO: Take into consideration a player's cosmetic preferences.	**DON'T:** Always choose the latest trends when selecting heads; many times heads that have been popular over time make good choices.
DO: Look to shot pattern and match heads that will help create a consistent and desireable pattern.	**DON'T:** Provide demo clubs that only the fitter likes; offer a variety of head demos.
DO: Consider a player's commitment to practice and improvement when recommending heads.	**DON'T:** Fail to consider all specifcations of a given head when offering it to a player.
DO: Offer the player a reasonable number of head choices during fitting.	**DON'T:** Neglect cost factors of heads during a fitting.
DO: Try to match cost considerations of clubheads and set make-up with player budget.	**DON'T:** Stop a player from hitting a demo club that you are fairly certain he will not hit well; allow him to prove this to himself.
DO: Make certain the selected head specs (loft, lie, face angle, etc.) are properly suited to the player.	**DON'T:** Fail to answer any player questions accurately and completely.
DO: Be aware of possible loft, lie and/or face angle limitations when altering certain heads.	**DON'T:** Overlook putters during any fitting.
DO: Realize that head design specifications may be influenced by other fitting parameters such as shaft flex, length, etc.	**DON'T:** Forget wedges as a vital part of a complete fitting.
	DON'T: Eliminate your own continuing education related not only to head design, but to other specifications as well.

Chapter 3
Length

The length of a golf club, be it a wood, an iron or a putter, has a directly quantifiable effect on distance and accuracy. Having the correct - or incorrect - length of club has an impact on just about every other golf club specification. Finding the proper club length should be the first specification determined during the actual static or dynamic fitting situation. The correct length club for a particular player will provide immediate and noticeable improvement in ball flight and feel. Conversely, if a player is playing with a club that is the incorrect length for him or her, just about all facets of their game may suffer as a result. The length of a club is one of the most obvious specifications when it comes to how a player addresses the ball. Correct posture and stance at address lead to improved play; conversely poor posture as a result of a mis-fit club length may be impossible to overcome during a typical swing.

It would seem that a definition of length would be fairly straight-forward. Surprisingly though, the definition may not be as obvious as one may think. Playing length is defined as the measure from the groundline to the end of the grip cap with the club placed in normal address position. This measure can be made with a 48" ruler, or can be made more accurately with a device called a True-Measure. The True-Measure ensures that the club will not move during measuring, eliminating a common problem when using the 48" ruler. There are a number of companies that measure club length without the grip on the club. The grip and its grip cap will add @1/8" to the club length; as the grip is part of the club, it should be included in the overall measurement of length. There are also manufacturers who measure length from a point at where the heel of the club transitions into the sole. This is very difficult to measure consistently and may lead to a different measure than the True-Measure will yield. It is important to realize that not every club that is claimed to be 38" long may, in reality, measure as such.

What is important when measuring length is to be consistent at all times. Always use the same method of measuring for any and all clubs. In the cases of a player asking you to make a club to a certain "standard" length, always inquire as to what that length actually is - try to get a club for measurement purposes to ensure what the player is talking about and what is reality are truly the same. Standards will vary from manufacturer to manufacturer. From a custom fitting point of view, there is no actual "standard". Standards are used for reference only and are not intended to be any type of concrete basis for custom fitting. Additionally, so-called standards have changed over the years. What used to be considered a standard length is now actually as much as 1" shorter than today's modern measures.

Why the changes in standards? Looking back to the days before 1970,

INDUSTRY AVERAGE GOLF CLUB LENGTHS THROUGH THE YEARS

	1950's & 60's	1970's & 80's	1990's	2000's
WOODS				
Driver	43"	43.5"	44"	45"
3	42"	42"	43"	44"
5	41"	41"	42"	43"
7	N/A	40.5"	41"	42"
9	N/A	N/A	40.5"	41.5"

N/A indicates clubs were not produced during those years

Notes:
1) During 1990-2000's, Titanium drivers were 45" and beyond depending upon manufacturer."
2) Graphite shafted clubs in the 1970's and 1980's were at least ½" longer than the above standards.
3) Ladies lengths are typically 1" less than the above standards.

IRONS			
1	39"	39.5"	40"
2	38.5"	39"	39.5"
3	38"	38.5"	39"
4	37.5"	38"	38.5"
5	37"	37.5"	38"
6	36.5"	37"	37.5"
7	36"	36.5"	37"
8	35.5"	36"	36.5"
9	35"	35.5"	36"
PW	35"	35.5"	35.5"
SW	35"	35.5"	35.5"
UW	N/A	35"	35.5"
AW	N/A	N/A	35.5"

N/A indicates clubs were not produced during those years

Notes:
1) Irons with graphite shafts produced in the 1970's through the present are at least 1/2" longer than the above standards.
2) Ladies lengths are typically 1" less than the above standards."

If a club is either too long or too short for a player, his posture will be compromised leading to inconsistency.

just about all irons were forged blades and all woods were blocks of persimmon or laminated maple. Karsten Solheim produced some very limited sets of cavity backed irons (which were actually made by drilling forged blade clubheads) in the 1960's, but these were certainly the exception. Most clubs before 1970 were all about the same length and were similar in design. The traditional clubs featured #5 irons at an average of 37" in length. (Ladies #5 irons were most likely to be 36" long.) The majority of drivers were 43" long for male golfers and 42" for

Karsten Solheim's early cavity back design was ahead of its time in the mid-1970's.

females. Most of the shafts in these clubs were heavier steels shafts, further limiting their length. Enter the 1970's and a growth in technology. Investment casting began to gain a foothold; irons were cavity-backed instead of blades and light-weight shafts came onto the scene courtesy of True Temper's TT Lite. Woods were not made of wood any longer, but were cast from 17-4 stainless steel. These innovations allowed clubs to be made longer. Cavity backed cast clubs and metal woods permitted more forgiveness on less than perfect shots and the lighter shafts reduced the weight of the clubs. The majority of manufacturers increased the "standard" length of their clubs 1/2" as a result. In theory anyway, these longer, lighter clubs could be hit a bit farther without any compromise in accuracy - a decided advantage for most players. This newer, longer standard is known as the "Modern Standard."

Graphite shafts entered the golfing scene to a degree in the late 1970's as

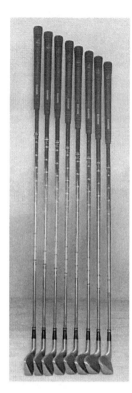

A set of irons following a typical length progression.

well. As these shaftss were noticeably lighter than even the lightest steel shafts by as much as 40 grams, club manufacturers faced a dilemma of how to manage the lighter weight of these shafts when actually assembling clubs. Some companies cast heads to heavier weights to accommodate the lighter weight shafts, but most do not. The vast majority of club producing companies simply made the graphite-shafted clubs longer in order to maintain the balance and weight of the clubs. Most graphite-shafted clubs are 1" longer in drivers and fairways and ½" longer in irons with steel shafts. For example a standard steel-shafted #5-iron is 38" long and a standard graphite-shafted #5-iron is 38.5" in length.

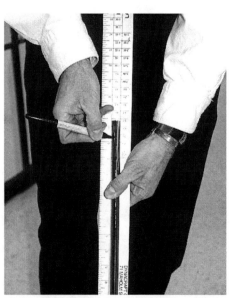

One method by which to mark a shaft for proper club length cutting.

A True Measure very accurately measures the length of irons or woods.

Standard lengths for woods are 43 1/2-44" for males; with ladies' clubs, 1" less.

As casting technology improved into the 1980's, 90's and into the 21st century, head designs became larger and more forgiving. Plus, the amount of lighter weight steels shafts expanded several-fold. Club manufacturers correspondingly made club lengths longer as a combined result of the greater forgiveness of the larger heads and the lighter weights of the newer varieties of steel shafts. These steel lengths are typically 1/2" longer than the Modern Standards mentioned previously, making #5 irons 38" long for men and 37" long for ladies. This means that when compared to most clubs produced in the early 1970's and previous, today's steel-shafted irons are a full 1" longer. Still, graphite-shafted irons are generally assembled at 1" longer lengths than are their steel counterparts. Today's modern woods, with their very high-volume titanium heads designed for maximum forgiveness are often shafted as long as 45+" and called "standard" by some manufacturers. It is unusual to find any drivers for men to be shorter than 44" with a steel shaft or shorter than 45" with graphite. Driver lengths for lady players are again generally 1" shorter as a standard.

Do be aware that these standard lengths are used by foundries when determining the specific weights to use when casting heads. As standards have become longer, many club head weights have become lighter. This is in order to create an average swingweight and total weight for the clubs. Combining the length with the head weight, a resulting men's swingweight of between C9 and D3 usually results; this would be considered to be in the norms of most steel shafted clubs. (Normal ladies' swingweights are considered to be C3-C7.) While this is not always the case, it is important when fitting a player for length that you are aware of what components will be used. If longer clubs are required, perhaps lighter heads will be needed and vice-versa. As club length has an effect on club weight, it is important to know the weight of all of the components of the club - head, shaft and grip - as suggestions are being made during the fitting.

The length of a club is one of the very first things a player is aware of when holding that club. If a club is much too long, it will most likely feel very unwieldy to the player. It is important in fitting a player to a given length, that the player's hand position is comfortable on the club and that he or she does not have to alter hand position or posture to adapt to the new club. Think about 50+" drivers used by some. For most players, even finding a comfortable address position is a challenge. Even in the case of a club that is only an inch or so too long for a player will cause changes in the address position, often creating ball flight problems as a result. A club that is too long will most often yield one of two address problems. Initially, it may cause the player to stand more upright than normal, thus altering his perception of the ball and usually leading to inconsistency. The player tries to get the center of the sole on the ground and as a result, his hand (and probably his entire body) are in a higher position than is comfortable. Comfort and posture are key elements involved in length fitting. If the club does not feel good to the player, it may not allow him to perform to his fullest potential.

A second thing a club too long may cause is a lie angle (Lie angle is simply defined as the position of the shaft as it leaves the clubhead relative to the groundline.) problem. If the player holds a longer club while keeping his hands in their normal position, the toe of the club will most likely be more off the ground than desired. With the 50+" type of club, the toe may be off the ground nearly a full inch! The initial impression of a club that is too long for a player - even if it is only slightly too long - is not a positive one. On the other hand, a club that is too short will pose potential problems as well. Such a club will create a posture for the player that is too "bent over" or is in a non-athletic position, reducing his swing arc substantially. The player may feel constrained since he will not be able to take what he perceives to be as long of a swing as normal. Lie is affected when a club is too short also. The toe of the club will often rest on the ground if the club is too short, creating a poor visual image as well as causing accuracy problems as we will more further discuss in Chapter 4, "Lie".

EFFECT ON BALL FLIGHT

A club's length is perhaps the most important fitting parameter related to shot distance, accuracy, consistency and feel. It is also perhaps the most important club specification related to the actual posture and address position of the player. Determining the correct length of club for a particular player early in the fitting will make all subsequent fitting steps more concise. A best-fit length situation will have the golfer matched with the longest shaft that he or she is able to hit consistently. Anything less than achieving this goal may compromise the performance of the clubs once the player reaches the course.

DISTANCE

The distance a shot flies is directly related to how long the club is assembled. A longer club, provided the weight of it is not too great, will yield a longer swing arc. The longer the arc, the more potential for increased swingspeed, and thus increased distance. As a club's standard length has increased through the years, manufacturers' claims of more distance are easy to substantiate through the use of robot-testing. But, even so, if the longer length clubs do not fit a player's posture, all to often this longer distance simply means longer shots into the woods.

How much longer will a change in length affect a shot? There is no definite numerical calculation for this, but for each increase of 1/2" in length, swingspeed only increases 1-2 miles per hour. At best, this produces a shot that goes less than 2 1/2 yards longer than with the shorter club. But, if distance is a

Long clubs require a change in address posture for best results.

result of a longer-length club, why aren't all players best-fit with these types of clubs? There are at least two key reasons. First, as a club is made longer, it becomes heavier unless some material in the club is changed. Heavier clubs may be too difficult to swing for some players, especially slower-swinging ladies and seniors. The result will be fatigue during play, as well as a loss of consistency and accuracy on the course. A second factor is directly related to this consistency. If a player can swing a longer club in the same manner as a shorter one, distance will increase. But, as a longer club is more often difficult to return to impact in the same manner, if the ball is not contacted in the center of the face, distance may actually suffer. Thus, there are definitely times when the longest length club will not produce the longest length shots.

Another misleading factor related to longer-shafted clubs involves the testing methods used by manufacturers to substantiate their distance claims. Most often clubs are tested on some type of robotic machine, often at artificially high club-head speeds. These machines swing the club the same way every time and hit the ball in the face center every time. If a player is able to swing in the same manner every time as does the robotic machine, longer clubs will produce more distance with no sacrifice in accuracy. But, as any experienced clubfitter or logical golfer knows, no golfer - even the best in the world - can come close to matching the repeatability of a robot.

The quest for distance is often the key motivating factor in the purchase of new clubs. Very seldom will a person enter a clubmaker's shop and directly ask for clubs that hit the ball straighter. In almost every instance, the golfer will be seeking that magical club that will add 10-20 yards to their drives. It is those very same golfers, who, if they could hit the ball straighter - and possibly even shorter - would score better due to improved accuracy and not improved distance. The fitter must be acutely aware of this "distance mentality" and not let it overly influence club length selection. In fairness to most golfer's they really don't know how far they hit an average drive. They watch television and hear announcers relaying details of a player's 300+ yard drive. With 270 yards or more

becoming a low-average PGA Tour drive, it's no wonder most golfers may develop an inflated concept of just how far they hit a drive. Plus there are no yardage markers leading from the tee to the fairway for which a player can accurately judge driving distance. In most cases, finding the proper length club for a player will improve distance as a result of getting the club face more accurately positioned at impact - a goal of any fitting session.

ACCURACY

How often a ball finishes where it is intended to finish is accuracy. Improved accuracy is a result of fitting the proper club length to a player. The proper length club can be returned to impact more consistently than can a length that is too long or too short. The drawbacks of a player having shaft that is too long have already been documented. It may seem logical that a shaft that is shorter will be more accurate. This is true to a degree, but there will be a point of diminishing returns. The shorter shaft may be able to be swung more consistently, but once the shaft becomes too short for the player, accuracy will actually suffer due to the poor posture and resulting swing plane the too-short shaft creates. Further, once a shaft becomes noticeably too short for a player, distance will be lost because the person will no longer be in an aggressive position - he will, in effect, be in a non-athletic posture. There is a fine line at times between distance and accuracy. Most players are seeking distance, but most will actually be helped more with an improvement in accuracy.

Let's say a player currently hits an average drive 235 yards. The number of fairways hit per round is 4. This player hits the ball plenty long enough, but the second shots most often come from the rough - or worse. If this golfer could be matched with a shaft that is more accurate, but only allows him or her to hit the ball 215 yards, the player's game would actually improve. If that shorter drive lands in the fairway 8 times or more instead of 4 times in any given round, the odds of the second shots being on or near the green will increase substantially. The number of penalty strokes as a result of errant drives will quickly diminish. The fact that the player is more accurate will

instill confidence; they he may actually perceive that he is hitting the ball longer simply because it is easier to find in the fairway than it is in the rough or trees.

CONSISTENCY

Consistency is a result of the proper combination of distance and accuracy. Ask any player whose scores are suffering and they will tell you one of their main problems is "consistency." By matching the longest club that a player can return to impact in the proper position, consistency will be increased, and at the same time distance and accuracy will improve as well. Being able to return the club squarely to impact often produces confidence knowing the shot will go approximately where it was intended. Improperly fitted club length makes consistent swings very difficult. If clubs are too long, the shot that is hit on-center (probably by accident) will travel much longer than was intended. Most other shots will be off line and shorter than anticipated. In cases of clubs being too short, shots may be marginally consistent, but distance will suffer. If the player tries to compensate by swinging harder, consistency suffers, creating a "catch-22" in which the player's game suffers to some degree. Thus distance and accuracy combine to yield consistency.

FEEL

Feel is an intangible characteristic resulting from impact between golf ball and clubface. When a ball is struck solidly on the face center, the shaft transmits positive feel feedback to the golfer. Shots hit on the heel or toe or high or low on the clubface will produce less positive feedback and may actually "sting" the player's hands. What does club length have to do with feel? In all actuality, a great deal. If the length of the club is such that it allows a player to swing the club consistently and make consistent impacts, it will feel acceptable to the player. One of the few ways a player might be able to communicate a dismay or satisfaction with a given club length is through his or her comments of how the club feels. A player complaining of a non-solid feel at impact is probably communicating indirectly that the ball is not being struck on-center. Selecting a club of the proper length very often cures the negative feel of which the player speaks.

LENGTH AND OTHER FITTING PARAMETERS

Club length is perhaps the one specification that, when changed, will have some effect on more specifications than any other. As the length of a clubs increases or decreases, just about all other measurable specifications are affected in some manner. This is the key reason for establishing the proper playing length early in the fitting session. Once length is established correctly, any change in a future-fitted specification will not have nearly the widespread effect on other specs as will length.

SWINGWEIGHT

Any change in the length of a club will alter swingweight. A change in length by 1/2" as compared to the "standard" length of a given club will alter swingweight approximately 3 points. This change is regardless of whether the shaft is steel, graphite, titanium or some other composite material. A length increase will raise the swingweight; any shortening of the club will reduce it. This @3 point per 1/2" applies to woods, irons and putters. For example, if you are using the Modern Standard #5 iron length of 37 1/2", and the player requires a 38" length, expect the swingweight of that club to be 3 points higher. From a fitting point of view, if a player is fitted to either a longer or shorter shaft, certain factors must be taken in to account.

If a club is going to be made longer, the swingweight will increase. In order to reduce this increase, the fitter may look to a lighter head and/or lighter shaft. If a lighter head can be found that fits the player's needs, that head should be in the neighborhood of 6 grams lighter to account for a 1/2" addition of length. Should a head not be able to be located, a change in shaft weight (again provided

The weight of the club head is a key factor in a club's final swingweight.

that it fits the player) is a possibility. Approximately each 9 grams in shaft weight will result in a 1-swingweight point change in a club. Thus if the swingweight needs to be reduced by three points, a 27-gram lighter shaft may do the trick. Keep in mind the shaft's balance point will have an effect on its weight distribution, thus making the 9-gram change an approximation. A heavier grip is a possibility as well. Each @5 grams of grip weight will induce a 1-swingweight point change. Thus, if a 15-gram heavier grip can be located that will meet the player's needs, this is also an acceptable method by which to obtain the desired swingweight. (The chart on page 56 shows the relationship between compoenent weight and swingweight.)

If the club is to be made shorter, say by 1/2", weight must be added to the club. An addition of 6 grams to the head will maintain the same swingweight a compared to before the length decrease. This 6 grams may be found in the raw weight of a head or may be garnered by the addition of some type of lead or tungsten weight in the hosel of the club. Shaft weight may be increased also. But, if the player is being fitted with steel shafts, it is unlikely there will be a big enough difference in shaft weight from the heaviest to lightest steel shaft to achieve a three-swingweight addition that requires the approximate 27 grams. A lighter grip will yield a swingweight increase. Here again, approximately 5 grams will be 1 swingweight. To obtain the desired 3-swingweight increase when shortening a club 1/2", it will take a grip 15 grams lighter to do the job.

In the cases of very overlength clubs or very short clubs, swingweight ceases to become an issue. For example, if a 50" driver is being fitted, it is for certain that the swingweight will be in the "E" or "F" range at least. This is simply a function of the length of the shaft. There is little that can be done to change this, regardless of how light of a shaft or head that you may find. An opposite situation occurs when fitting clubs 2" underlength of more. Such clubs will swingweight in the low "C" or even into the "B" range due to their shorter lengths. Again, you will not be able to add enough weight to bring these club up to the norm of C8-D1. The same thing happens when working on

junior clubs. Very often it will be impossible to achieve normal swingweights due to the shorter nature of the clubs. In the cases of very short junior clubs, they may not even be heavy enough to cause the swingweight scale to register at all.

TOTAL WEIGHT

Also known as static weight or overall weight, the total weight of the club is just that - what the club weighs as expressed in ounces or grams. Much like swingweight, any change in club length will have a direct effect on total weight. Longer clubs weigh more than do shorter ones, assuming they are constructed from similar components. It may be necessary when fitting longer length clubs to find lighter components; the opposite would be true when fitting shorter clubs. Typically very long clubs are best fit with graphite shafts in order to maintain an approximate desired weight. Shorter than normal clubs may be best constructed with steel shafts to do the same thing. Since head weights do not vary a great deal from manufacturer to manufacturer, shaft weight becomes the overriding component when addressing club length.

One key factor when considering the total weight of the club is the player's ability to swing the club consistently and accurately. If a club is too heavy, the player may alter his or her swing due the feeling that they must swing harder to get the club back to the ball at impact. Such situations often lead to the player swinging outside-in or "over the top", and in doing so reducing consistency. In cases where the club may be too light, the player loses all feel of the club. He or she may feel like there is not enough weight in the club to maintain any swing balance. This phenomenon is known as "Zorro Golf", where the player seems to have the feeling that the club is waving about during the swing in much the same manner as Zorro's sword. While it may be argued that a lighter club can be swung faster or that a heavier club will put more mass behind the ball at impact, either leading to added distance, there is a point of diminishing returns. It is up to the fitter to match the weight of the club to the player's feel and consistency for a best fit situation.

LIE

Lie is defined as the angle between the shaft and the groundline with the club in playing position. As a club is made longer, it effectively becomes more upright. Each 1/2" addition of length yields a club that is effectively 1 degree more upright. The opposite is true when going to shorter shafts; a 1/2" reduction in length yields a lie that is effectively 1 degree flatter. Think of it in this manner...if you hold a long shafted driver as you would a shorter driver, what happens to the toe of the club? It is well off the ground; it is effectively more upright. In order for it to sole properly, it would have to be bent to a flatter lie. The opposite is true as well. Hold a short junior club in with your normal stance and address position. The toe of the club is on the ground, but the heel is raised. It is effectively flatter. It must be bent more upright to sole correctly. Thus longer clubs usually need to be bent flatter and shorter clubs usually need to be bent more upright to maintain consistency through the set. (There will be instances during custom fitting in which perhaps a longer length and more upright lie is required. That is why it is "custom" fitting - what fits each individual is what should be recommended.) The length versus lie factor is precisely why wedges, which are the shortest clubs in the set, have the most upright lies at @64 degrees and drivers, which are the longest clubs in the set have lies much flatter, in the 56 degree range.

SHAFT FLEX

As a club is made longer, it typically becomes firmer in flex. This is because the butt end of the shaft is the stiffest portion of the shaft. But, as a club becomes longer, its swingweight increases as well, thus offsetting the added stiffness of the shaft. In situations of making shorter than standard clubs, they will most likely be stiffer than anticipated, unless heavier, graphite-weighted types of heads are being used. This is due to the butt of the shaft being cut to make them shorter (The stiffest part of the shaft is removed.) and the swingweight of the club being less since it is shorter. When fitting a player with shorter shafts, it is a wise idea to look for a softer flex shaft to counteract this stiffness increase. If club length causes the swingweight of the club to be

higher than typical, the shaft flex will decrease slightly. If the club length causes the swingweight to be lower than typical, the club will play stiffer. For a full explanation of length versus weight and flex, see Chapter 7.

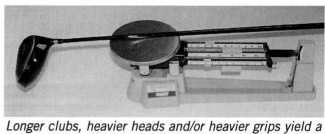

Longer clubs, heavier heads and/or heavier grips yield a higher total weight club.

The longer the shaft, the more it will tend to bow downward during the swing. A longer shaft, or one that is more flexible, will tend to bow downward as much as several degrees as a club is swing. This will have the effect of flattening the lie of the club as it reaches impact. Longer clubs will bow as much as a couple of degrees. Wedges, as they are shorter and stiffer, will tend to bow less than a degree. In any event, as length becomes longer, shafts will tend to bow downward more and will consequently effect a club's lie more as well. Shorter shafts do not exhibit this tendency to bow a large amount, making the bowing effect not so great on those clubs.

BALANCE POINT

The balance point of a club is the point at which its weight is evenly distributed relative to the head end and grip end of the club. It can easily be determined by balancing the club on a piece of angle iron or even by balancing the club on your finger. In any instance that a club is

A club with a lower balance point will feel heavier to most golfers.

made longer, its balance point will shift slightly further from the grip end of the club. Just how much depends upon factors such as shaft weight, shaft balance point, head weight and grip weight. If a club is fitted to a shorter length, the balance point of it will be moved toward the grip end of the club. Most minor alterations in length will not cause noticeable changes in balance point that a player will actually be able to feel.

EXTRA LONG DRIVERS

Here again, "long driver" is not a true head specification, but such clubs certainly do deserve discussion. Certain players may request a specific driver to be used for long drive competitions, scrambles, etc. In all reality, they would be much better simply using their "normal" driver, but, as a fitter, these "long driver" requests should be addressed. Driving the ball like John Daly, Tiger Woods or National Long Drive Champion Jason Zubak is a dream for just about everyone. While not many "mortal" golfers can honestly claim a great many 300-yard drives - except perhaps on downhill holes with the wind behind them - it is a goal that may not be totally out of reach provided a specialized driver is utilized. Does that mean a golfer can buy a 300-yard drive? Not exactly. But, with the right overlength driver, players may be surprised at the looks on their playing partners' faces when they drive the green on that short par 4!

A number of short stature players use long drivers. These drivers actually create arc that the shorter player's body cannot. Senior PGA Pro Gary Player, at 5'3" tall used an overlength "long" driver throughout his career. Many lady players will also benefit from longer drivers.

A typical driver is somewhere in the neighborhood of 44-45" inches long in today's golfing world. It has a lightweight graphite shaft and most likely has an oversize titanium head. The companies who make these clubs tout them as being able to produce long and straight drives. But, in all reality, none of these "stock" clubs will suddenly qualify you for the next Remax Long Drive Championship. So, how then, can a new driver add some distance to your long game and make you the envy of your playing competitors?

First, let's look at physics. A longer driver will, as a result of its length, create

COMPONENT WEIGHTING VERSUS SWINGWEIGHTING

Clubhead Head	Weight	Raw Shaft Weight	Grip Weight	Club Length	Swingweight
1 wood	198 grams	125 grams[1]	52 grams[2]	43"	D-0
3 wood	208 grams	125 grams	52 grams	42"	D-0
4 wood	213 grams	125 grams	52 grams	41.5"	D-0
5 wood	218 grams	125 grams	52 grams	41"	D-0
7 wood	228 grams	125 grams	52 grams	40"	D-0
1 iron	230 grams	125 grams[1]	52 grams	39.5"	D-0
2 iron	237 grams	125 grams	52 grams	39"	D-0
3 iron	244 grams	125 grams	52 grams	38.5"	D-0
4 iron	251 grams	125 grams	52 grams	38"	D-0
5 iron	258 grams	125 grams	52 grams	37.5"	D-0
6 iron	265 grams	125 grams	52 grams	37"	D-0
7 iron	272 grams	125 grams	52 grams	36.5"	D-0
8 iron	279 grams	125 grams	52 grams	36"	D-0
9 iron	286 grams	125 grams	52 grams	35.5"	D-0
PW[3]	293 grams	125 grams	52 grams	35.5"	D-3
SW[3]	300 grams	125 grams	52 grams	35.5"	D-6

NOTES

[1] Raw shaft weight is based on a 45" UDWS (parallel tip Dynamic S-flex for woods) and a 39" UDIS (parallel tip Dynamic S-flex for irons). Under proper trimming and installation, each shaft's weight will drop slightly through the set.

[2] Grip weight is based on an average weight of an M58 Men's Victory or Tour Wrap rubber grip.

[3] Traditionally, the pitching wedge and sand wedge are designed to be played at slightly to significantly higher swingweights that the #1-9 irons.

By computing swingweight prior to assembly, it allows accurate construction of custom fit clubs.

a longer swing arc, potentially adding to clubhead speed. This speed can, if the club is delivered squarely at impact, add considerable distance to a drive. The amount of added driver length we are talking about here is substantial when making the finished club in the 50" or more range. This driver will likely be more difficult to "time" properly at first since the longer club will actually take a longer time to swing due to the added length. Any situation in which the clubhead is not delivered in the square position will result in severe off-line shots. (There is always a trade-off when making alterations to clubs. The longer the golf club, the more distance potential...but also the more potential for off-line shots.) For many players though, once proper timing is established, they - and any onlookers - are surprised at the gain in sheer distance as a result.

There is a catch though. The reason that everyone is not running to their local pro shops or clubmakers has to do with the number of limitations encountered when constructing these longer drivers. The vast majority of driver heads on the market today, be they OEM clubs or component clubs, weigh 200 grams, give or

Dynamic fitting for length outdoors ensures the proper conbmination of distance and accuracy.

take approximately 5 grams. What this means is that as a club's shaft is extended, the swingweight of the club will become noticeably heavier since no weight can be removed from the club head. Why, you ask, aren't lighter clubheads available? The answer is twofold: If a clubhead is made lighter, it will have to be made to a smaller volume or its walls will have to be made thinner, neither of which is acceptable. Overlength drivers need a large head to compensate for the potential of less on-center hits as compared to a standard length driver. If the other option is exercised and the walls of head are made thinner, the risk of head breakage is increased - again, an unacceptable scenario. A second reason that few, if any, drivers are much lighter than 195 grams is that there simply is not a huge demand for extra length drivers. This long driver market, while viable for some seeking the most possible tee shot distance, is a small segment of the golfing population.

Long clubs may be effective in adding distance to shorter stature players and slower swingers.

For each 1/2" a driver is made longer, its swingweight increases 3 points. So, for example, a favorite driver right now is 44" long and weighs D-1 and a player wants to experiment with a longer 50" shaft on this driver, the swingweight of the club will increase 36 points, making it G-7. The major reason that many longer drivers feel somewhat awkward is due to this weight distribution factor. The majority of the mass of the club is very far from the player's hands and the club may feel unwieldy as a result. Another consideration when looking at a 50+" driver is the lie angle of the club. As a club is made longer, its effective lie increases at a rate of 1 degree per 1/2". Checking out the 44" driver when it is made to 50", we find its effective lie angle to be 12 more degrees upright. If this driver is placed in playing position, the toe of the club will be considerably off the ground. Unfortunately, most drivers today have lie angles of at least 54 degrees, with many approaching 60 degrees - making these 50" long will certainly create some interesting optics for the golfer. Fortunately though, the driver is the lowest lofted club in the set, with the exception of the putter. As loft decreases, the effect of an incorrect lie is diminished; thus, while there is reason for concern with the lie of a 50" driver, it is not as important as if we were making a 50" wedge.

LENGTH DEMO CLUBS

The number of clubs needed to do a basic job of fitting iron length include just a few clubs. To accomplish a much better fit, the number of fitting clubs will be expanded accordingly. For basic men's length fitting, three #6 irons will be utilized. These irons will be shafted with lightweight steel shaft and some type of standard grip. The heads will all be the same type; a popular cavity back model is a good choice. The three demo clubs will be assembled to three lengths: 36.5", 37.5" and 38.5". By having a player choke down on these clubs, lengths of 36", 37" and 38" can effectively be created. A more advanced iron demo set would include demo #6 irons of all six of these lengths. Be sure to specifically label all of the demos as to what length they are and to what fitting parameter they apply. More advanced demos would include length clubs for ladies, in lengths 1" shorter than men's lengths. These would be fitted with more flexible shafts and ladies' grips. A left-hand demo section would be a recommendation also. This would match the men's RH section in number of clubs and specs.

In fitting wood lengths, the same parameters apply. Use something at 43", 44" and 45" if possible. The longer clubs may have to have graphite shafts due to weight considerations. You may also be able to use the clubs that are shaft fitting demos for length demos as a result of this weight consideration. Ladies' wood demos would be 1" shorter, with more flexible shafts; a lefty section should match the men's RH demo wood selection. The only other materials you will need for length testing is face impact tape. This tape will provide concise records of where on the face the player makes contact with the ball.

FITTING LENGTH

DYNAMIC FITTING INDOORS

Dynamic fitting of length indoors is a key element in the complete fitting scenario. Making certain that the length of a player's clubs is correct for him or her is paramount to the remainder of the fitting session being done efficiently and accurately. While changes can be made to the recommended length of a player's clubs later in the session, determining length as

a first step provides a definitive building block for all future fitting steps.

The required materials for accurate indoor lie fitting are a lie board of some type and face impact labels. Begin with the "standard" length #6 (37 1/2") with a face impact label affixed to it and have the player hit a couple of shots. Note the position of the ball impacts. Is the position consistent or does it vary greatly? (Be sure to not use any impacts that the player relayed to you as "bad" shots.) If the pattern is consistent, try going with a longer club, the 38 1/2" #6 iron. See if the impacts on the labels change at all. If they are still consistent, the longer length is probably a good fit for the player. If they are not as consistent at the longer length, try the 38" club. What you are trying to determine is what the longest length the player can hit consistently. In cases of the player not being able to hit the standard length club consistently, go to a shorter club. If the player complains about the feel of the club, it is probably due to the impact locations being inconsistent. Feel will improve noticeably when face impacts become consistent. Do be aware that as a club is made shorter, the player may lose distance; always try to maximize distance potential with the longest, most accurate club possible. It is equally important to test both wood lengths and iron lengths; just because a player is able to hit longer than standard irons accurately, he may require standard length woods or vice-versa. Be sure to rely on player feedback as to which length club is most comfortable in the cases of when different lengths are selected. The player is the only one who knows how the clubs feel - feedback from the player is a key element of a good fit.

Save the impact labels in order to show the player a clear visualization of how length had an effect on impact position. This will solidify in the player's mind that he is on the right track toward properly fitted clubs and will correspondingly increase his trust in your ability. There will be times that the impacts are consistent, but may not be in the face center. While not an ideal situation, it does show an element of consistency. If the player hits consistently toward the toe of the club, perhaps a head design with more mass toward the toe will help feel and shotmaking; shots toward the heel may call for a more heel-weighted clubhead. While center impact is the goal of length fitting, consistency is a close secondary mark to achieve.

DYNAMIC FITTING OUTDOORS

Outdoor length fitting is very much like indoor fitting. The exception is that the player and fitter will be able to see the direct relationship of distance, accuracy and length. By combining the visual record of the impact labels on the face with the observed ball distance and direction, it will be easy for the fitter and player to agree on which length is best for him or her. While the longest-hitting club may be fun to watch, seeing it produce less accurate shots than a shorter club will prove it is not the best choice. Again, consistently accurate distance is the goal. By testing a number of demo clubs, this length will be quantifiably determined.

An important note related to the dynamic fitting of length: As any change in length may often cause a change in the effective lie of the club, it is recommended that length and lie be tested at the same time both indoors

Lie lables are used on the soles of irons during length fitting.

A lie label showing proper lie (left) and one showing a flatter lie is required (right).

The desired face impact position of a properly fit shaft length.

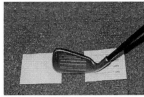

File cards under a club's sole are not an accurate way to determine lie.

and out. Impact labels will be placed on the club's sole in addition to the club face. The resulting impacts will not only determine where on the face the ball hits, but where the sole hits the ground (or lie board) as well. By combining the results from length and lie testing, an accurate picture of both specifications can be determined concurrently. Plus, fitting both specs at the same time will provide further visual reinforcement of the effect length has on lie. The lie board will provide evidence that as a longer test club is hit, the effective lie of that club becomes more upright; the marks on the sole will confirm this. In the same manner, the lie labels will confirm that as a club becomes shorter it effectively becomes flatter.

By matching lie and length at the same time, an adjustment in lie may help to position the ball impacts in the center of the face. Many times a more upright club will help move face impacts from the toe toward the face center; flatter clubs may help move heel impacts toward the center of the face. By utilizing both length and lie clubs at the same fitting juncture, the close interaction of these two specifications will be best fit in a very visual manner through the use of impact labels. For a discussion of how to properly dynamically fit lie, please refer to the next chapter.

STATIC FITTING

Static fitting related to length involves using a series of tables and charts to help provide a general idea of what the given player requires. By measuring such things as fingertip to floor, wrist to floor, or end of grip to ground, a general idea of club length can be developed. By studying things such as a player's ability, it may be determined that length can be increased for better players or perhaps even decreased for less consistent players. The concept here is that a better player will usually be more consistent and may benefit from the added distance potential of a longer shaft. Perhaps

FINGERTIP TO FLOOR FITTING	
LENGTH	#5-Iron Fitting Recommendation
24" to 25.5"	1" underlength
25.5" to 27.5"	.5" underlength
27.5" to 30"	Standard
30" to 31.5"	.5" overlength
31.5" to 33.5"	1" overlength

the best example of this is LPGA professional Emilee Klein who is only 5'4" tall, but who uses a 50" driver. Unfortunately when using static fitting there is no way to verify this since you will not actually see the player hit balls. An opposite example is PGA Tour player Jay Williamson, who, at 5'8" tall uses only a 40" driver. If either Jay or Emilee were fitted to a driver statically, neither would likely be fitted with the driver they are currently using successfully. There are a variety of charts from numerous manufacturers related to static fitting. Be certain when using such charts that you know what standard lengths these companies are referring to - remember what is standard for one company may not be standard - or even be measured the same - as from another company.

The fitter may be able to use existing clubs as a basis for fitting. The player may be able to describe if the clubs are

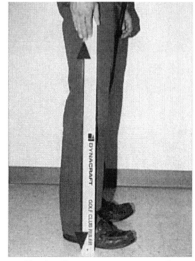

Fingertip to floor measurements are a part of static fitting.

too long, too short or just right. While the player may not know the specific lengths, they can be accurately measured provide the fitter has the opportunity to see the clubs. Once the clubs are measured, then any length adjustments based upon player comments can be made.

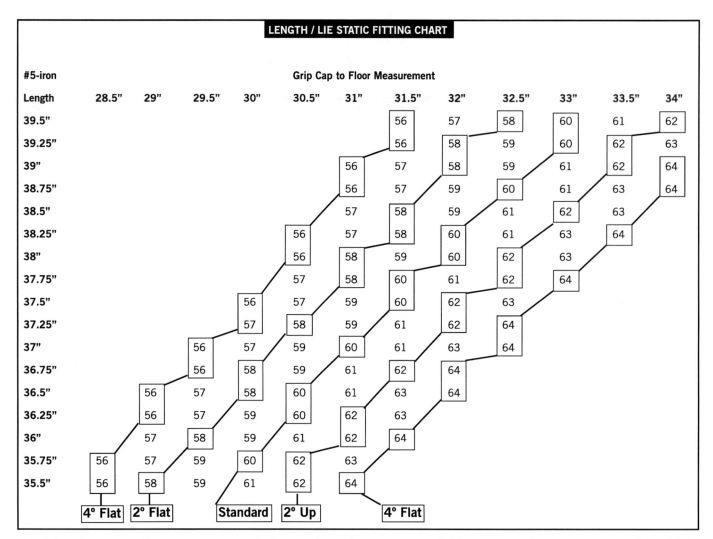

To determine proper lie, measure vertically from end of grip cap to ground. Then cross reference to length of the #5-iron.

Junior golfers, especially beginners may be last fit by using a height based-club length chart. As a junior progresses, dynamic fitting will provide more accurate fitting, but from a beginner's perspective, the chart will suffice.

Static fitting will usually provide a player with an acceptably fitted set of clubs. While this type of fitting is a marked improvement over buying clubs off the rack at a pro shop or department store, there is no substitution for actual dynamic fitting, particularly related to length. Seeing precisely where on the face the ball is hit is by far the best way to determine the proper length for a player. It is quantifiable and accurate...something static fitting may approach but will not always accomplish.

ABILITY & LENGTH CONSIDERATIONS

Handicap	Recommended Length
8 or less	+.5"
24 or more	-.5"

Lie	Recommended Length
2° Flat	+.5"
2° Upright	-.5"

HEIGHT BASED LENGTH FITTING

Height	Driver Length	#5-iron Length	Deviation From Standard
6-7 to 6-11	45"	39 1/2"	+2"
6-5 to 6-7	44 1/2"	39"	+1.5"
6-2 to 6-5	44"	38 1/2"	+1"
6-0 to 6-2	43 1/2"	38"	+.5"
5-9 to 6-0	43"	37 1/2"	0"
5-7 to 5-9	42 1/2"	37"	-.5"
5-4 to 5-7	42"	36 1/2"	-1"
5-2 to 5-4	41 1/2"	36"	-1.5"
4-11 to 5-2	41"	35 1/2"	-2"

JUNIOR HEIGHT BASED FITTING CHART

Height	(Inches)	Driver	3-wood	3-iron	5-iron	7-iron	9-iron & Wedge	Putter
3'-0"	36"	27.5-28.5"	6.5-27.5"	23-24"	22-23"	21-22"	20-21"	19.5-20.5"
3'-2"	38"	28.5-29.5"	27.5-28.5"	24-25"	23-24"	22-23"	21-22"	20.5-21.5"
3'-4"	40"	29.5-30.5"	28.5-29.5"	25-26"	24-25"	23-24"	22-23"	21.5-22.5"
3'-6"	42"	30.5-31.5"	29.5-30.5"	26-27"	25-26"	24-25"	23-24"	22.5-23.5"
3'-8"	44"	31.5-32.5"	30.5-31.5"	27-28"	26-27"	25-26"	24-25"	23.5-24.5"
3'-10"	46"	32.5-33.5"	31.5-32.5"	28-29"	27-28"	26-2""	25-26"	24.5-25.5"
4'-0"	48"	33.5-34.5"	32.5-33.5"	29-30"	28-29"	27-28"	26-27"	25.5-26.5"
4'-2"	50"	34.5-35.5"	33.5-34.5"	30-31"	29-30"	28-29"	27-28"	26.5-27.5"
4'-4"	52"	35.5-36.5"	34.5-35.5"	31-32"	30-31"	29-30""	28-29"	27.5-28.5"
4'-6"	54"	36.5-37.5"	35.5-36.5"	32-33"	31-32"	30-31"	29-30"	28.5-29.5"
4'-8"	56"	37.5-38.5"	36.5-37.5"	33-34"	32-33"	31-32"	30-31"	29.5-30.5"
4'-10"	58"	38.5-39.5"	37.5-38.5"	34-35"	33-34"	32-33"	31-32"	30.5-31.5"
5'-0"	60"	39.5-40.5"	38.5-39.5"	35-36"	34-35"	33-34"	32-33"	31.5-32.5"
5'-2"	62"	40.5-41.5"	39.5-40.5"	36-37"	35-36"	34-35"	33-34"	32.5-33.5"
5'-4"	64"	41.5-42.5"	40.5-41.5"	37-38"	36-37"	35-36"	34-35"	33.5-34.5"

LENGTH
Summary: Do's and Don'ts of Length Fitting

DO'S

DO: Use Dynamic Fitting for length whenever possible

DO: Fit for the specifications of length and lie together as they directly influence one another

DO: Know that as a club is made longer, it effectively becomes more upright, at the rate of @1 degree per 1/2"

DO: Keep in mind that as a club's length increases, it becomes heavier; as it is shortened, it becomes lighter

DO: Realize that shaft flex changes as a club is lengthened or shortened

DO: Observe that a longer club's shaft will bow downward more during the swing than will a shorter club's shaft

DO: Consider that better players may be candidates for longer clubs due to their ability to return the club to the same position at impact consistently

DO: Communicate that a longer club may offer the potential for more distance, but at a possible sacrifice of accuracy and consistency

DO: When fitting juniors, make the clubs a bit overlength so the junior may grow into them as he or she ages

DO: Determine what lengths are your standards and label demo clubs accordingly

DON'T'S

DON'T: Fit a player for length without concurrently looking at the required lie

DON'T: Assume that a tall player requires longer clubs or that a shorter player will best hit shorter clubs

DON'T: Fail to consider that length impacts other fitting parameters, such as shaft performance and weight, in addition to lie

DON'T: Overlook the effect of club length on a player's consistency

DON'T: Assume all companies and fitters utilize the same length standards; always be certain of the club's actual length rather than a so-called "standard"

Chapter 4
Lie

The lie of a golf club plays a key role in shot direction, particularly related to mid and short irons. By definition, the lie of a golf club is the angle formed between the centerline of the shaft and the groundline with the club in normal playing position. A club's lie is either considered to be standard, flat or upright. These measures are based on industry norms. For example, a typical #5 iron has a lie angle of 60 degrees. One that is flatter than this will have a lie angle of less than 60; its shaft will closer to the groundline than the standard club. A more upright #5 iron's lie angle will be greater than 60; it's shaft will be more vertical related to the groundline. Each individual club a set has a specific lie angle; generally the shorter the club's length, the more upright its lie angle.

A lie that is best suited to a player will position the plane of the club's face toward the target at impact, making it easier to hit straighter shots. Improper lie angles may cause improper set-up positions, pushed or pulled shots and/or a club that does not feel solid at impact. Players and fitters are often inclined to believe a player's shot difficulties are a result of poor swings. Lie angle has such a great influence on shot direction, that a player making a perfectly good on-plane swing with a short iron that may have a lie angle that is incorrectly matched to him, can actually miss his intended target by several yards. Improper lie angles will, in effect, cause the plane of the face of the club to tilt to one side or the other, yielding shots pushed or pulled in relation to the target - all at no fault of the player.

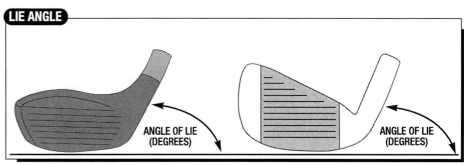

LIE ANGLE

ANGLE OF LIE
(DEGREES)

ANGLE OF LIE
(DEGREES)

If the lie angle of a player's clubs is not properly matched to him, he must attempt to compensate for this problem either by altering his swing somehow or by altering his alignment; neither of these situations leads to consistent play. Often changes as small as 1 degree can make a noticeable difference when it comes to accuracy with a player's irons. If the lie angle of a player's clubs is correct, accuracy results. A lie angle that is incorrect for a right handed golfer results in shots that tend to go straight to the left (called a pull) or straight to the right (called a push) of the target. A club that is too flat for a player results in shots that often miss the target to the right due to the tilt of the too-flat club's face plane. If a club is too upright for a player, it's face plane in tilted to the left, causing errant shots in that direction. This is not to say that a player cannot hit clubs with incorrect lies on target; but certainly the percentage of time that happens is much increased with clubs that have properly matched lie angles to the player's swing.

The more lofted the club, the more any negative effects of an improper lie are noticed. Let's look for an explanation as to why the wrong lie on a wedge will be more detrimental to accuracy than will an incorrectly fitted lie on a #3 iron. The loft of a wedge will be in the neighborhood of 50 degrees, while the #3 iron will have an average of perhaps 20 degrees. The higher lofted club will effectively tilt more from an equal amount of lie change than will a lower lofted one. To prove this, take a right handed #3 iron, hold it in your hands and aim it toward a specific target, say a clock on the wall. Now, effectively change the lie of this #3 iron by tilting the toe counterclockwise (right-handed club.) This creates the same effect as making a club too upright. Notice where the face points; it will point to the left of the clock. A ball struck with the clubface in this upright position will be directed to the left of the target as a result of this face plane tilt.

Now, start with that same right-handed club aimed to the clock again, but this time rotate it clockwise. This tilts the face plane to the right, effectively creating a flatter golf club. A ball struck from this clubface position will be directed to the right of the target. Be sure to note how much the face plane of the #3 iron tilts in both the flat and upright positions. Now, do the same thing with the wedge.

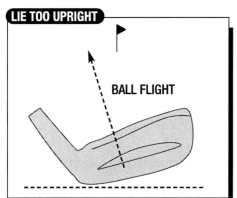

LIE TOO UPRIGHT

BALL FLIGHT

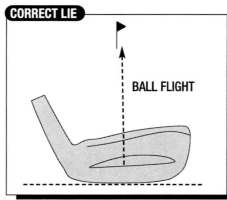

CORRECT LIE

BALL FLIGHT

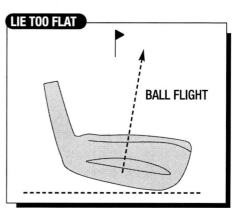

LIE TOO FLAT

BALL FLIGHT

Lie has a tremendous influence on face plane angle and ball direction.

Anticipated ball flight of an iron with a lie that is too upright is left of target.

Anticipated ball flight of an iron with a lie that is too flat is right of target.

Holes drilled in the center of club faces can be used to slow the effects of proper lie in address position.

Moving it counterclockwise will tilt the face plane to the left, just as moving it did with the #3 iron. But, notice how much more quickly the face points to the left - this will cause the ball to move much more noticeably to the left if it is struck on this type of lie. A lie "problem" of only a couple of degrees will thus have a much greater effect when the club has greater loft. If you then reposition the wedge toward the target and then rotate it clockwise, note how quickly the face points to the right. This effectively flat lie will cause a much more obvious misdirection as compared to the same amount of clockwise rotation of the #3 iron. The proven conclusion: Lie has a much more noticeable and quantifiable effect as the loft of a club is higher. This is why any lie problems are more recognized in shorter irons than in longer irons or woods.

Loft has a further effect on ball direction related to face plane tilt. The more loft a club has, the more backspin it will produce on the ball when it is struck. Thus a ball hit from the wedge will have substantially more backspin (approximately 12,000 rpm) than will one hit from the #3 iron (approximately 5,000 rpm.) If the lie of the club is properly matched to

the player, this backspin will have little or no effect on ball direction. But, if the lie is not matched to the player, any backspin from a shot may have an influence on ball direction. In other words, as there is more backspin from a wedge shot, this added spin will create a situation where this backspin actually counteracts any negative sidespin imparted as the result of the face plane tilt. When discussing higher lofted wedges, the amount of backspin actually helps to "correct" the negative impact of face plane tilt as the result of improper lie angles. As a #3 iron does not impart as much backspin as does a wedge, the negative effects of an improper lie will not be magnified as greatly when compared to middle irons and short irons; the added spin of the higher lofted wedges also tends to help reduce the influence of face plane tilt. These facts further substantiate the necessity for proper lie fitting, especially when considering the middle to short irons in a set.

A similar type of demonstration in a static form can be done with a couple of irons that have holes drilled in the center of their faces. This hole should be the same diameter as a golf shaft. Insert a shaft cut to a length of 12" into the hole. You may want to glue a plastic golf ball

onto one end of the shaft for a more noticeable visual effect. Have the right handed golfer place the club in address position as he or she normally does, aligning the club with a specific target. If the static lie is correct for the player, the shaft (and ball) will point directly toward their target. If the lie is too flat, the shaft/ball will be aligned to the right of the intended target; if the lie is too upright, the direction of the shaft/ball will be to the target's left. This is not to say that lie should be fit to a player in this manner - on the contrary, the position of the club in a static position such as in the demonstration may not be an accurate picture of the face position at impact during an actual swing. This demo is only meant to show what could happen if the club were in a similar position at impact related to what it was at address.

To add to this demonstration, a driver could be drilled and the shaft/ball inserted. The amount that the driver points left or right will be less than the #3 iron. If there still exists any doubt, use a putter, bent to zero degrees of loft and drill it in

DIRECTION DEVIATION DUE TO A CHANGE IN THE LIE ANGLE					
CLUB	LOFT (degrees)	LIE CHANGE (degrees)	DISPERSION ANGLE (degrees)	TYPICAL DISTANCE (yards)	SPREAD (feet)
1	17	2	0.6	215	7
2	19	2	0.7	205	7
3	22	2	0.8	195	8
4	25	2	0.9	185	8
5	28	2	1.0	175	9
6	32	2	1.1	162	9
7	36	2	1.3	148	10
8	40	2	1.4	135	10
9	44	2	1.5	122	10
PW	48	2	1.7	110	10
SW	55	2	1.8	85	8
UW	60)	2	2.0	60	6

from Golf The Scientific Way, 1995, Carl Scheie

the same manner as the irons and/or driver. Any rotation of this 0 degree-lofted putter will result in no change in the direction the shaft/ball points. This firmly illustrates that if a club has zero loft, lie has virtually no effect on ball flight. When the putter demo is compared to the wedge demo, the opposite ends of the lie/length spectrum can easily be seen. Once again, to summarize, the more loft a club has, the more lie will potentially affect ball flight from that club - especially if the lie is not properly matched to the player.

The lie angle of a club, be it a wood iron or putter, is measured in the same manner. The club will be positioned in some type of specifications gauge. To properly measure the club's lie angle, it must be positioned so that it rests on the center of its sole, also called its normal playing position. The center of the sole (or the face centerline) will be determined by sliding some type of file card or business card under the clubhead from the heel side and the toe side. When these cards, which are slid under the club simultaneously, meet equidistant from the center of the face, the club is in what is considered to be its normally soled position, or its playing position. At this point, the lie angle can be read directly from the gauge. There is no other way to accurately measure the lie of a club other than using some type of specification gauge. Once club lies are determined, they can then be compared to a standard or compared to other clubs in a set to determine information concerning the player's clubs related to his shot pattern.

Once a fitter determines the proper lie for a player, that lie is set through the use of a loft/lie machine. This machine

A loft/lie machine is used to calibrate lies and change them if necessary.

A club properly positioned in a specifications gauge allows its lie to be measured accurately.

securely holds the iron, allowing it to be bent two degrees. Thus if the player requires a club that is 1 degree upright, a loft/lie machine is used to accomplish that alteration. It is very important to know the measured lie of the clubs that you are using to fit the player; without knowing these numbers, the lie could be mistakenly made too upright or too flat. Remember that not all club designs have the same lie. In other words, one #5 iron model may be 60 degrees as its manufactured specification, while another may have 62 degrees. By knowing what is being worked with prior to bending, the

The specs gauge shows the lie of this club to be 60°.

proper amount of bending (if any) is accurately determined.

NOTE: The loft of a club can be altered through the use of this same machine. Most loft/lie machines are not set up to bend woods; most woods do not have hosels that are long enough to permit bending. For all practical purposes, club lie related to irons can be altered, lie for woods cannot.

EFFECT ON BALL FLIGHT

As previously mentioned in the introduction and explanation of lie angle, a

properly fit lie angle positions the clubface consistently toward the target at impact. This should provide more accuracy for all players. If a player is having difficulty with shots that travel right or left of target, particularly with mid and shorter irons, the lies of those clubs deserve investigation. Consistent inaccuracies to the left indicate a lie angle that may be too upright, while shots often pushed right of target may show evidence that the lie of the club(s) is too flat. Also, as previously mentioned, most irons can be adjusted easily for lie at a maximum of 2 degrees. Most woods, due to their shorter hosels, cannot be adjusted. This is not all that big of a problem since woods typically are among the lowest lofted clubs in a set. Plus, the design of most of today's woods includes a radiused sole, allowing the club to be positioned in a variety of lies at address due to this radiused sole configuration. In essence, the radius sole make the metal wood somewhat self-adjusting related to lie.

Just how much does an incorrect lie cause a change in ball direction? Not considering backspin as a factor, each degree will elicit a 2-3 yard variation between when the club was aligned and where the ball will travel, assuming an on-plane swing is made from flat ground. 2-3 yards may not seem like much - and on a #3 iron it really isn't. That is, most professionals would be happy to "miss" every long iron by only a few yards. But when hitting a wedge, the 2-3 yards can mean the difference between being on the green or in a greenside bunker. Now, if

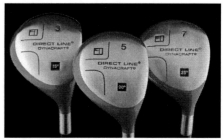

A club with a radiused sole accomodates a variety of lies easier than does a flat soled club.

TERRAIN, LIE & EFFECT ON BALL DIRECTIONS

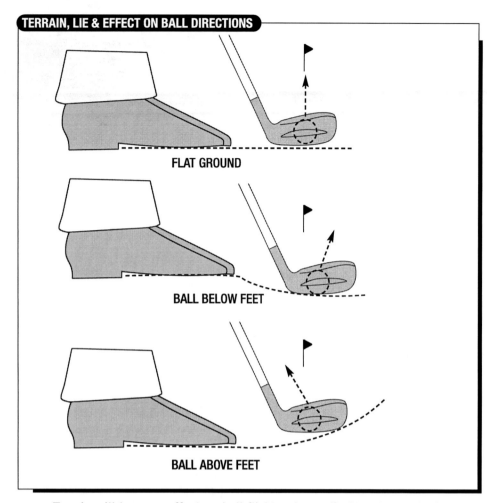

FLAT GROUND

BALL BELOW FEET

BALL ABOVE FEET

Terrain will have an effect on ball flight unless adjustments are made.

INDUSTRY AVERAGE GOLF CLUB LIES THROUGH THE YEARS

	1950's & 60's	1970's & 80's	1990's & 2000's
WOODS			
Driver	55	55	56
3	56	56	58
5	57	57	59
7	N/A	58	60
9	N/A	N/A	61
IRONS			
1	55	56	59
2	56	57	59.5
3	57	58	60
4	58	59	60.5
5	59	60	61
6	60	61	62
7	61	62	63
8	62	63	63.5
9	63	64	64
PW	63	64	64
SW	63	64	64
UW	N/A	64	64
AW	N/A	N/A	64

N/A indicates clubs were not produced during those years
Notes:
1) All numbers are measured in degrees
2) Ladies lies are typically 1° flatter than the above standards

the added effect backspin has on a more lofted club is considered, it may be very difficult for even a very good player to hit a club with the improper lie either accurately or consistently.

Let's utilize another example to illustrate how lie causes shots to stray from their intended target. A player is faced with a shot from the side of a hill with the ball below his feet. The club will be soled on the ground in a flatter position than from a level lie. The ball hit from this type of side hill lie will tend to go to the right of the target as a result of the club's face plane being tilted in the same direction as the ground. From a lie with the ball below his feet a player must guard against hitting shots to the right by making a very conscious effort to maintain the face plane on the target line. What if the player is faced with the opposite situation, with the ball being above his feet on a side hill lie? The club will tend to follow the position of the ground, effectively making it more upright and tilting to the left. The tendency from this type of lie is to pull shots to the left of the target. The player must be aware of this tendency of the terrain influencing effective lie angle prior to playing a shot. Any shot played from a level lie will tend to not influence the properly fitted lie angle in any direction other than toward the target.

At this point, it may be a good idea to mention a trend among many club manufacturers related to lie. There is a consistent trend toward making the lies of all clubs, with the exception of putters, more upright. Why is this? Think about it for a moment...what is the shot pattern common to most players? Nearly 90% of all golfers have a tendency to slice the ball. Having a more upright lie angle engineered into new club designs helps to tilt the club's face to the left, assuming a right-handed player. If the face is angled left, perhaps the slice to the right will not be so severe. While this may, in theory, help the slicing player, it may not help - and in fact hurt - the ball flight characteristics of the player who hits the ball straight or who draws the ball. This trend is another key reason that the fitter must be cognizant of the lie angle of the clubheads being recommended. If the player will require flatter lies and the clubs are

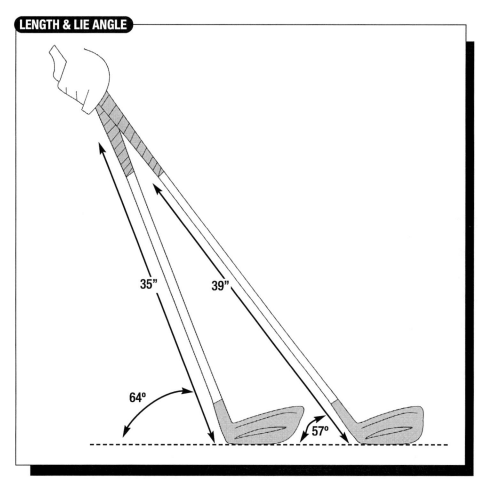

LENGTH & LIE ANGLE

35" 39"

64°

57°

As a golf club is made longer, its corresponding lie angle will be flatter.

engineered with a lie angle a few degrees more upright than the norm, the heads may not be able to be bent on a loft/lie machine enough to properly fit the player. As a result of this trend toward more upright clubs, the player requiring clubs a few degrees flat, unfortunately, may be somewhat limited in his or her choices.

LIE AND OTHER FITTING PARAMETERS

LENGTH

Lie and length have a direct relationship with each other. As a club becomes longer, its specified lie becomes flatter. This is the reason that a driver will have a lie in the 55° range and a wedge will be in the 64° range. Drivers are the longest clubs in the set; wedges are the shortest. Any time that the lie of a club is altered, either flat or upright, that change potentially will cause a change in the way a player normally or naturally holds his or her hands at address (and impact.) Any properly fitted lie angle should not change the player's hand position in any notice-

able manner. In fact, it should allow the hands to be in a position most comfortable to the player, allowing the most consistent swings possible. Incorrect lie angle will cause alterations of hand/address position; properly fitted lie will create the situation where address/hand position is assumed normally and repeatedly by the golfer.

As noted in the previous chapter, any time a change in length is recommended, a club's lie should be checked as a result. Each 1/2" increase in length will require the lie to be made flatter by 1 degree in order that the club sole in the same position. The 1/2" longer length effectively made the club 1 degree more upright than it was prior to the length increase. Unless this change in lie is made, the player will have to raise the position of his hands (move them away from his body) in order to sole the club properly. If length is shortened, the lie is effectively made flatter, again 1-degree of lie per 1/2" of length. A club that has been shortened will cause a player to reposition his hands lower (closer to his body) to properly sole

the club. A lie adjustment upright should be made in order to maintain the same hand position of the player prior to any length reduction of the club. Just as a length change repositions the hands and address position, a lie change does as well. This direct relationship is an important consideration as fitting modifications are made for the player

SHAFTS

A golf club shaft bends, flexes and twists a number of ways during a swing. The one way that it bends related to a club's lie is the downward bowing of the shaft during the swing. As a club is swinging, centrifugal force acting on the head of the club will, in effect cause the shaft to bow downward. This will tend to flatten the lie angle at impact. The longer the shaft, the more downward bowing that will occur. A club that is fitted properly to a player will seem to have the toe slightly off the ground at address. This is perfectly acceptable as the club's shaft will tend to bow downward during the swing, flattening its lie effective angle. Longer irons and woods, may exhibit bowing as much as 4 degrees (or more in very long drivers), while shorter clubs such as wedge may only approach a 1-degree effect on lie from shaft bowing.

A second consideration related to shafts and lie relates to a shaft's flexibility. The more flexible the shaft, the more it is likely to bow downward during the swing as well. Thus, a very flexible ladies shaft will show more bowing than will an extra firm shaft, provided both are assembled to the same length. If a player is fitted to either very flexible or very stiff

A longer shaft will bow more than a shorter one, effectively flattening the lie as it is swinging.

shafts as compared to the tested demo clubs, it is imperative to check the lie of these clubs after they are assembled to take in to account the bowing or non-bowing properties of these shafts. Perhaps another reason for the trend toward more upright lie angles in most of today's clubs is the trend toward more flexible shafts in these same clubs. As the shaft bows downward more, the lie, in effect, becomes flatter. If the lies are more upright to start, the increased bowing may make them sole in the proper position at impact. Shaft bowing and its effect on lie is a classic example of how one fitting parameter has a directly quantifiable effect on another parameter.

A shaft that has a tip firm design versus one that has a tip flexible design may influence lie angle at impact as well. Much in the same manner as softer shaft will bow downward more during the swing, a tip flexible design will do the same. The tip flexible shaft may cause the lie angle of the club to be effectively flatter. Conversely a tip firm shaft will not have as great of an impact on the lie of the club as will the less firm tip.

WEIGHT

While perhaps a minor factor related to lie, when the lie of a club is changed significantly, that change has an effect of the swingweight of the club. In the case of a lie change of 3 degrees, an approximate 1-swingweight change will occur in the club. The reason behind this change is the fact that as a club is flattened or made more upright, the toe of the club is moved either farther away or closer to the butt end of the club. Thus, in the situation where a club is made flatter by 3 degrees, its swingweight will increase by approximately 1 point as the toe of the club is a longer distance from the butt end of the shaft. The converse is true as well; when a club is made more upright by 3 degrees, it's toe moves closer to the shaft butt, reducing swingweight by a point.

The weight - and the distribution of that weight - can also have an effect on the lie of a club. A club head that is significantly heavier than typical will have the effect of flattening the club lie more than a head of standard weight due the added force exhibited by the heavier weight of the head. As most clubheads of the same number weigh within a few

grams of each other, the overall effect of head weight on lie may be negligible, but does perhaps deserve consideration if working with extremely heavy or very light club heads. The weight distribution of a club head may also influence a club's lie angle. As a head becomes larger, it center of gravity moves away from the centerline of the shaft. A higher percentage of its weight is thus moved toward the toe of the club. As weight moves in the manner, it will increase the amount the shaft bows, again due to centrifugal force. Thus, larger headed clubs or clubs that are longer from heel to toe, may add to the effect of shaft bowing and its corresponding cumulative effect on the lie of the club at impact.

LIE DEMO CLUBS

A basic demo selection of clubs to adequately fit lie will be limited to a selection of three mid-irons. The middle-iron of choice will be the #6 iron. The demos will include a standard lie #6 iron, one that is 2 or 3 degrees upright and one that is 2 or 3 degrees flat. Thus, if the standard club has a lie of 61 degrees, the upright will have, for example, 64 degrees and the flat demo will have 58. Each club should be labeled specifically as to the lie angle and to the testing parameter. As with all demo clubs, the lengths should be whatever standard the fitter is utilizing throughout the demo selection of clubs. Shafts are to be lightweight, R-flex steel and grips are to be a standard size selection. No woods are needed for lie testing due to the fact that their lower lofts do not show negative effects of lie as greatly as do higher lofted clubs. Further, most woods have radiused soles to allow for various address positions and the shorter hosels of most woods do not permit lie alteration in the first place.

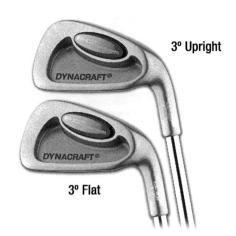

3° Upright

3° Flat

Irons with flat and upright lie angles are key components of a complete demo selection.

A more advanced demo selection would add a long and a short iron to the above. Three #3 irons and #9 irons (2-3 degrees upright, standard and 2-3 degrees flat) will allow dynamic testing of a variety of irons in the player's set. There will be times when a player swings short and/or long irons in a different manner than he swings mid-irons. The recommended lie of the mid-iron may not always apply to the long or short irons. By testing several different clubs, it can be assured that lie angle of all clubs in the set in correct for the player. To even better offer a complete demo choice, ladies' clubs of various lies should be added. These will have shorter, more flexible shafts and ladies' grips. A beginning demo assortment will be #6 irons only; more advanced test clubs will include long irons and short irons. Left-handers will also justify the same demo club choices as will right-handers or ladies. The demo clubs required to concisely fit lie are fairly extensive. There will be nine clubs needed for each section (three #3's at upright, standard and flat, three #6's and three #9's in the same specs.) These requirements for advanced fitting are the same for right-hander, ladies and men's length left-handers, making a total of 27 clubs necessary for the most accurate possible fitting of lie. (If a ladies' left hand section is also included, it would bring the total of required demo clubs to 36.)

In addition to the demo clubs, the fitter will need some type of lie board from which to hit balls. This may be as "low-tech" as a plywood board, or as high-tech as a Plexiglas mat surrounded by artificial

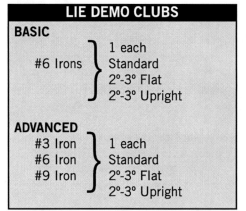

LIE DEMO CLUBS	
BASIC	
#6 Irons	1 each Standard 2°-3° Flat 2°-3° Upright
ADVANCED	
#3 Iron #6 Iron #9 Iron	1 each Standard 2°-3° Flat 2°-3° Upright

grass. A good compromise is a Lexan plastic lie board that costs less than $20.00 and can be used indoors or out. The board, approximately 1' x 2' x 1/8" in size, is simply placed on the floor or the ground, a ball placed on it, and shots struck from this point. Impact labels are applied to the club's soles prior to hitting from the board; these labels are marked when the club strikes the lie board. It may be a wise idea when purchasing lie boards to buy two of them. If a player makes an extremely poor swing (which is guaranteed to happen eventually), they may hit the side of the board, shattering it into many pieces. The fitter, should another lie board be available, will not have to stop the fitting process, making

Some type of lie board is used to accurately determine proper lie during dynamic fitting.

the player feel less-embarrassed by breaking the board.

FITTING LIE

DYNAMIC FITTING INDOORS

When fitting lie, there is no substitute for some type of dynamic fitting in which the player actually hits balls during the fitting session from a lie board of some type. Prior to hitting from the board, sole impact labels are applied to the club. When the club's sole strikes the lie board, the impact labels are torn or marked at the impact point. These marks are analyzed related to the position of the marks. The ideal situation has the mark in the center of the sole. If a club is too upright for player, the mark will be toward the heel; if the lie is too flat, the mark will be toward the toe side of center.

Begin the testing with the standard lie #6 iron. Have the player make 2-3 swings that he or she considers to be representative of the way they swing on the course. Observe the label marks. If they are centered, this lie is good for the player. But if the marks are toward the toe,

give the player the more upright club to try. (Remember marks toward the toe indicate the club is too flat.) The marks after a few hits should now be closer to the center of the sole. If they still tend toward the toe, the club is still too flat for the player. For each 1/4" the sole marks are toward the toe, the club needs to be made upright by one degree. Thus, if the player marks the 3-degree upright demo club 1/2" toward the toe, the final upright specification for this club will be 5 degrees upright. (3 degrees from the original standard plus 2 more degrees from the 1/2" toe marking)

If, on the other hand, the golfer marks the original standard lie #6 iron toward the heel of the club, this club is

LIE ALTERATIONS	
Impact mark on sole	**Proper Lie**
1" toward heel	4° flat
3/4" toward heel	3° flat
1/2" toward heel	2° flat
1/4" toward heel	1° flat
on center	no change
1/4" toward toe	1° upright
1/2" toward toe	2° upright
3/4" toward toe	3° upright
1" toward toe	4° upright

too upright for the player. The flatter test club should be tried. This club should bring the sole impacts more toward center. Again, the 1/4" equals 1 degree formula can be used to accurately fit lie if necessary. Once the lie for the #6 iron is determined, the same test is done for the #3 iron and the #9 iron if those demo clubs are available. In this case any differences in the manner in which the player holds his hands at address - and much

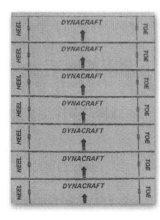

Lie labels are placed on a club's sole prior to lie testing.

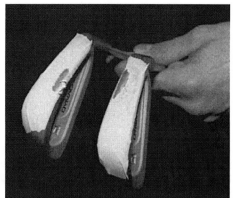

Lie impact labels showing properly and improperly matched lie angles.

more importantly at impact - are accurately fitted to him through the matching of the proper lie club to his swing.

It is possible (and recommended) to fit lie and length at the same time. By combining the length fitting procedures (see Chapter 3, pages 56-57) with these lie fitting processes, the lie-length relationship is easily seen and is more accurately fit. Remember that as length changes, the effective lie changes. It makes sense to fit length and lie at the same time as any change in one has a direct effect on the other. The goal of center impacts on the face and sole are likewise achieved in the fitting of lie and length. If a player has trouble at a given length in finding the center of the club face during length testing, an alteration of lie often can move the impact marks where they should be. If a player seems to be marking the clubface toward the toe, this may be an indication that a more upright lie is necessary. Testing a more upright club will often show these face marks moved more toward the face center. The opposite is true as well. Face

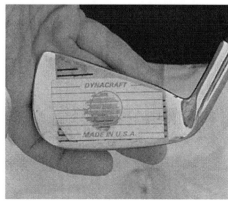

Face marks on the toe indicate possibly a more upright lie is required; proper impacts (shown) in the center of the face.

impacts favoring the heel are often recti-fied with a flatter lie angle club. Doing the fitting of both lie and length concur-rently makes the process less time-con-suming and more accurate as well.

DYNAMIC FITTING OUTDOORS

To dynamically fit lie outdoors, the same theories apply as when accomplish-ing the indoor fitting of lie. The same lie board is used, the same demo clubs are utilized and impact labels are placed on the club's sole and face. It is recommend to fit both lie and length together out-doors, just as that is a wise move to do so indoors. The advantage that outdoor fit-ting may provide is that ball flight is observable as a part of accurate fitting. Should shots noticeably head left of tar-get, chances are the club being tested is too upright for the player; the sole marks should be toward the heel. If the club is too flat, ball flight should be to the right

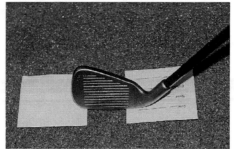

Placing file cards under a club's sole is not an accurate method of fitting the lie of an iron.

and the sole marks toward the toe. The observable ball flight, reinforced by the sole markings ensure proper lie fitting based on the combination of observing ball flight and impact marks together.

STATIC FITTING

The static fitting of lie is accom-plished through a combination of compar-ing a player's physical characteristics (and perhaps address position) with charts of

average fitting parameter generally com-piled based on dynamic fitting. Measurements very similar to those made when fitting length are used. Here again, lie and length are fitted concurrently, uti-lizing similar charts in the process. The goal of static fitting is the same as that of dynamic fitting - to achieve consistent impacts in the center of the face and in the center of the sole. Perhaps you have seen a fitter use some type of tool that they have the player hold in playing posi-tion that has a gauge on it that is designed to show the lie of the club. While this tool may show what the static lie of a given club may be, it does not allow the golfer to make a swing and thus can only loosely approximate what the actual lie of the club should be. Another, all too often seen method of static lie fitting involves having the player hold the club in playing position with the fitter placing file cards under the sole. Here again, if there was some way to ensure the player would (or

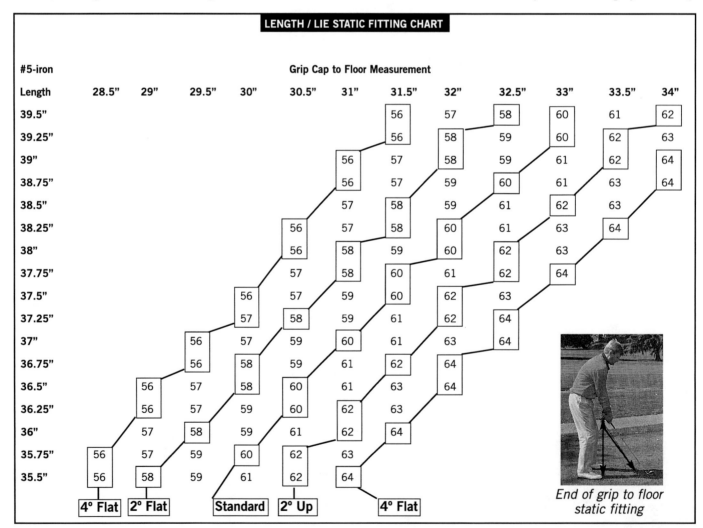

LENGTH / LIE STATIC FITTING CHART

#5-iron — Grip Cap to Floor Measurement

Length	28.5"	29"	29.5"	30"	30.5"	31"	31.5"	32"	32.5"	33"	33.5"	34"
39.5"							56	57	58	60	61	62
39.25"							56	58	59	60	62	63
39"						56	57	58	59	61	62	64
38.75"						56	57	59	60	61	63	64
38.5"						57	58	59	61	62	63	
38.25"					56	57	58	60	61	63	64	
38"					56	58	59	60	62	63		
37.75"					57	58	60	61	62	64		
37.5"				56	57	59	60	62	63			
37.25"				57	58	59	61	62	64			
37"			56	57	59	60	61	63	64			
36.75"			56	58	59	61	62	64				
36.5"		56	57	58	60	61	63	64				
36.25"		56	57	59	60	62	63					
36"		57	58	59	61	62	64					
35.75"	56	57	59	60	62	63						
35.5"	56	58	59	61	62	64						

| 4° Flat | 2° Flat | | Standard | 2° Up | | 4° Up |

End of grip to floor static fitting

To determine proper lie, measure vertically from end of grip cap to ground. Then cross reference to length of the #5-iron.

could) return the club back to this position at impact, this method is acceptable. But, since this is not the case, there is a definite deficiency in this method as well. Additionally, remember that a club flattens as it is swung as a result of centrifugal force, so the card placed under the toe should in reality go farther under the club than the one placed under the heel -

guesswork at best.

The obvious key drawback of static fitting is not being able to see the player swing the club. A player could have the "classic" address position of a Ben Hogan, but then might make a swing at the ball like wrestler Hulk Hogan. Static fitting would match this player's clubs to the address position; unfortunately when

the club is swing, these static measurements most likely would be very different than may be required by the player. Static fitting is better than no fitting at all, but, especially as lie and length are so closely related to how the club is actually swung, there really is no accurate substitute for dynamic player testing of these parameters.

LIE
Summary: Do's and Don'ts of Lie Fitting

DO'S

DO: Use Dynamic Fitting to best-fit lie to all players

DO: Always know that lie has a major effect on ball direction, especially related to irons

DO: Keep in mind that as a club's loft decreases (becomes stronger), any effect of an improper lie will decrease as well

DO: Fit a player to the specifications of lie and length at the same time as these specifications have a direct effect upon one another

DO: Be aware that as a club's length changes, so does its effective lie. A longer club is effectively 1 degree more upright per 1/2" of length

DO: Realize that a club that has a proper lie will appear to have its toe off the ground at address

DO: As a reference, realize that as a club's length is shorter, it's specified lie angle is generally more upright

DO: Create lie standards that will be used during fitting and label the demo clubs accordingly

DON'TS

DON'T: Use static fitting as an accurate method of lie fitting

DON'T: Fail to consider the profound effect that incorrect lies can have a ball flight

DON'T: Believe that tall players always require upright lies and that shorter players should have flatter lies

DON'T: Try to determine the correct lie angle for a player without considering the correct club length for a player

DON'T: Think that all companies use the same standards for lie specifications

Chapter 5
Face Angle

Face angle is the single most important determinant of ball direction related to wood clubs. It is defined as the position of the clubface in reference to the target. A strict definition of face angle is the angle of a wood's clubface to the groundline, with the shaft bore perpendicular to the intended line of flight. The club's face is defined as the area of the club on which the ball is intended to be properly struck. The groundline is a reference to where the club is soled; either on flat ground or on a perpendicular plane with the club's shaft line.

An important aspect of face angle is that, to be accurately determined or measured, the club must be in what is considered to be the "normal playing position." This position is the position at which the club comes to rest naturally on the ground at address. It is the way the club is designed to "sole" or rest on the ground. It is found by simply allowing the club to rest on the ground in playing position with the golfer's hands on the club and his body in the address position. The player must be careful not to manipulate the club in any manner. In the case that manipulation occurs, the club's measured face angle and the actual face angle now in play will be two different things - most likely negatively affecting the club's designed playability.

Face angles typically are labeled as either square, open or closed. (At times an open face may also be labeled as a

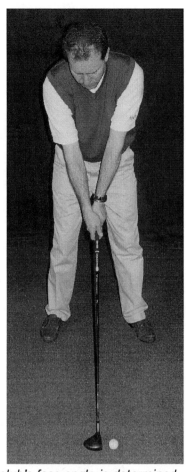

A club's face angle is determined related to how the club is held in its "soled" position at address.

slice face and a closed face may be called a hook face.) Each of these terms applies to the position of the face relative to the target when the club is in the soled posi-

tion. A face that is square points directly at the target at address; it is perpendicular to the target line at a 90-degree angle. A face angle that is open, aligns to the right of the target (for a right handed player); one that is closed, aligns to the left of the target (again for a right handed golfer.) Face angle is measured in degrees, with a square face considered to be zero (0) degrees. An open or closed face is also measured in degrees; the more open or closed the face is, the higher the number of degrees open or closed that it is. For example, a 3-degree open face points more to the right of the intended target than does a 1-degree open face.

The "look" of a particular face angle and its actual measurement may not always appear to be the same. That is, what a face angle appears to be to a player holding the golf club as compared to its actual measurement may differ by a couple of degrees. Why? Consider how a player correctly positions a wood in his stance at address. The head of the wood is positioned forward in the stance, the longer the wood (i.e., the driver), the more forward it is positioned. As a result of this forward positioning of the wood, a player's eyes actually view the head of the club from different angles. The left eye of a right-handed player will view the head at a more direct angle, closer to 90 degrees, than will the right eye, which will see the head from a much more angled view. These different angles of the

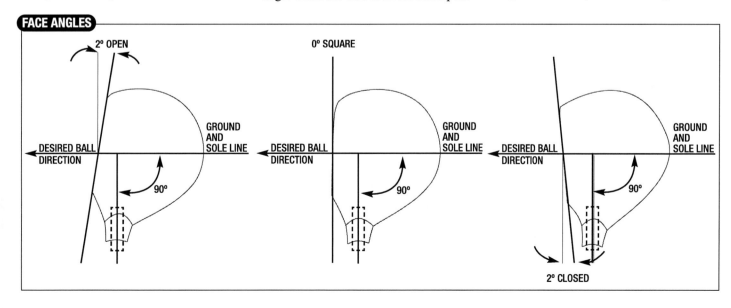

FACE ANGLES

2° OPEN

0° SQUARE

DESIRED BALL DIRECTION

GROUND AND SOLE LINE

90°

DESIRED BALL DIRECTION

GROUND AND SOLE LINE

90°

DESIRED BALL DIRECTION

GROUND AND SOLE LINE

90°

2° CLOSED

eyes will create a visual effect of the club appearing as if it more square to the target than it is. For instance, the golfer may state that the club "looks" square, or as if it is pointing directly toward the target but when measured, the club is actually 1-2 degrees open. This fact that a club appears more closed than it actually measures can sometimes be confusing to the player. Looks can be deceiving - that is why it is vitally important that that player understand that the club cannot be manipulated at address. Any such manipulation will change the specification of the club to something other than it was designed; this will most often be detrimental to both consistency and accuracy.

Face angle may be more accurately approximated by having a player hold the club in playing position while the fitter makes some observations. That is, the player and fitter together may be able to determine if the club is relatively square or whether it sits open or closed. The player takes his stance and soles the club. The fitter, positioned behind the player, determines where the club points by observing in which direction the face is aligned related to where the player is aiming. This process may be made easier if the club has an alignment arrow on its crown, but in cases of no alignment mark, the fitter can easily use another club, a pencil, or other straight object to indicate where the face is aligning. To do this, the face position is observed and the shaft, pencil, etc., is positioned against the face, pointing in its direction. At that point, both player and fitter will surely be able to see where the face is pointing and thus may be able to approximate face angle for the particular club.

By positioning a club on a tile floor in address position, an approximation of the club's face angle related to square, open or closed can be approximated.

A better way to obtain a "ball-park" face angle measurement is to move indoors to a room that has a tile-type of floor. Have the player position his feet perpendicular to a set of tile lines on the floor. Now have him sole the wood in its normal playing position. Check the relationship of the face position to a set of tile lines parallel to the player's feet. If the face points in the direction of the tile lines, it is square; if it points to the right, it is open and if it aligns left, it is closed. (This assumes the player is right-handed; for left-hander, an open face points to the left, a closed face points right and a square face points directly at the target, just as in the case of a right-handed golfer.) While perhaps exact degrees cannot be determined by this method either, it does allow for a more accurate judgment of whether the club's face is truly square, open or closed.

To more accurately determine the face angle of a wood, a machine known as a specification (or specs) gauge is required. These gauges, ranging in price from under $200.00 to upwards of several thousand dollars, very specifically quantify a wood's face angle (among other specs.) To properly utilize the specs gauge, a club is placed in the machine and its normally soled position is determined. This is done by positioning the club so that its sole center is resting on the base of the gauge. Once this soled position is found, a directional gauge is placed on the face to determine the face angle. It is important that this directional gauge be placed on the club equidistant from the heel and the toe of the club. This ensures that the proper face angle will be determined. The specific face angle measurement can be read directly from the gauge, typically in 1/2-degree increments.

The only truly accurate method of determining a club's face angle is through the use of a spcifications gauge.

EFFECT ON BALL FLIGHT

As previously mentioned, face angle is the single most important factor in ball direction for woods. This should be an obvious fact now that we have defined face angle as well as how it is measured. Let's assume that a right-handed golfer makes an on-plane, square-to-square swing. In such a case, a face angle that is square will propel the ball straight toward the intended target. If the club in this instance has an open face, the ball will tend to go to the right; if the club's face is closed, the ball will go left. The amount that the ball goes right or left of the intended target is a function of how many degrees open or closed the clubface measures. A 2 degree open face angle will direct the ball more to the right than will a 1-degree open face, and so on.

Next, let's take the example of a golfer who may not make the on-plane, square-to-square swing. This is a much more common occurrence than in the previous example. Let's say a golfer is using a square-faced club, but is having problems hitting shots to the right of the intended target. This would potentially indicate that the clubface certainly must be pointing to the right of the target at impact. If the player can be fitted with a wood that has a closed face angle, this may help straighten the player's shots. That is, the closed face wood will actually be positioned in a square face position at impact, resulting in straighter shots. The player had to make no adjustment in his swing in order to now hit the ball noticeably straighter; the club's face angle compensated for the player's swing path and pattern.

A similar scenario takes place for the player who tends to hit the ball to the left of target consistently. At impact, the clubface must be aligned to the left of the intended target. If an open-faced club is used, it will effectively position the face of the club in a more square manner in relation to the target, producing straighter shots. Looking closer at swing paths and face angles, it can be generalized that certain swing characteristics have a noticeable influence on a wood's face position at impact. Depending upon the swing characteristics and the golf ball flight pattern, face angle further has a quantifiable effect on a player's directional control.

Basically there are three types of swing paths. Each has a decided effect on the club's face position at impact as well as on the resulting ball direction. The three swing paths include:

* SQUARE...In such a swing path, the golfer takes the club back on a line perpendicular to the target and returns it on the same line to impact. The result of this type of path is typically a straight shot, assuming a square clubface is used.

* OUTSIDE-IN...This path is identified by the player taking the club back outside (to the right of) the intended target line

and then returning it toward impact inside that line. This swing path is more common than any other and typically produces shots to the right of target, assuming a square club is utilized. This type of swing may be labeled as "over the top" and is commonly the cause of sliced shots - the shot pattern 90% of average golfers see every time they step on the tee.

* INSIDE-OUT...Identified by the player swinging the club back inside (to the left of) the intended target line and then returning it to impact outside that line. This type of swing path, a characteristic of many better players, often produces

shots to the left of target, assuming a square-faced club was swung. A shot that curves from right to left, or a "draw" may be the result of an inside-out swing.

What happens when any one of the three possible swing paths combine with any one of the three possible face angle combinations? That is, a face angle can be either square, open or closed and a swing path may be either square, outside-in or inside-out. As these factors combine, each unique combination will produce an identifiable shot pattern. A square-faced wood, when swung in the square path, will yield straight shots. That same club, when swung outside-in will produce a shot that tends to curve to the right, or a "fade." An inside-out swing with the square face angle will promote a shot that curves left of target, or a "draw." But, if the path of the swing remains square and the face angle is changed, a different set of ball flight characteristics results. The more outside-in or inside-out the swing path, the more the shots will curve; the "fade" quickly becomes a violently curving "slice" and the "draw" can quickly become a "hook" if the swing path is dramatically one way or the other.

As noted in the example above, in the case of a square path and a square face, the ball flies straight at the target. But, if the path is square and the face is closed, the ball goes to the left, but it does not curve to the left. It will go in a straight flight to the left of the intended target. This straight-left flight is known as a "pull." The opposite is true when a square path and open club face angle meet at impact. The resulting flight will be straight right; this shot is called a "push." Here again, the more open or closed the face, the more right or left the shots will tend to travel. From an initial fitting point of view, when discussing a player's game with him, to determine what he believes the shot pattern to be. A sliced shot or a pushed shot may end up in the same position after they land, but they got to that position via different flight patterns. The slice got there through a curving pattern, the push was a much straighter shot, but aligned to the right. Do not just ask a player where his shots finally come to rest, try to determine their ball flight to get to that position.

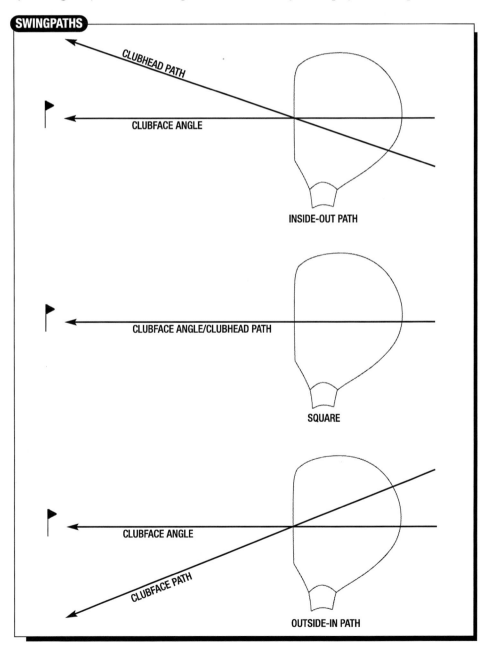

SWINGPATHS

CLUBHEAD PATH

CLUBFACE ANGLE

INSIDE-OUT PATH

CLUBFACE ANGLE/CLUBHEAD PATH

SQUARE

CLUBFACE ANGLE

CLUBFACE PATH

OUTSIDE-IN PATH

Swing paths may be one of three main types; each will have a decided effect on ball direction when combined with face angle.

TYPICAL BALL FLIGHT PATTERNS

Swing Path	Face Angle	Probable Ball Flight Pattern	Face Angle Recommendation
A. Square	Square	Straight	No Change
B. Square	Open	Starts right, stays right	Closed
C. Square	Closed	Starts left, stays left	Open
D. Inside-out	Square	Starts straight, draws	Open
E. Inside-out	Open	Straight right, draws	No Change
F. Inside-out	Closed	Starts left, hooks	Open
G. Outside-in	Square	Starts straight, fades	No change
H. Outside-in	Open	Starts right, slices	Very closed
I. Outside-in	Closed	Straight left, fades	More open

NOTE: Any changes in the degree of face angle, relative to the target, may cause the ball flight to vary from the above examples. Variations of inside-out and outside-in swing paths also may change expected ball flight patterns.

General guidelines for face angle and swing path shot patterns are shown in various diagrams in this chapter and charts on this page. By observing a player's ball flight or by listening to him honestly describe what is happen to the ball when it is in the air will help to determine the most likely face angle and swing path of the particular player. Once these charac-teristics are known, the accurate fitting of face angle may begin.

FACE ANGLE AND OTHER FITTING PARAMETERS

A properly fit golf club results from a series of fitting parameters that will best match a given player. Face angle is but one of those parameters. A change in the face angle of a club may have a notice-able effect upon the playing characteris-tics of that club. In the same manner, a change in another of a club's specifica-tions, may yield a change in the way the club's face angle influences play. The inter-relationship between one specifica-tion and another is a key consideration during the fitting of any and all specifica-tions to a given player.

LOFT

It may bear discussion at this point of a face angle phenomenon called "effective loft." Effective loft is a relationship between the club's face angle and its loft. (Loft is the specification that controls dis-tance and trajectory.) Effective loft is defined as the wood's loft when it is placed in a square (0-degree) position. Perhaps the best way to explain effective loft is through a series of examples that relate face angle and loft to create a cer-tain type of ball flight.

In the case of a wood that has a

BALL FLIGHT PATTERNS

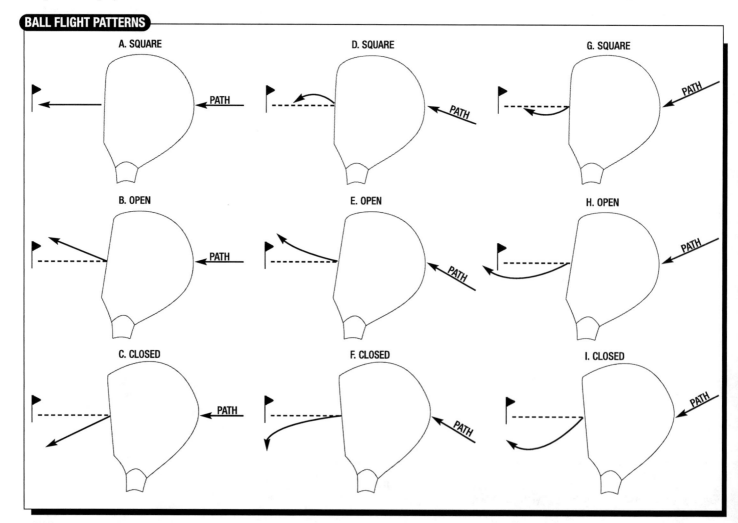

A. SQUARE	D. SQUARE	G. SQUARE
B. OPEN	E. OPEN	H. OPEN
C. CLOSED	F. CLOSED	I. CLOSED

square face, its effective loft is the same as its measured loft. That is, if the club has a loft that is measured at 10-degrees in a specs gauge, that will be its effective loft. But if that 10-degree lofted wood has a face angle of 2 degrees open, its effective loft will not be 10 degrees. If the face of the open club is aimed directly at the target, it will in effect be "closed-down." Its effective loft will decrease a corresponding amount to the number of degrees it was closed to move the face to the 0-degree position. If the 10-degree driver was moved 2 degrees to the square position, its effective loft would be reduced 2 degrees; it has an effective loft of 8 degrees.

If this seems a bit difficult to understand, take a clubhead and it in your hand, pointing it a specific target, say a clock hanging on the wall. Assume it has a square face and a 10-degree loft. If you want to hit an imaginary ball straight toward the clock, all you have to do is move the head on the line between you and the clock. Now, assume the club has a 2-degree open face. This means that when you hold it in your hand the face will point to the right of the clock. If you move the head straight back and forth, the face still points to the right and your imaginary ball goes right. In order to hit the imaginary ball straight, you have to turn the face counterclockwise (to the left - assuming a right-handed golfer.) In the process, the loft of the club will be reduced. You have effectively taken the 10-degree loft in the open position and changed it to 8 degrees in the square position. The club's effective loft is 8 degrees.

Following the same example, hold a 10° loft head that is 2 degrees closed. Thus it would be pointing to the left of

the target clock. Moving the head straight back and forth down the line would shows the face pointing to the left of the clock. In order for the club to be positioned toward the target, the face must be opened (and your hands turn the club clockwise to the right) so that it indeed points where it should. You will now be able to actually see more of the face when this is done; the effective loft of the club has been increased. Instead of playing to its measured loft of 10 degrees, the club now plays to an effective loft closer to 12 in a square position.

A clubfitter needs to be acutely aware of the effective loft phenomenon. If you fit a player with either an open or closed face and that face returns to impact in that same open or closed position, the effective loft does not change. But, if the club returns to a square (or a more open or closed position) its effective loft will change. Remember the term, "normal soled position?" A club's loft is designed to perform in this position. If a club measures 10 degrees in this position, that is the loft to which it was designed. If a player manipulates the club at address due the his trying to compensate for some type of swing deficiency or unacceptable optics, he effectively will change the loft of the club. If he turns it to close the face, the effective loft is reduced; if he opens it, the effective loft increases. There is a very close one-to-one relationship between the amount of opening or closing of the face and the change in effective loft of the club.

TORQUE

Face angle and shaft torque pose a relationship that must be considered by the clubfitter as well. Shaft torque (the resistance to twisting of a shaft) has the

effect of positioning the club's face at a specific direction at impact. A higher torque shaft will twist more; a lower torque shaft will twist less. A shaft that has a good deal of torque may help to close the face of a club for a player who tends to swing slowly or smoothly. That same high torque shaft may close the face excessively in the hands of a fast swinging player. While torque is but one factor in a shaft's performance, it does have the effect of helping to close (or open) a club's face at impact. Thus, shaft torque has a very profound effect on the club's face position (or face angle) at impact.

If the shaft's torque closes the face for a given player, the actual face angle at impact may be more closed than intended, resulting in shots to the left of target. In the cases of faster swingers, this may be detrimental to performance, but in the case of slower swingers who have difficulty squaring the face at impact, it may actually help. In general, most quick swinging players are better fitted with lower torque shafts, in the 3.5 degree or lower ranges, while smooth swingers or less-strong golfers or better matched with torques certainly at 4 degrees or more. Keep in mind that there will be much more torque variation from high to low when using graphite shafts than when using steel shafts. Most steel shafts have a torque somewhere in the 2-degree area; graphite can range from less than that to well over 10 degrees.

There will be instances of a player being actually best-fit with a closed face angle who simply does not like the way the club looks at address. He constantly wants to manipulate the club so it looks good - probably opening the face angle and increasing the effective loft in the process. He could potentially be matched

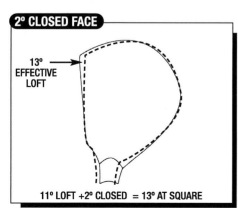
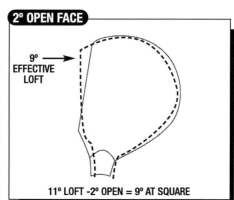
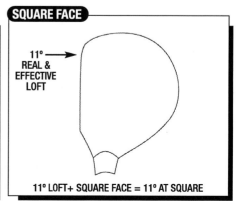

Effective loft is a combination of a wood's face angle and its relationship with the target.

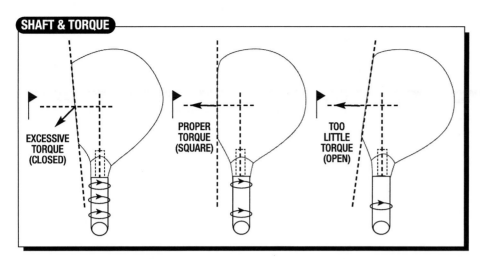

SHAFT & TORQUE

EXCESSIVE TORQUE (CLOSED)

PROPER TORQUE (SQUARE)

TOO LITTLE TORQUE (OPEN)

Regardless of where lead tape is placed on a club head, it will not alter the CG any appreciable amount.

to a square face angle (assuming he is less likely to manipulate this club) and a higher torque shaft. The higher torque may help close the square face into a similar position as the original best-fit closed face positioned it. Another type of situation can occur when a strong player likes the look of, for example, a square face club, but hits too many shots to the left. By matching this player to a lower torque shaft (one that does not twist as much), the club face may effectively be more open at impact than it previously was, leading to more accurate drives and eliminating the tendency of shots to the left.

A number of graphite shafts feature graphics that indicate the torque of the shaft.

In a similar manner that shaft torque may have an effect on the position of the club's face at impact, a shaft's flex (it's bending properties) may influence face angle as well. As a shaft is swung, it bends and twists in a number of ways. If it bends too much or too little, the face may be out of position at impact, yielding errant shots. It was previously believed that if a shaft was too soft for a player, their shots would tend to be "hooked" to the left and if the shaft was too stiff, slices resulted. This has been proven to not be correct in all cases and will vary from player to player. Often times a shaft that is too soft may actually lead to faster swinger not being able to square the club's face to the target, causing shots to the right. In essence, if a shaft is either

too soft or too stiff for a player, expect the club's face to be out of position at impact - exactly in which manner will vary from player to player.

CENTER OF GRAVITY

The center of gravity of a club head can have an effect on the club's face angle as well. As a club's center of gravity, or CG, moves closer to the shaft, the required face angle is more open as a club tends to rotate around its center of gravity. This is a reason why most wooden woods were produced with open faces; if they were square or closed, shots will be hit to the left more often. As technology changed and metal woods become the norm, the CG of the head moved away from the shaft somewhat. Thus, most metal woods have face angles that are not so open. As titanium became the main material for clubhead production and the resulting heads approached and exceeded 300cc's, the club's center of gravity moved even farther from the hosel. The required face angles for these larger clubs are more closed than are those for smaller metal woods and as many as 3-4 degrees more than for wooden woods. The key reason the larger heads will have more closed face angles is the effect of the CG being moved away from the shaft - do not be alarmed at heads that are over 300cc's having closed face angles - if they did not, the face would be nearly impossible to return squarely to the target.

One final note here. Related to the use of lead tape to change the center of gravity of a golf club, it would take a tremendous amount of tape to have a noticeable effect on the CG of any club, be it a wood or an iron. Lead tape can be used to increase the weight of a club, but

as far as it being able to be placed on the head so that is has a noticeable effect on ball flight, it just will not happen under normal conditions. It will take between 10 and 15 grams of tape to have any effect on CG whatsoever. As each 4 1/2" strip of lead tape 1/2" wide weighs 2 grams, it would take upwards of 40" of tape on a club to have even a slight effect. There is simply not room on a club for that much tape. Even so, if lead tape is to be used on a club in an attempt to influence ball flight, it would be placed as follows: For potential closing of the face, place it on the heel. For possible opening of the face, it would go on the toe. In cases of attempting to increase trajectory, it would be placed on the sole. If lower ball flight is being sought, place it on the top part of the club head. Again, lead tape is best used for adding small amounts of weight to the club, not for altering its center of gravity or having any noticeable effect on face angle at impact.

FACE ANGLE DEMO CLUBS

The number of clubs specifically designated to fit face angle are not numerous or expensive. To accurately fit face angle, demo clubs of varying face angles will be required. Drivers are most often used when fitting face angle. To accurately match face angle and player, three clubs will be needed...one with a square face angle, one with a face angle 1-2 degrees closed and one correspondingly 1-2 degrees open. As offset clubs tend to help a player square the clubface, a wise addition to your driver demo section for face angle might be an offset driver. Try to find heads that are similar in lofts and looks. While this might not be totally possible, try to be as "uniform" as possible. In other words, if the square face demo is a 220cc stainless model, do not use a 325cc head for the closed test club, and so on. All of the demo clubs will be fitted with the same types of shafts - a lightweight steel in "R" flex will provide good results - and will be the same length (43-44"). Likewise all clubs will have the same grip type and size. If you so desire, you may expand your demo club selection with individual degrees of face angle as suggested below.

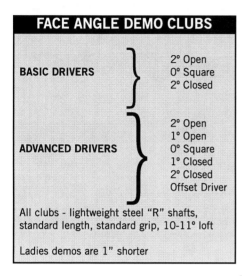

FACE ANGLE DEMO CLUBS	
BASIC DRIVERS	2° Open
	0° Square
	2° Closed
ADVANCED DRIVERS	2° Open
	1° Open
	0° Square
	1° Closed
	2° Closed
	Offset Driver

All clubs - lightweight steel "R" shafts, standard length, standard grip, 10-11° loft

Ladies demos are 1" shorter

FITTING FACE ANGLE

DYNAMIC FITTING INDOORS

To accurately dynamically fit face angle indoors, some type of computer will be a prerequisite. There is no way that a fitter, regardless of his or her ability, will be able to determine the specific position of the club face without some type of computerized measuring device. These computers begin in the several hundred-dollar price range and continue to those approaching $50,000.00. What the computer does is identify the position of the club's face at impact. Most analyzers will

Face angle can be accurately measured indoors using a GolfTek swing analyzer.

also indicate the player's swing path in some graphic manner. Advanced analyzers also utilize this face positioning to provide an interpretation of ball flight due to swing path and face angle. By looking at the position of the face and the resulting ball flight according to the computer, the fitter will be able to recommend an open face perhaps in the case of a player hitting shots to the left and vice-versa. Do remember though, that the shaft and head size that will be selected will have an effect on the face angle; it is thus important not to "officially" select a face angle until shaft testing is completed as well.

Assuming a computer is available, have the player hit a few balls with the club that you believe he will hit least effectively or perhaps the club closest to the spec that he is playing currently. Why? Most players have a problem with accuracy - with their current clubs. If the player slices (as do most players) start with the most open face angle demo club available. It is also a wise choice to have the player hit a few balls with his own club to see where the face angle of that club is at impact. While this will not help the player (obviously), it will provide

Smaller computers measure golfer traits such as swingspeed, path and face angle.

reinforcement that this face angle is not best suited for the player. Next, test the square face angle club. The computer will show an improvement in face angle position...whether this face angle is ideal, it is not known just yet. As there was most likely improvement in face angle position, next try the closed demo club. This may or may not show even more improvement in face angle position. If it

does, this would be a best fit selection. If, however, it positions the face too much closed (as per our example), the square face angle is a more wise choice.

DYNAMIC FITTING OUTDOORS

Dynamic fitting outdoors is very similar to dynamic fitting indoors. The same demo clubs are used, the same steps in using the demos are used, but instead of looking a computer screen, actual ball flight is observed. As in any fitting, watching actual ball flight is most often a better way to fit. Combined with an indoor computer, it provides very definitive data toward a complete fit. When fitting for face angle outdoors, follow the process of having the player hit his own club, then the series of demos. Watching ball flight may produce a "gee-whiz" effect. In other words, by hitting just a few demo clubs, the player will see a noted change in ball flight. As in the previous example, going from the most open to a more closed face angle, will certainly cause the slicing golfer to see an immediate difference in shot direction for the better. At that point, you become a "hero" to the player as the only way he ever hit the ball straight before was by accident - he was so used to having to play a slice, you have now potentially opened up a whole new game for him. The confidence he has in you as a fitter has grown exponentially due to the simple fitting of face angle through a few demo clubs.

Outdoor fitting permits the player and fitter to observe ball flight for a best-fit face angle recommendation.

A couple for cautions to remember when dynamically fitting face angles, whether indoors or out, include any possible tendency of a player to manipulate the club at address, effectively altering the club's face angle and effective loft. It is imperative that the player not reposition the club in any manner prior to testing for face angle, otherwise results may be skewed. Another key concern was mentioned before; that of making certain that when a shaft is fitted to the golfer, the torque of the shaft is not so much or so little to effect the face position at impact. Always, regardless of what parameter is being fitted, be aware that other parameters may very well have an effect on that one, making it a key element of fitting to consider the interplay of one specification effect on another.

STATIC FITTING

When it comes to static fitting of face angle, the player's discussion of his or her game will be the only source of information related to what might be a best-fit situation. Without having the opportunity to see the player actually hit balls, accurate face angle fitting is, at best, subjective. What can be done (hopefully) is to measure the face angle spec of the player's current driver and then ask questions, such as " Do you tend to miss more shots to the right or left?" "Describe your typical ball flight? Is it straight, left or right?" "Is there a distinct side of course you tend to hit most shots to and from?" Assuming the player is telling you the truth and he claims to be hitting the ball fairly straight, recommend a face angle close to what the current club has now. If he claims to be having trouble missing

most shots to the right, perhaps a more closed face than current will be a better choice. Correspondingly, if the player complains of missing a high percentage of shots to the left, go with a more open face than his present clubs.

Unfortunately, if the current driver cannot be measured, it is up to the discretion of the fitter to arbitrarily select a face angle based upon player discussion and evaluation of his game. This is the key reason why static fitting has distinct limitations. If at all possible, dynamic fitting of any specification, especially face angle, will provide more accurate best-fit scenarios.

FACE ANGLE
Summary: Do's and Don'ts of Face Angle Fitting

DO'S	DON'TS
DO: Keep in mind that face angle is the single most important factor related to ball direction in woods	**DON'T:** Overlook the cosmetic effect that face angle has on a club
DO: Know that swing path plays a key role in face angle fitting	**DON'T:** Fail to consider the relation between shaft torque and face angle
DO: Realize there is no substitution for the Dynamic Fitting of face angle	**DON'T:** Forget that irons do not have face angle
DO: Be aware that a shaft's torque and stiffness will have a potential effect of the club's face angle at impact	**DON'T:** Offer to modify face a club's face angle without knowing if it has a long enough hosel to permit alteration
DO: Consider that face angle and loft produce the effective loft of a wood	
DO: Take into account that an open face angle may look square to a player, that square looks closed and that closed may look "very closed" when fitting	
DO: Stay abreast of the trend toward most oversize drivers having a closed face specification	
DO: Know that nearly all 300+cc drivers will have face angles at least square or slightly closed to help square them at impact	

Chapter 6
Loft

Loft is, by definition, the angle formed between club face and groundline. The higher the loft measurement of the club, the higher the resulting ball flight. Conversely a lower-lofted club will tend to hit the ball lower, provided all other specifications of the club remain the same. Loft is the primary reason a ball becomes airborne. Typically through a set of clubs, the longer the club, the lower the loft. That is, a #1 iron will have less loft than a #2 and so on through the set. Putters will have the least amount of loft in the set, wedges will have the most. Determining the proper loft for a given player is an important consideration in fitting. In addition to helping get the ball airborne, loft has a secondary influence on accuracy. Lofts exist in conjunction with lengths of clubs to create different distances as well as trajectories. The goal of loft fitting is to optimize carry and roll distances related to woods; related to irons, the goal is to determine a trajectory that will hold the ball on the green without sacrificing distance.

All clubs that are the same number are created equal, right? A driver is a driver is a driver - not so fast. Driver lofts in today's marketplace range from lower than 5 degress as used by strong touring pros and long drive champions to as high as 14 or 15 degrees on certain lady and senior models. Yet all of these clubs are considered to be drivers. In this 9-degree range of driver lofts, some are separated by as little as .5 degrees. It is easy to see how two different drivers may provide very different playing characteristics related to ball flight and to accuracy as well.

Fairway woods follow the same trend in club number and club loft. For example, there are certain "strong" fairway clubs that have 12 or 13 degrees of loft - less than some drivers. Similarly, #3 woods vary from 13 to over 17 (or more) degrees of loft. The same applies to all fairway woods; the loft of one company's #5 wood may be the same as another manufacturer's #7. In short, it cannot be assumed that any metal wood with a certain number engraved on its sole will play similarly from one company to another.

The matter of loft versus playability becomes further clouded as some manufacturers do not use numbers on their clubs, but refer to them instead by name. "Rescue", "Jackaroo", "Heaven Wood", "Hypersteel", "Ely Wood", "Baffler" or "Machete" are monikers given to particular types or models of woods. These names often are not directly correlated with a loft. That is, sometimes the club will have no loft indication whatsoever on its sole, possibly confusing the golfer - and sometimes even the fitter. This poses unique choices for both player and fitter. Due to the proliferation of the variety of head designs, lofts and names given to them, it is sometimes confusing as to which loft is best for a player on a given head. The key element is to be aware of the actual lofts of the clubs being fitted and to not worry so much about their names.

Equally variable in today's world is the inconsistency of lofts from one company to another. What was formerly called a "standard" loft is now much weaker in many cases than lofts of clubs today. Even from current manufacturers, it is not uncommon for lofts of the same club number as indicated on the sole to vary by as much as 4 degrees. That is, the loft on a forged blade #5 iron may be 28 degrees, while the loft on an oversize cavity back may be 24. Just as with woods, not all irons are created equal. As a result of this great disparity of lofts, it is

A wide variety of clubs use names instead of lofts as shown by this "Rescue" and "Tri-Metal".

not uncommon for a player to claim they hit one #5 iron as much as 15 yards longer than another. It is important that the fitter realize this difference between lofts of the specific models that he is using for fitting and make recommendations accordingly.

Loft "standards", if there are such specifications, have changed noticeably over the past quarter-century. The decided trend is toward stronger (lower) lofted irons in the quest for added distance. This is not always a negative as head designs over the past 30 years have changed from non-forgiving blades to larger, improvement-oriented cavity backs. These perimeter-weighted designs have a higher percentage of their weight toward the sole. The lower the weight, the lower the center of gravity and the

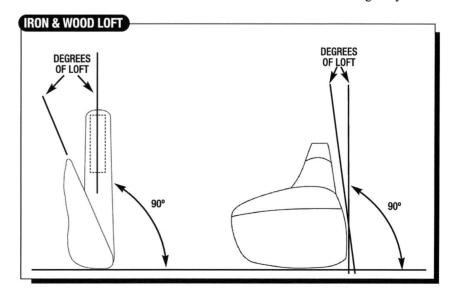

IRON & WOOD LOFT

DEGREES OF LOFT

DEGREES OF LOFT

90°

90°

INDUSTRY AVERAGE GOLF CLUB LOFTS THROUGH THE YEARS

	1950's & 60's	1970's & 80's	1990's & 2000's
WOODS			
Driver	11°	10°	9.5°
3	16°	15°	14°
5	22°	21°	18°
7	N/A	27°	21°
9	N/A	N/A	25°
IRONS			
1	17°	16°	15°
2	20°	19°	18°
3	24°	22°	20°
4	28°	25°	23°
5	32°	28°	26°
6	36°	32°	30°
7	40°	36°	34°
8	44°	40°	38°
9	48°	44°	42°
PW	52°	49°	46°
SW	56°	55°	55°
UW	N/A	60°	60°
AW	N/A	N/A	50° & 52°

N/A indicates clubs were not produced during those years

TRADITIONAL VS MODERN LOFTS

Club	Traditional	Modern
WOODS		
#1	12°	11°
#3	17°	16°
#5	23°	22°
#7	29°	28°
IRONS		
#1	17°	16°
#2	20°	18°
#3	24°	21°
#4	28°	24°
#5	32°	28°
#6	36°	32°
#7	40°	36°
#8	44°	40°
#9	48°	44°
PW	52°	48°
SW	56°	54°
UW	60°	60°

higher the ball flight. Today's lower lofts combine with the cavity-backed design to create a ball flight that is neither too high nor too low for most players. Thus the concept of "standard" is used more for reference than specific application; yet the variety of lofts available today does provide the golfer with a myriad of custom fitting options. The challenge for the fitter is to combine the most playable head design for the golfer along with the loft that will generate the combination of the best distance and accuracy - the goal of any best-fit situation.

CAVITY BACK VS. BLADE LOFT SPECS

Loft Cavity Back	Loft Blade
17°	19°
20°	22°
23°	25°
26°	28°
30°	32°
34°	36°
38°	40°
42°	44°
46°	49°
55°	55°

A club loft that is too strong (too low) for a player will usually precipitate two problems. Initially, there will be a loss of accuracy. As a club has more loft, it will tend to create more backspin. Remember that backspin helps to counteract "negative" sidespin. That is, if a ball is hit with an outside-in swing, it will tend to spin clockwise, resulting in a slice. If the club has more loft, the spin generated by the loft will tend to reduce the negative sidepsin; loft in essence, provides a corrective factor. When the loft of a club is too strong for a player, there will be less correction related to off-path swings. The net result will be an overall loss of

Changing the loft of an iron in a loft/lie machine.

accuracy. Make sure the terms strong and weak are understood related to loft. "Strong" indicates a lower lofted club, as a club becomes stronger, its loft decreases. The term "weak" related to a club with more loft. As loft is added to a club, it becomes weaker.

Loft will also have a direct effect on distance. Slower swinging players will tend to need more loft in order to help them get the ball airborne. Faster swingers will be able to generate enough clubhead speed to get lower lofted clubs airborne. A misconception exists that the lower the loft, the longer the ball flight. This simply is not true; often slower swinging players may benefit by using higher lofted clubs. Dynamic fitting will determine exactly what loft a player will be able to hit the longest and most accurate.

Feel deserves mention here as well. If the loft of a club is too low for a player, often he or she will describe the club as being "dead." This is most likely due to the combination of a less than perfect swing, combined with a lack of forgiveness of the low loft. Consistency will suffer; any time consistency is compromised, feel is usually compromised as well.

A club's loft can be measured by using a variety of methods. Perhaps the simplest (and least accurate) method is through the use of a loft gauge. This four-position gauge has openings matching 4 specific lofts. When measuring a driver, these openings may correspond to 8, 9, 10 and 11 degrees of loft. The gauge is placed onto the club with one side on the center of the face and the other on the sole's center. (Remember that a wood's face will have face curvature from its top to sole called roll; it is important to position the gauge in the face center for measuring accuracy.) If the two sides match the sole center and face center, the loft is the degree indicated on the gauge. If the sides do not match, another position in the gauge may be tried. The two drawbacks to this method are the fact that if the club is not one of the four lofts on the gauge, it cannot be measured; the other is the difficulty of positioning the club precisely on face and sole center when holding both the gauge and the club. Loft gauges exist not only for drivers but for fairways. Their use and characteristics are the same as the driver gauge. Such loft gauges do not exist for irons or putters.

In much the same manner that the face gauge was used, a protractor can also be used to measure a wood's loft. The technique of finding the face and sole center is the same; the drawback of being accurately able to position the protractor is also much the same as when using the gauge. The advantage the protractor has over the gauge is that all lofts are able to be determined; there is no limit in loft choices as there is with the gauge. Plus, if used carefully, the protractor can be used to determine the lofts of irons and putters. While the protractor is a better way to measure loft, a specifications gauge is by far the best method of accurately determining a club's loft.

The specifications gauge will hold

This type of loft gauge really does not provide adequate loft choices for a variety of clubs.

The only truly accurate way to measure a club's loft is through the use of a specs gauge.

any club securely as it is being measured. This is the same gauge that is used to measure lie and face angle. The club is positioned in the gauge with the sole center resting on the base of the gauge. Once this position is determined through the use of file cards as described in detail in on page 63 of Chapter 4, the loft (as well as the lie and face angle) can be accurate-

ly determined. To measure loft, a protractor is slid along the base of the specifications gauge until it meets the center of the face. The process is the same for all clubs; the only consideration that should be made is for face roll when measuring woods. Once the gauge is against the face, loft is read directly from the gauge. There is a thumbscrew that can be tightened so that the loft can be locked in place for reading after it is taken off the gauge. Due to the stability of holding the club in the gauge, this becomes the preferred method of measuring not only the loft of a club, but is lie and face angle (in the case of woods) as well.

EFFECT ON BALL FLIGHT

TRAJECTORY AND DISTANCE

How high a ball goes at its apex is defined as its trajectory. The higher the loft on a club, the higher the resulting trajectory. Thus if we compare two drivers, one with 8 degrees of loft and one with

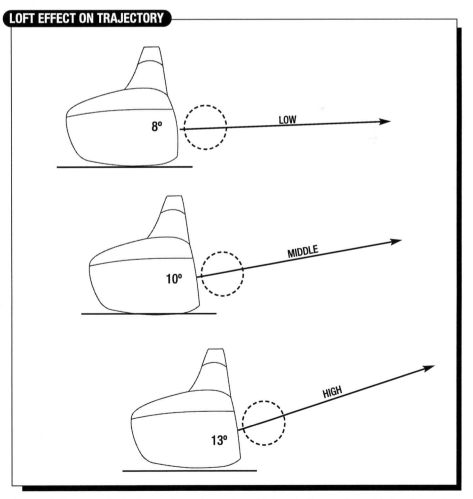

LOFT EFFECT ON TRAJECTORY

8° LOW

10° MIDDLE

13° HIGH

Lower lofts equate to lower launch angles; higher lofts produce higher launch angles.

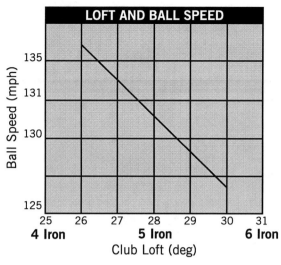

The lower the loft on a club, the higher its ball-speed tends to be.

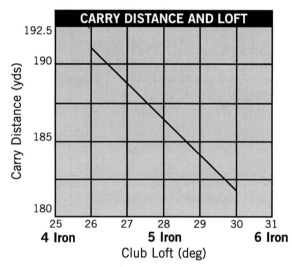

Generally as club loft becomes stronger, the carry distance produced from that club increases.

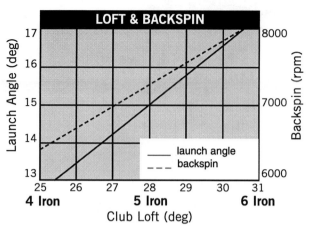

As loft increases, launch angle and backspin increase as well.

10, the 10 degree lofted club will fly higher, assuming the same head design, shaft type and material, club length, etc. Generally for faster swinging players (90 or more miles per hour with a driver), the higher trajectory will result in a slight loss of distance. This is due to the higher flight of the ball resulting in less roll after the ball hits the ground. But, for a slower swinger, a ball that travels higher may actually carry a longer distance than one hit lower, thus resulting in more distance. While loft does have an effect on distance, it is a different effect when compared to fast and slow swingers.

When discussing irons, the same may hold true, but there will not be as large of a discrepancy between trajectory and distance as there is with woods. This is due to the added backspin helping to get the ball into the air with an iron. Shorter irons (#9's and wedges) spin the ball more than any other irons. That is

part of the reason that these clubs fly higher than any others. But, if iron lofts are decreased, there will be the distinct possibility that the ball will run farther after it hits the ground. This can be beneficial if overall distance is desired, but may detrimental if the ball is supposed to stop reasonably close to the hole. Thus more loft equates to higher and shorter flight in irons, regardless of swingspeed; less loft equates to longer and lower shots - assuming all shots are struck on-center with an on-plane swing.

ACCURACY AND BACKSPIN

The more loft a club has, the easier it is to hit straight. The primary reasons are backspin and club length. A higher lofted club puts more spin on the ball. The higher loft actually causes the ball to remain on the face a fraction of a millisecond longer. The longer the ball stays on the face, the more it spins. The more backspin a ball has, the less likely it is to travel off line. Backspin has a negating effect of any sidespin; thus the more backspin a club has, the less likely it is to travel off course. The other factor involved in accuracy is club length. Shorter clubs are easier to return squarely to impact than are longer ones. They are, as a result more accurate. Add to this the fact that the shorter irons have more loft (which further promotes accuracy) and it is no wonder the shorter, more-lofted clubs in a set are the easiest one to hit most accurately.

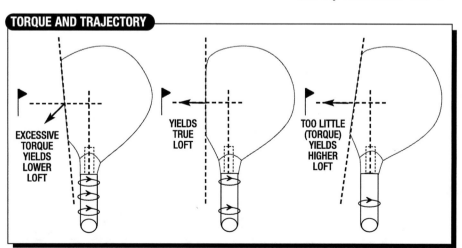

The torque of a shaft has a correlation with the dynamic loft of a club.

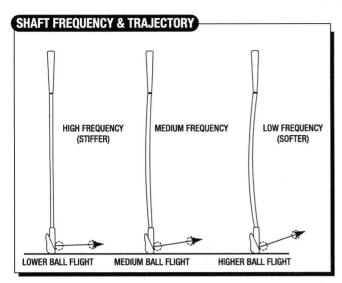

SHAFT FREQUENCY & TRAJECTORY

HIGH FREQUENCY (STIFFER) MEDIUM FREQUENCY LOW FREQUENCY (SOFTER)

LOWER BALL FLIGHT MEDIUM BALL FLIGHT HIGHER BALL FLIGHT

DYNAMIC LOFT

The term Dynamic Loft refers to the actual position of the club face at impact. If the club shaft were an inflexible rod, and the player made an on-plane swing, the actual loft and dynamic loft of the club would be virtually the same. But, as the shaft is not a solid rod, it may tend to bow forward at impact, having the effect of increasing the loft of the club. The more flexible the shaft, the more the potential there is for this to occur. A shaft's torque may also have an effect on dynamic loft. If a shaft has a higher degree of torque, it is most often a tip-weak shaft. Tip weak shafts may tend to bow forward more at impact, perhaps leading to more dynamic loft. But, there is a fine line between a high torque shaft bowing forward and closing down at impact. Any closing down could result in a low hooking shot, rather than a straight, higher one. Lighter weight shafts, due to the fact they move the club's balance point farther from the player's hands, also promote higher shots.

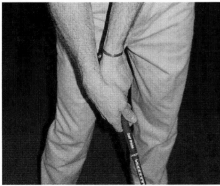

A "wristy" swing adds dynamic loft to a club - it also leads to consistency concerns.

The golfer himself has an impact on dynamic loft. A player who may tend to supinate or "flip" his or her wrists may actually position the club in a more lofted position than it was at address. This type of swing characteristic may either result in higher shots than perhaps are expected or can yield thin, unsolid feeling shots. The opposite is true as well. A shot hit with the wrists in an unhingned (pronated) position will effectively reduce dynamic loft, resulting in lower than desired trajectories. During dynamic fitting ball flight will be observed taking into consideration any tendency for a player to either add or reduce dynamic loft as a result of his swing.

SWING PLANE AND ANGLE OF ATTACK

A player who has an upright swing plane will tend to hit the ball higher than a player who has a flatter plane. This is due to the increased angle of attack from the upright plane. The more upright the swing plane, the higher the ball will fly. Many seniors may possibly require lower lofts as they do not generate a great deal of head speed and hit the ball on the upswing. Depending upon ball position, there is not a direct relationship between angle of attack and recommended loft. If the ball is positioned forward in the player's stance, there is more chance for a sweeping type of swing, which actually may add loft to the club (and require a lower-lofted club as a result.) In the cases of the player playing the ball back in the stance, perhaps a higher-lofted club will be in order as a result of the steeper angle of attack in this position. Thus, at times, a strong player may actually be best-fit with a higher loft due to his steep angle of attack and rearward ball position.

OFFSET

Offset (the distance from the leading edge of the club to the leading edge of the hosel) causes a change in a shot's trajec-

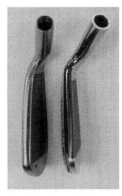

Examples of offset and non-offset irons.

tory, thus influencing loft. A club with more offset will tend to hit the ball higher than will one with a lower offset. (It will also tend to help square the face for straighter shots.) The added offset will effectively position the club at impact so that it adds backspin to a shot, causing it to fly higher. Irons are more offset than woods; this keeps a player's hands forward, possibly creating a lower launch angle but more backspin. Offset also tends to instill confidence at address as the club seems easier to hit. Psychology does play a role in performance; if a club seems like it will be easy to hit, chances are the true results may improve.

CENTER OF GRAVITY

While center of gravity and loft will vary from club to club, the CG will have the effect of positioning the face (and loft) in a certain manner at impact. If a club's center of gravity is equal to or higher than the center of the ball, expect a lower trajectory. If the CG is lower than the equator of the ball, expect the ball to get airborne more easily. If a club has a low CG and heavy sole, during the swing centrifugal force will be working to cause the area on the club where the CG is most highly concentrated to seek the ground. The heavy sole will be forced toward the ground. At the same time, the club will

A club with brass sole inserts has a low center of gravity.

LOFT COMPARISON FAIRWAY WOODS-LONG IRONS		
Loft	Iron	Wood
15°	#1	#3
18°	#2	#4
21°	#3	#5
24°	#4	#6
28°	#5	#7(26°)
32°	#6	#9(31°)
36°	#7	#11(35°)
40°	#8	#13(39°)
44°	#9	#15(43°)
NOTE: All lofts based on modern standards		

often be positioned in a more lofted position, resulting in higher ball flight. During a fitting, any club with a heavier sole should be studied carefully to ensure it does not add excess trajectory to the shot. A clubhead that has a higher CG will yield a correspondingly lower ball flight as its sole is not so heavy and the forces of physics that are exerted on it will not be so great.

The same type of concept applies to woods that are broad from front to back. Their CG is more rearward than that of most smaller woods. The rear part of the head is forced to toward the ground, resulting in added dynamic loft to the club. Shallow faced woods have a low CG due to their compact size. The reason they are easier to get airborne is due to the lower weight distribution and the physical effects of centrifugal force upon those types of clubs.

FACE ROLL

Face Roll has a minor impact on ball trajectory. While it could be argued that a ball hit high on the face of a club will fly higher than expected due to the face curvature, or roll, any such differences are inconsequential. The same could be figured for a shot hit lower on the face. The face roll will cause it to go lower than anticipated. The fact is any shot hit high enough or low enough on the face for roll to have an effect will be a poor shot regardless of roll. Face roll is much more important in the cosmetic look of the club than it is in trajectory.

SOLE ANGLES, OFFSET AND BENDING

Anytime a fitter may recommend a change in the loft specifications for a given iron (Remember wood lofts cannot be changed by bending.), there will be a resultant change in two other specifications; sole angle and offset. An iron, by design, will rest flat on the ground on its sole center provided it is properly addressed. If the loft of an iron is changed, this sole angle will correspondingly change. If an iron's loft is decreased (made stronger), it's leading edge will be more tilted toward the ground, creating what is known as a dig or scoop sole. A dig sole will tend to lead to the potential of more fat shots or at least to the tendency to hit behind the ball slightly. As the club is bent stronger, its offset increases as well. In effect, the leading edge is bent back toward the hosel, adding to offset.

If a club is bent so that its loft is increased (made weaker), offset is reduced and sole angle changed. When loft is added, the leading edge is moved off the ground, causing what is known as a bounce sole. Such a sole design will make the leading edge of the club appear to be noticeably off the ground at address. At impact, unless adjustments are made by the player, a bounce sole will tend to produce thin, low shots. The leading edge of the club hits the ball first, causing these undesirable, low running shots. The maximum amount that loft should be changed is 2 degrees; any more than that will definitely create a dig or bounce sole, rendering the club less playable than its design would dictate.

LOFT AND SET MAKEUP

Set makeup related to loft is defined as how many clubs will be in the player's bag and what the specifications of those clubs will be. The goal in determining proper set makeup for a player is to provide him or her with 13 clubs that will provide all of the distance and accuracy requirements likely to be encountered during a typical round of golf. Thirteen is used as the number of clubs, making the assumption that the fourteenth club is a putter. A fitter is able to tailor the set makeup to a particular course if necessary, or to a particular style of play. For example, most touring pros have a couple of different wedges; they select which ones they will use during a given tournament based on the particular grass and sand conditions they will encounter that week. The player being fitted can do

much the same.

Let's begin with the driving club. Note the term "driving club" is used. Not all players (especially beginners and slow swingers) may be fitted with a driver, but instead with a # 3 wood. In any event, the goal of this club is to hit the ball as long and as accurately as possible. Every player will have a driving club in his or her set. These driving clubs can be specifically tailored to the course the player plays most often. Let's say the player plays a course with few trees and no watering system. On such a course, a low-loft driver may be a good choice. While it may not provide as much carry as higher lofted woods, the added roll on the hard ground will lead to longer shots; the lower loft may not provide the best accuracy, but as there are not many trees or rough on the course, this does not pose a great problem.

At least one fairway club should be part of a player's set. This club is used for long shots from good lies in the fairway. Most players will also benefit from one or two more woods; one to be used for long shots from the rough and one to be used for more accurate distance shots from either rough or fairway. These woods may have lower centers of gravity, shallow faces or rails to help them perform well from less-than-ideal conditions. In many cases, the CG of woods makes them a better option than long irons for slower swinging and less accomplished players. It is not uncommon for a player to carry a full complement of woods, including a driving club, a #3 wood for good lies, #5 and #7 woods for lies in the rough or fairway and even a #9 or #11 wood for shots form very bad lies of for those closer to the green. LPGA professional, Liselotte Neumann carries six or seven woods, proving that high-lofted woods are not just for lesser ability players. In any event, each of these woods that a player carries, from the driving club through highest-lofted wood, are designed with a certain distance parameter in mind.

Part of a player's set makeup may be some type of "transition" club, also known as an "iron/wood" or a "wood/iron." These clubs have become popular replacements for long irons in many players' bags. In addition, these clubs, due to their smaller heads and lower CG's than even many high-lofted fairway woods, are easier to hit from the rough for a number of players. These clubs are sometimes built to long iron specifications using .370" shafts and some are sometimes built to #5, 6 or 7 wood lengths using wood (.335") shafts. If the player is interested in these types of clubs, be certain that the lofts chosen do not overlap either the lofts of the player's long irons or high-lofted woods. Let's say, for example, a golfer has a #7 wood of 24 degrees of loft, a #4 iron of 23 degrees and is interested in a transition club of 22 degrees of loft. In this situation, the player has three clubs that will hit the ball very similar distances. The fitter and player need to make some decisions about what club(s) stay and what are removed. One suggestion might be to keep the #7 wood, drop the #4 iron and select a transition club in the 22-degree range.

Moving to irons and set makeup, no longer is an eight iron set the standard. In years past, a set of irons included eight clubs, #3 iron through pitching wedge. The advantage the custom fitter has is that he or she can make certain all of the distances are "covered" during the selection of set makeup. Thus if the player hits high-lofted woods or transition clubs better than long irons, the #3 and #4 can be eliminated from the set. The key is to have clubs that match in distance and trajectory requirements...not necessarily those that match in name or number. Most probably, unless adjustments are made for some reason, irons will have 4 degrees of loft from one to another in a set. Exceptions occur related to wedges, but most irons show this 4-degree variation or something very close to it. Thus in choosing irons, there is not a great need to worry about the degrees between each, but more to be concerned with the design of the irons and how well the player hits them.

Related to wedges, we find a huge difference in lofts from one wedge to another. Pitching wedges of 45 degrees exist, as do models exceeding 50 degrees. Sand wedges range from just above 50 degrees to over 56. There are wedges known as utility wedges, gap wedges, and all-purpose wedges, just to name a few. The key element in wedge fitting is to find a pitching type of wedge with 4-5 degrees more loft than the #9 iron. Add

another wedge 4-5 degrees less-lofted than that as a sand or all-purpose wedge. Another wedge or two of higher loft may be added, again going in 4-5 degree increments, depending upon how many other clubs are in the player's bag.

The magic number is fourteen clubs in a set to comply with USGA Rules. Statistically more than half of a player's shots are hit with 110 yards of the green. Having only two clubs, for example a pitching wedge and sand wedge for use in this range may limit the player's ability to score as well as he possibly can. Adding wedges that have lofts other than the PW and SW can make for more accurate shot-making in this 110 yard area. Many professionals actually carry three wedges and some have even four. These wedges are typically a 50-degree PW, a 54 or 55-degree SW, a 59 or 60-degree lob type of wedge and for those carrying a fourth wedge, a 64-degree model. These lofts will allow a player to make a full swing - which is easier to do - on a number of shots near the green, increasing the possibility of getting the ball close to the hole. For a complete discussion of wedge fitting, including specifications other than loft, please consult Chapter 10.

Both fitter and player need to be aware that there are literally hundreds of clubs that will help his game. The key is to narrow the selection to the 13 of them, plus the putter, that will provide the potential for lower scores. Through knowledge of club lofts and their effect on performance, the fitter will be able to guide the player toward an assortment of clubs that will provide incremental distance and accuracy through the set.

LOFT AND OTHER FITTING PARAMETERS

FACE ANGLE

A review at this point reminds us of the loft face angle phenomenon called "effective loft." Effective loft is a relationship between the club's loft and its face angle. (Face angle refers to the direction of the club face, either at address or at impact.) Effective loft is defined as the wood's loft when it is placed in a square (0-degree) position. Perhaps the best way to review effective loft is through a series of examples that related face angle and loft to create a cer-

tain type of ball flight.

In the case of a wood that has a square face, its effective loft is the same as its measured loft. That is, if the club has a loft that is measured at 9-degrees in a specification gauge, that will be its effective loft. But if that 9-degree lofted wood has a face angle of 2 degrees open, its effective loft will not be 9 degrees. If the face of the open club is aimed directly at the target, it will in effect be "closed-down." Its effective loft will decrease a corresponding amount to the number of degrees it was closed to move the face to the 0-degree position. If the 9-degree driver was moved 2 degrees to the square position, its effective loft would be reduced 2 degrees; it has an effective loft of 7 degrees.

EFFECTIVE LOFTS - DRIVERS		
Stated Loft	Face Angle	Effective Loft
8°	1.5° Open	6.5°
8°	0° Square	8°
8°	2° Closed	10°
10°	1.5° Open	8.5°
10°	0° Square	10°
10°	2° Closed	12°
12°	1.5° Open	10.5°
12°	0° Square	12°
12°	2° Closed	14°

Following the same example, what happens if the head were 2 degrees closed? It would be pointing to the left of the target, assuming a right handed club-head. In order for the club to be positioned toward the target, the face must be opened so that it indeed points where it should. You will now be able to actually see more of the face when this is done; the effective loft of the club has been increased. Instead of playing to its measured loft of 9 degrees, the club now plays to an effective loft closer to 11 in a square position.

A clubfitter needs to be acutely aware of the effective loft phenomenon. If you fit a player with either an open or closed face and that face returns to impact in that same open or closed position, the effective loft does not change. But, if the club returns to a square (or a more open or closed impact position) its effective loft will change. Remember the term, "normal soled position?" A club's loft is designed to perform in this position. If a club measures 9 degrees in this position, that is the loft to which it was designed. If a player manipulates the club at address due the his trying to compensate for some type of swing deficiency or unacceptable optics, he effectively will change the loft of the club. If he turns it to close the face, the effective loft is reduced; if he opens it, the effective loft increases. There is a very close one-to-one relationship between the amount of opening or closing of the face and the change in effective loft of the club.

SHAFT LENGTH AND LOFT

Typically a club fitted with a longer and lighter shaft will provide a higher ball flight as a result of the longer arc and potentially higher swingspeed such a club may produce. If the player being fitted is matched to an overlength driver with a lightweight shaft, it may be wise choice to select a club whose loft is a degree or two less than originally planned. In other words, if the player is using a 60-gram graphite shaft at 45", instead of choosing a 10-degree loft, perhaps a 9 or even an 8.5 loft will produce a ball flight that will be similar to what the player desires or is used to. In most cases larger heads are used on these longer shafted drivers. Most of the large heads have deeper centers of gravity, further potentially adding to the trajectory of the drives. The combination of these factors cause loft choices to tend toward the lower lofts in order to "equalize" ball trajectory. This is why more and more OEM's are offering lower and lower lofted clubs. It is not uncommon for even the average player to use an 8 or 9 degree, longer and lighter shafted

oversize titanium driver with a good deal of success. Longer length and ultralight shaft weight, when combined with 300+cc heads yield higher ball flights; lofts must be fitted accordingly.

Most golfers have seen evidence of this. When titanium drivers came onto the scene in the mid-1990's, players who hit them complained that they went too high. They believed it was the titanium that somehow caused this. What they did not realize was the longer and lighter shafts that these clubs employed created more arc and speed, causing the higher flight. Manufacturers did not realize this effect initially and made lofts on titanium drivers in much the same manner as they did on steel headed (and shorter, heavier-shafted) drivers. Quickly, manufacturers began producing titanium heads with lower lofts; these new heads lowered ball flight to a similar trajectory of a stainless metal wood - one to which the player was accustomed. Two possible demo clubs to use in order to prove this include two titanium driver heads of the same spec, one with a 43" steel shaft, the other with a 45" 60-gram graphite shaft. The longer, lighter shafted model will produce noticeably higher flight, proving that lower loft is a potential consideration when fitting these types of clubs.

LOFT DEMO CLUBS

In a basic setup, loft demo clubs will be focused on woods only. As in other demo setups, all shafts will be lightweight steel, regular flex, standard length and grip. All demo clubs will be labeled accordingly. As there are a number of loft ranges for drivers, a basic demo would include one each in the low, mid and high loft ranges. A wise start to a loft demo program would be an 8, 10 and 12 degree

All loft demo clubs should be specifically labeled.

model. If possible, head design on all should be approximately the same. Do not use a shallow, a deep and a standard head. Also, volumes, face angles, etc. should be the same for all loft demo heads if possible.

As the demo program becomes more complete, the addition of other lofts is an initial consideration. Perhaps a very low-lofted driver and a higher lofted one (even a #3 wood) will make for a more complete fitting option. Advanced demos may include a shallow driver and a very large or deep driver in order to show the player the potential impact of center of gravity on loft. Two titanium drivers shafted differently (as previously discussed) are a good choice testing. In an advanced demo selection, perhaps some #6 irons of various lofts should be includ-

LOFT DEMO CLUBS	
BASIC (woods only)	
8°	
10°	
12°	

ADVANCED (woods & irons)	
Woods	**#6 Irons**
7°	28°
8°	32°
10°	36°
12°	
13+°	

All clubs assembled with lightweight steel "R" shafts, standard length, standard grip

Ladies 1" shorter

ed. Remember that if all of the #6's are of the same design, two of them will have to have their loft changed by bending. (One should be bent 2 degrees stronger, one 2 degrees weaker.) If this is done, play close attention to any sole angle changes due to the bending. It may be better to find three irons of similar design that have different loft specs by design to eliminate the possibility of sole angle influencing playability and loft selection.

EFFECTIVE LOFTS-FAIRWAY WOODS		
Stated Loft	**Face Angle**	**Effective Loft**
15°	1.5° Open	13.5°
15°	0° Square	15°
15°	2° Closed	17°
21°	1.5° Open	19.5°
21°	0° Square	21°
21°	2° Closed	23°
26°	1.5° Open	24.5°
26°	0° Square	26°
26°	2° Closed	28°

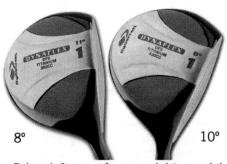

8°   10°

Driver lofts vary from model to model and must be fitted accordingly.

FITTING LOFT

DYNAMIC FITTING INDOORS

The fitting of loft indoors becomes somewhat subjective unless very sophisticated computerized equipment is available. There are few, if any, computers that factor loft into their on-screen data. Launch monitors do exist which will provide definitive launch angle data, but these, which may cost nearly $10,000, are cost-prohibitive is most shops. That said, when fitting loft indoors in a dynamic setting, look for the angle of attack as an initial guideline. A player who has a steep angle of attack may hit the ball higher than desired, thus requiring a lower loft driver. As previously mentioned, longer and lighter shafts tend to promote higher trajectory; if a player is being fitted with such a shaft(s), lower loft on the driver might be a wise option. Specific comments by the player about whether he or she hits the ball too high or too low will help you make a suggestion related to loft - especially when combined with the results of the loft measurements taken during the equipment evaluation.

In an indoor fitting situation, without a launch monitor, much the same observations will be made when fitting irons as when working with drivers. Steep angles of attack or upright swing planes generally yield high shots. If the player complains that his shots are too high, look to a set of irons that are engineered with lower lofts or a higher center of gravity as a first choice. Lofts can be altered, but again, no more than 2 degrees - and as not as good a choice as finding heads that have lower lofts as part of their design.

DYNAMIC FITTING OUTDOORS

The best place for most fitters to determine the most accurate loft specification is definitely outdoors. Here both player and fitter can actually monitor ball flight and make comments as to which trajectory is most desirable and which loft produces it. Generally as lofts are decreased, ball flight will become lower; also, accuracy may suffer at some point. Remember, the lower the loft, the less backspin that is produced. Thus, any swing "flaws" become recognizable as errant shots as loft is reduced. What is desired in an outdoor fitting is the realization of a loft that will produce the trajectory that is preferred by the player with no loss in accuracy. The player may want to hit his drives lower, but if when hitting the 8-degree demo club he can't hit the ball consistently, this is not a good choice. It is best to hit test the 10-degree head. This should improve accuracy, even though the trajectory may be a bit higher than the player initially desired - or at least thought he desired.

By hit testing a number of loft selections, both player and fitter will be able to see a point of diminishing returns. That is, a point where the lower loft, even if a lower ball flight is desired, will begin to cause accuracy problems. At whatever loft this is, the fitter should give the player the two loft clubs on the weaker side of this selection. For example, if the 8-degree driver is somewhat inconsistent, try the 10 and 12-degree driver. Probably the 12-degree will produce shots that are accurate, but too high. The 10-degree model may be the best-fit compromise to achieve both accuracy and trajectory for the player. The player should hit a couple of irons models of varying lofts and head designs (related to center of gravity) as well, here again looking for the best blend of trajectory and distance.

STATIC FITTING

The static fitting of loft will somewhat have to rely on player comments concerning how high or low he thinks he hits the ball. Especially in situations that the fitter may not be able to measure the loft of a player's current clubs, the static fitting of loft is somewhat guesswork. The ability of the player can be taken into account; that is, the better the player, the lower the recommended driver loft. The higher handicap player who complains of hitting the driver poorly may better be recommended with a 12-degree (or higher) driver. Keep in mind these are generalizations only and may not be accurate. When static fitting for the specification of loft, unfortunately the fitter's abilities are compromised due to lack of definitive data.

LOFT
Summary: Do's and Don'ts of Loft Fitting

DO'S	DON'TS
DO: Remember that loft is the most important element in ball trajectory	**DON'T:** Always assume all #5 irons (for example) have the same lofts
DO: Be aware loft standards may vary noticeably from one company to another	**DON'T:** Fit a player by a club's sole number, but rather by its loft specification
DO: Know that a club's specific loft characteristics may be influenced by shaft specifications	**DON'T:** Ignore the effect of other specifications (face angle, length and shaft) on the effective loft of a club
DO: Keep in mind the effect of face angle on the effective loft of woods	**DON'T:** Fail to consider the effects of shaft length, flex and weight on loft.
DO: Look to higher lofts for slower swinging players	
DO: Fit juniors and beginners with more generous lofts	

Chapter 7
Shafts

With several fitting specifications set, our fitting program now moves onto the other components of the golf club, starting with perhaps its most mysterious element - the shaft. Shaft fitting in the 21st century is a more complicated process that any time in the history of golf. Not because clubfitters know less about shafts, but because there is so much more to know, and more from which to choose.

Beginning in the 1980's and continuing through today, shaft technology has been changing at an unprecedented rate. The R&D departments of the world's shaft manufacturers are continually developing new products to match specific player needs, all the while refining their production techniques as well. The result? The highest quality most consistent shafts ever - including steel, graphite and unique composite materials!

But the boom of golf shaft development has created some confusion in the process. If a club fitter is truly committed to providing his customers with the best-fit golf equipment, no longer can he simply stock just a handful of shafts. Now he must keep up to date with the latest technology trends and offer choices based on specific swing characteristics. At the present there are well over 1,500 individual shaft models available to clubmakers. Given that incredible variety, how is the club fitter to be reasonably certain that his recommendations are correct?

Since 1992, Dynacraft Golf Products, Inc. has provided part of that answer with its revolutionary Dynacraft Shaft Fitting Index (DSFI). This guide, based upon

Shafts come in a variety of materials, weights and colors.

matching the performance characteristics of a shaft to a golfer's swing speed, tempo, length of swing, etc., has helped to eliminate much of the guesswork. Because of the time it saves and its accuracy in pairing the "right" shaft with the golfer, DSFI is a vital part of the Total Clubfitting program.

EARLY SHAFT FITTING

For as long as the game has been played, golfers (and clubmakers) have been searching for the "perfect" shaft. Despite incredible technical advances through the years, the pursuit still remains. Early clubmakers had few options with regard to shaft matching. Hickory was the material of choice from the mid-1800's through the 1930s. Woods such as lancewood, ash, lemonwood and greenheart also found there way into golf shafts.

The obvious drawbacks of wood shafts, besides inconsistency, included warping, moisture absorption and variations in feel and torsion. Because of these, steel shafts were initially introduced in 1894 as Thomas Horsburgh patented a solid steel rod for the first shaft design. While this shaft gained little acceptance, it did provide the impetus for Arthur Knight of New York, who patented the first tubular steel shaft in 1910. The American Fork and Hoe Company subsequently produced the first step down steel shaft in 1927. And, about the same time, the USGA and R&A lifted the ban on steel shafts, thus effectively ending the era of wood-shafted clubs.

The basic construction of steel shafts remained the same from their introduction in the 1920's through the 1950s. During that era, shafts were fitted to a player's golf swing based solely on flex. The flex was determined by the weight of the shaft, with heavier shafts being stiffer than lighter ones. Golf professionals of the day fit players based only on this shaft weight characteristic. "Hitters" were given more rigid shafts, where "swingers" received softer shafts. In short, clubs were fit totally based upon an L, A, R, S and X-flex system of shaft classification.

While steel shafts remained the dominant shaft material for nearly half a century, experiments with other materials were frequently tried in an effort to reduce the shaft weight. The 1950's saw the advent of a lighter weight shaft manufactured by the Golfcraft Corp called the Glasshaft, comprised of a fiberglass material bonded around a thinner-walled steel tube. Later in the 1950's, the first all-fiberglass shaft, called the Wondershaft, was developed . In 1965, LaFiell Products produced the first true lightweight shaft made from aluminum. While this shaft did succeed in reducing weight, PGA Tour pros rejected its soft feel, and soon too did the playing public.

In the early 1970s, graphite first appeared as a shaft material. These "miracle" shafts promised tremendous distance gains, better feel and lower scores. However, these shafts were very inconsistent. If a player was lucky enough to find one graphite shaft he liked, the chances of finding a shaft with similar feel - even of the same model - were quite slim. This consistency problem caused the demise of graphite, almost as quickly as its emergence. It did prompt graphite shaft producers to find better ways to make their shafts, resulting in the high-quality graphite and composite models of today.

MODERN SHAFT FITTING

By the late 1970's to early 1980's, clubfitting progressed to the point that three variables could be considered for each golfer. Flex had been refined as a parameter into which five categories could be configured on virtually any design. That gave shaft producers the opportunity to introduce lighter weight designs that offered varying flexes. Shaft weights subsequently were grouped into three categories: standard weight (121 - 132 g), lightweight (110 - 120 g) and very lightweight (70 - 109 g). Golfers who swung harder or faster were matched with standard weight models in stiffer flexes, while slower swingers were recommended for lighter weight, weaker flexes.

As the 1980's progressed, so did shaft technology - at an incredibly rapid pace. Shafts were soon being produced and fitted with another consideration - bend point. A high bend point shaft was believed to launch the ball on a low trajectory, while a low bend point was thought to yield a high trajectory and a mid bend point produced a trajectory in-between. Now a given player could receive a shaft in a variety of flexes, with a specific weight characteristic and either a high, mid or low bend point, depending upon his desired ball flight.

By combining shaft flex, weight and bend point specifications, golfers could be

facets of that publication and introduce the DSFI method of shaft selection as we begin our discussion of properly fitted shafts.

THE SHAFT AND THE SWING

The golf shaft is the only dynamic part of a golf club as it moves through the swing arc. The grip does not change shape during the swing, nor does the clubhead. (It may be argued that the faces of certain larger volume drivers flex, but when compared the flexion of the golf

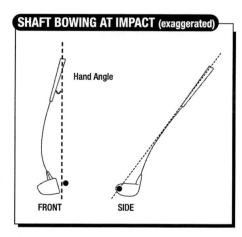

SHAFT BOWING AT IMPACT (exaggerated)

Hand Angle

FRONT   SIDE

the center of gravity of the club is away from the centerline axis of the shaft. The shaft also bows downward during the downswing and flattens the lie angle of the clubhead.

Because the shaft is not totally rigid, the swing sequence shows that the shaft has loaded (stored energy) and unloaded (released energy) during the swing. The correctly fit shaft will unload with the maximum energy at impact and allow the clubhead to be in a square position at impact. A shaft that is too stiff will limit the amount of stored energy, which can also cause a lower ball flight and lack of feel. A shaft that is too flexible will unload too early causing problems squaring up the face at impact and causing less than desired results.

SHAFT FITTING VARIATIONS		
Standard Weight	**Lightweight**	**Very Lightweight**
High bend point (L,A,R,S,X)	High bend point (L,A,R,S,X)	High bend point (L,A,R,S,X)
Mid bend point (L,A,R,S,X)	Mid bend point (L,A,R,S,X)	Mid bend point (L,A,R,S,X)
Low bend point (L,A,R,S,X)	Low bend point (L,A,R,S,X)	Low bend point (L,A,R,S,X)

fitted with any one of 45 different combinations of shafts. Yet, other parameters were soon to be added. As technology continued to grow by leaps and bounds, new specifications regarding the proper fitting of shafts evolved as well, particularly related to graphite and composite shafts. Today's shafts not only consider the three parameters (weight, flex and bend point) noted above, but also take in account torque - the amount of twisting in

shaft, it is minor in comparison.) The shaft, on the other hand, changes shape in various ways and at different points in the swing - it is on these changes that our shaft fitting will be based.

At address, the shaft is a straight connection between the grip and the clubhead. As the backswing begins, the shaft bows, causing the clubhead to lag behind the shaft. Additionally, torque begins to cause the shaft to rotate in a counter-

It is the shaft that will ultimately control the position of the clubhead at impact. It is through a combination of factors that this influence will evidence itself. The shaft's frequency has a definite effect. The higher a shaft's frequency, the stiffer it will be, thus a greater force must be applied to make the shaft work properly.

Torque has a definite effect. The torque of a shaft should help in aligning the clubface square to the target precisely at impact for the best results. A shaft with too low of a torque will resist the head from closing, thus leaving the face open. At the same time, higher torque values can help less-abled players achieve a square clubface position at impact.

SHAFT WEIGHT CLASSIFICATIONS (1980)	
Standard weight	Steel shafts weighting between 4.25 and 4.65 oz.
Light weight	Steel, alloy and composite shafts weighing between 3.9 and 4.2 oz.
Very lightweight	Steel, alloy and composite shafts weighting between 2.5 and 3.8 oz.

the shaft.

In the definitive industry text referencing the growing complexity of the proper shaft, an entire volume of research, "The Modern Guide to Shaft Fitting, Featuring the Dynacraft Shaft Fitting Index," was devoted to this subject. This book and its fitting guide represent the clearest and most concise shaft fitting procedure available in the game today. This research, originally available in book form, is now available for downloading at www.dynacraftgolf.com. As a key part of shaft fitting, we will explore the major

clockwise position (assuming a right-handed golfer). As the club reaches the top of the backswing, the clubhead has overtaken the shaft and has caused it to bow the opposite direction. When the player begins the downswing, the head lags even further behind the shaft and torque creates a clockwise rotation. Just before impact, after the hands have released, the shaft is then bowed slightly forward causing a slight increase of the dynamic loft of the clubhead. The head is also rotating closed, depending upon the torque resistance of the shaft and how far

Bend point will have a minimal effect. A shaft's bending qualities have an influence on clubhead position at impact; a lower bend point shaft may force the head to contact the ball with an increased amount of loft. Conversely, a high bend point shaft will tend to resist the forward bowing of the shaft and decrease the

SHAFT TERMINOLOGY: A SUMMARY

Balance Point: The point at which the shaft achieves equilibrium; the point where a shaft has its weight evenly distributed in both directions.

Bend Point: The point of maximum bending on a shaft as measured by compressing both ends of the shaft inwards.

CPM: Cycles Per Minute. A unit of measurement for shaft frequency. The number of oscillations than can be counted during a 60-second interval. Measured by a frequency analyzer.

Deflection: The deviation of the tip from the butt centerline after a known unit of force is applied to the tip in order to create a curve in the shaft.

Flex: The designation assigned to a shaft based on its stiffness, or ability to resist bending. Designations include ladies (L), amateur or senior (A), regular (R), stiff (S) and extra stiff (X).

Frequency: The number of oscillations of a shaft over a known period of time as the tip is pulled and released when the club is mounted in a frequency-measuring device. Measured in cycles per minute (cpm).

Kick Point: The point of maximum bending on a shaft as measured by deflecting the tip end of the shaft with the butt secured in a static position.

Parallel Tip: A type of shaft construction in which the shaft possesses one constant diameter in the tip section.

Pattern: This design of a particular shaft, indicating the distribution of flexibility about the shaft. A shaft described as stiff tip/weak butt is a low bend point design. A medium tip/medium butt is a mid bend point shaft, while a flexible tip/stiff butt is a low bend point design. Pattern is used to designate a particular model of shaft, e.g. Dynamic, Microtaper, TT Lite.

Raw Shaft: A shaft that has not been cut to length, either from the tip or butt.

Relative Stiffness: The stiffness of a given shaft when compared to another.

Taper Tip: A shaft that is produced to form a non-parallel tip. In effect, such shafts form a mechanical lock in a correspondingly sized hosel. Once the norm in the golf industry, taper tip shafts are used only by a select number of manufacturers. Taper tips are not used when designing component heads.

Torque: The twisting of a shaft that occurs as the club is swung and impacts the ball. Evaluated by clamping the butt end of the shaft and applying an angular force on the tip end. Measured in degrees.

---

effective loft. It should be noted, however, that research has found the overall effect of bend point to be extremely limited. The flex of the shaft will have a more predominate influence on actual trajectory of the ball.

Shaft weight has a definite effect. The weight of the shaft has a direct relationship on how fast the club can be swung. Faster swing speeds as a result of a lighter overall weight and potentially longer assembly length may yield greater distance, but usually at the cost of some accuracy. Lighter weight shafts may be swung faster, a plus for older players, ladies or those who may lack swing speed or strength.

It is up to the clubfitter and player working together to match all of the parameters of a shaft that best fits his or her individual swing. In considering each performance quality individually, howev-

er, the clubfitter must not lose site of a most important quality - feel. A shaft's performance and feel involves the interrelationship of many factors. Attempting to isolate each factor and its specific effect upon performance is a difficult process. Each factor can be defined on its own merit, but it is important to realize that in each swing all the factors combine to define the shaft's playability.

FLEX

The term "flex" is the single most often used word to describe shafts. As noted previously, a shaft labeled as one flex by a particular manufacturer may be quite different than a product with the same flex designation by another company. Instead of relying on these genetic letter designations, flex can be more accurately determined by measuring it in

either of two methods: deflection and frequency.

Deflection: A Static Measurement

Deflection is a static measurement that is taken by hanging a known amount of weight from the tip of a shaft while the butt end is secured. The amount the shaft bends from the horizontal position is its deflection (measured in inches). The more the shaft bends or deflects, the more flexible the shaft. Thus, a very stiff shaft will not deflect nearly as much as a flexible shaft. Deflection boards have been used for many years and are based on the deflection characteristics of steel shafts.

There are a few difficulties encountered when using a deflection board to measure consistent shaft stiffness. As these boards were designed with steel shafts in mind, shafts made from graphite, titanium and other "non-steel" materials

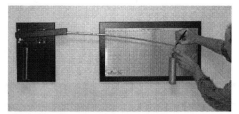

A deflection board shows the relative stiffness of shafts when compared to one another.

often exhibit unusual deflection readings. In addition, there is no pattern to these deviations. In other words, certain graphite shafts will deflect less than steel shafts, while others will deflect more - even from the same manufacturer and same generic letter flex designation.

The length of a given shaft may also cause misleading deflection board readings. The shorter the raw length of two shafts of the same type, the less the shaft will deflect. For instance, a True Temper Dynamic parallel tip R&S shaft (UDWC) is 47" in its uncut form, will deflect more than a Dynamic Gold R300 in a shorter raw length (46"). With no trimming, the Dynamic Gold R300 will appear stiffer on the deflection board due to its shorter length. But when the UDWC is trimmed 1" from the butt end, the deflection reading will be the same as the Dynamic Gold R300. A similar discrepancy in readings may occur when testing completed clubs on the deflection board. The weight must be hung from the same location in all tests. This may be difficult when comparing a no-hosel metal wood to a long hosel wooden or metal wood head. If the weight attached to the shaft - usually 4-7 lbs. - is not placed in the exact same spot on both clubs, the comparison cannot be considered valid.

Deflection boards provide a measure of relative stiffness, but do not offer exact flex readings. Some shafts may be "in-between" flexes, in which case a 1/4" interpretation in either direct could yield determinations of two different flexes. Thus, it is important to realize that the board is best used to ascertain comparisons between identical patterns and lengths of shaft, rather than a strict determination of flex.

Frequency: A Dynamic Choice

A second method for measuring relative stiffness is frequency analysis. Frequency is a dynamic measure of flex

obtained by securely clamping the butt of the shaft or gripped club and oscillating the shaft between sensors on a machine known as a frequency analyzer. These sensors yield a calculation of how many times the shaft would oscillate in one minute when the shaft is secured by its butt in the analyzer and the tip is set in motion. The resulting number is expressed in units of cycles per minute, or cpm.

The higher the cpm reading of a shaft, the stiffer the shaft or club. For example, a 265 cpm driver reading would indicate a stiffer club than another driver with a reading of 255.

Frequency measurements may be obtained for either completed clubs or for raw shafts. When measuring completed clubs, frequency readings take into account club length, head weight, shaft weight and shaft material (steel, graphite or other non-steel alloys). Frequency readings for a raw shaft will be completely different than those from an assembled club. Just as when using a deflection board, for a true shaft-to-shaft compari-

Frequency analyzation was a key paramenter in the development of the Dynacraft Shaft Fitting Index (DSFI).

son, it is vital that the same incrementally precise testing procedure be used for each shaft to be tested.

In analyzing frequency measurements, it is important to recognize that the frequency readings of clubs made from different shaft materials may not have the same progression. Some steel shafts, for example, exhibit a frequency progression of 4-5 cpm from one club to the next. In other words, a steel-shafted #5-iron may have a frequency of 300 cpm, the #4-iron would have a frequency of 296, the #6-iron would have a 304 cpm reading, a 7-iron would have a 308 cpm reading and so on. The rate frequency changes from one club to the next, is referred to as fre-

quency slope. If the frequency change from one club to the next is the same, that concept is referred to as frequency matching.

In clubmaking today, there is much debate about frequency matching. Royal Precision was granted a patent regarding a slope line frequency as described above, and claims this progressive frequency scale is ideal for steel shaft assembly. True Temper, on the other hand, sorts shafts by weight to assure an increasing rate of stiffness as the set progresses from long to short. Other manufacturers have endorsed flat line frequency, where every club in the set has the same frequency reading (for example 290 cpm for all the irons and 245 cpm for all the woods). In some cases the frequency falls in-between the traditional sloped frequency and the flat line depending upon the method of trimming. Many graphite shafts fall in the later two categories due to the relative shorter parallel tip sections when compared to steel. Each of these systems could be possibilities to a proper fit, but is up to the clubfitter to decide which is best for their customer.

Torque

Torque is a common term relating to today's graphite shafts. While it is generally discussed in regard to graphite shafts, steel shafts do exhibit torque as well.

True Temper Dynamic Gold R300 parallel tip Project CPM Values (D-1, standard length)		
Iron	CPM	
#1-iron	288	
#2-iron	292	
#3-iron	296	
#4-iron	300	
#5-iron	304	
#6-iron	308	
#7-iron	312	
#8-iron	316	
#9-iron	320	
PW	318	D-3
SW	315	D-6

Torque is defined as the amount of rotational twisting of the shaft during the swing. Again, just as when measuring frequency or deflection, torque-testing parameters must be consistent. The same beam length of shaft must be measured

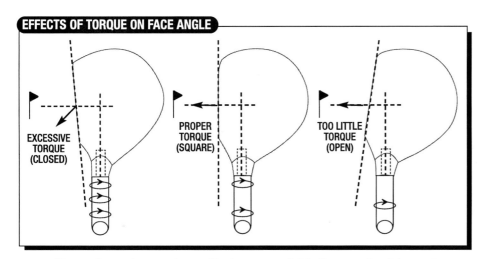

EFFECTS OF TORQUE ON FACE ANGLE

EXCESSIVE TORQUE (CLOSED)

PROPER TORQUE (SQUARE)

TOO LITTLE TORQUE (OPEN)

Torque has a tremendous effect upon a club's face angle at impact.

and the same weight or force be applied to the shaft. What is often confusing is that nearly all graphite shaft manufacturers have their own unique testing parameters. In effect, what one certain company states is a 3-degree torque shaft may actu-

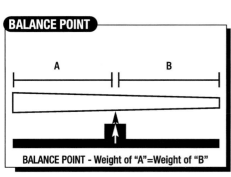

Torque testing added a key second consideration to DSFI testing.

ally be a 5-degree shaft on another's machine.

In the traditional method of measuring torque, the butt end of the shaft is clamped and the tip end is supported. A bar is attached to the shaft tip and a given weight is suspended from it. A protractor then is used to measure the angular deflection of the shaft, with the results expressed in degrees. A lower torque measurement of a shaft indicates that shaft twists less, and is considered torsionally stiffer. This does not mean that a low torque shaft is "better". Too little torque may be every bit as detrimental (or advantageous) to a player as too much.

Balance Point

A third specification influencing shaft feel and performance is balance point. Also known as center of gravity, the balance point is defined as the equilibrium at which one-half of the shaft's (or club's) weight is on one side of a given point and the other half is on the opposite side of that point. The construction of the shaft has a great deal to do with the location of the balance point of the shaft or completed club. Related to raw shafts, the majority of parallel tip shafts have balance points slightly toward the butt end of the shaft. Many taper tip shafts have the balance point in the center of the shaft. There are certain graphite shafts produced that have been designed to be tip heavy. This creates a standard swingweight without the use the heavier heads or longer assembly lengths. In each case, the balance point of the shaft, coupled with the

shaft weight, influences how much head weight is necessary to achieve a given swingweight.

The length of the club, balance point of the shaft and the amount of head and grip weight influence the balance point of the completed club. A club that is considered "head heavy" has a greater percentage of the weight of the club positioned closer to the head. This can usually be achieved by using heavier heads. However, there is a special group of shafts designed with a larger sized butt end, typically 0.865". These shafts require special, lightweight, thin-walled grips, which do not counterbalance the club as much as a standard grip, thus shifting the balance point closer to the head. These very large butt shafts saw great popularity in the late 1990's, but seem to have gone out of favor recently. The use of tip heavy graphite shafts keeps the balance point closer to the butt because no additional head weight is needed to increase swingweight.

Bend Point and Kick Point

The terms bend point and kick point relate two further specifications used in describing a shaft. Though often used interchangeably, they are in fact two very different measurements. Bend point is the area of maximum bending of a shaft as measured by compressing the ends of the shaft toward each other. Kick point can be defined as a location of maximum bending as well, but in this case it is measured by applying a force to the tip of the shaft while the butt end is affixed in a holding device (just as when measuring deflection). The two points are not located in the same place on the same shaft. Yet both are described in misleading terms of "high", "mid" or "low".

These descriptions would lead one to believe that a "high" bend point and kick point might be located under the grip, "mid" in the center of the shaft and "low"

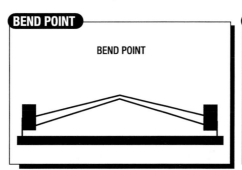

BALANCE POINT

A   B

BALANCE POINT - Weight of "A"=Weight of "B"

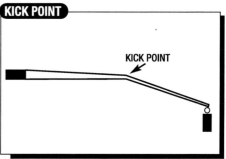

BEND POINT

BEND POINT

KICK POINT

KICK POINT

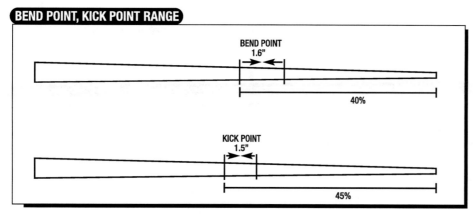

BEND POINT, KICK POINT RANGE

BEND POINT
1.6"

40%

KICK POINT
1.5"

45%

The importance of bend and kick point related to trajectory is most often overstated.

near the hosel. However, independent testing has verified that the actual bend point location is within a 1.6" range up 40% of the shaft length from the tip, while kick point is within a 1.5" range 45% of the length from the shaft tip.

While the terms low, mid and high may still be used, the difference between a high and low bend point / kick point are actually much smaller than golf equipment professionals have been led to believe. Additionally, the effect of bend point and kick point on ball flight now is considered marginal. However, bend point and kick point do play a role in shaft "feel" - a primary factor to keep in mind when fitting a shaft. Lower bend point / kick point shafts provide a softer feel than do mid or high bend points / kick points.

EFFECT ON BALL FLIGHT

There are many "cause and effect" relationships that occur between the shaft and ball flight. These relationships start in the personal interview portion of the

fitting process and carry over into the club evaluation part of the fitting session. Understanding how the shaft reacts and the resulting ball flight as caused by the shaft allows the search for the proper shaft can be narrowed considerably.

The first parameter one needs to understand is how shaft flex affects ball trajectory. The more flexible a shaft, the more it will bend forward prior to impact, resulting in increased dynamic loft. The trend today is the use of more flexible shafts; this one of the many reasons why the loft standards of most clubs have progressively become stronger.

Shaft flex not only determines ball trajectory, but also influences direction. The use of stiffer or more flexible shafts depends upon the swing path of the golfer. A golfer who slices or fades the ball typically has an outside-in swing path. In order to reduce the amount of left-to-right movement on the ball, the shaft needs to be stiffer. The stiffer shaft usually produces a lower ball flight. But if the shot is a slice, the face is open at impact and the effective loft of the club will be increased. A more flexible shaft will only compound the sliced or faded shot.

The opposite holds true for the golfer that draws or hooks the ball. This type of golfer has an inside-out swing path that produces that kind of ball flight. A stiffer shaft than what the golfer already has will restrict the ball from going right-to-left. A more flexible shaft will bow the shaft forward and at the same time most likely close the face down, creating a "low, duck hook".

Shaft weight also plays an important role in the ability for the golfer to square the clubface at impact. A good rule of thumb to apply in shaft fitting is the quicker or harder the player swings the club, the heavier the shaft they should use for control. Shaft weight impacts the overall weight of the club as well as the balance point of the club. If two clubs are of the same length and swingweight, then the club with the lighter shaft will have a balance point closer to the head. This is because a greater amount of head weight is usually required to achieve the swingweight; a greater percentage of the overall weight of the club is positioned farther from the golfer's hands.

Balance point can alter the golfer's swing path. If the club is head-heavy, or the balance point is farther from the hands, there is a tendency for golfers to cast the club causing an over-the-top swing, resulting in a slice. A club with the balance point closer to the hands could help those who slice or fade the ball because it is easier for them to move the club faster through the impact zone. To illustrate why this phenomenon works, think about a figure skater spinning in a circle. With the arms close to the body, the skater is able to spin faster. When the arms are spread out away from the body, the skater spins more slowly. Therefore, clubs with a balance point farther from the hands should be reserved for golfers who draw or hook the ball; the club fitter may also select a more closed face angle to counter the this effect of balance point.

In addition, the farther the balance point is from the hands, the higher the resulting ball trajectory. If a high-ball hitter were to use a shaft that is much lighter than what he is currently using, a stronger (lower) lofted club will most likely be required. Not only is the industry trend toward the use of more flexible shafts, but also to shafts that are lighter weight. Again, this is one of the many reasons why lofts are stronger today than years ago.

Torque is another factor that effects ball flight. Typically, shafts with higher torque are usually more tip flexible. This

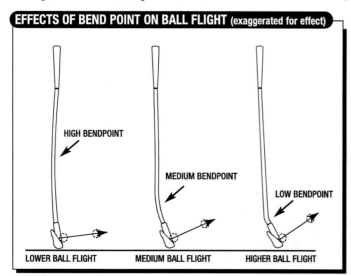

EFFECTS OF BEND POINT ON BALL FLIGHT (exaggerated for effect)

HIGH BENDPOINT

MEDIUM BENDPOINT

LOW BENDPOINT

LOWER BALL FLIGHT   MEDIUM BALL FLIGHT   HIGHER BALL FLIGHT

would cause a higher ball flight. However, many of the higher torque shafts are generally manufactured stiffer to compensate for this. Golfers who normally slice the ball may be better off with the stiffer, higher torque shaft as it tends to limit the amount of left-to-right movement on the ball. Remember, torque is the amount of rotation of the shaft. A shaft that has a low torque rating actually inhibits the head from closing or squaring up at impact. This is yet another reason why golfers who slice the ball would benefit from a stiffer/higher torque shaft. The converse would hold true for golfer who hooks the ball. Look for shaft with a lower torque rating, in conjunction with an open face angle and center of gravity location toward the toe of the clubhead.

Bend point and kick point, as mentioned before, have very little effect on actual ball flight, but more on feel. Clubhead loft and center of gravity have far greater impacts on ball trajectory. There are a byproducts of the stiffness distribution (or bend point) of the shaft: a high bend point shaft indicates the shaft has a stiff tip and a weak butt, while a low bend point shaft has a weak tip, but a firm butt end. A softer tip shaft may have the effect of flattening out more during the downswing and requiring a more upright lie angle on the clubhead. The weaker tip may also allow the shaft to bend more into a closed position at impact, further reducing a slice.

SHAFT FITTING DEMO CLUBS

Depending upon the size of your clubmaking shop and the amount of custom building you perform, you may wish to tailor your test shaft program accordingly. Using DSFI ratings can help you create a demo program for any budget. Shaft "feel" is a very subjective part of the game of golf. As a result, the following recommendations are based solely on swing speed, not manufacturers' specific designs and not so much on feel. To compile your series of test clubs, look through the DSFI ratings in the on-line "Shaft Fitting Addendum" and select at least one shaft from each swing speed range. Keep in mind the current trends in the golf industry so you will have products that customers are most likely to request. Assemble the test shafts with the most popular wood and iron heads in your product line. Make sure to keep all the lengths, swingweights, grip sizing, etc. the same so the customer is comparing only the shaft performance and feel. Now you are ready to let your customers experience dynamic shaft fitting, using the DSFI method.

Also as part of the demo program, some type of swingspeed indicating device must be utilized. Swingspeed gauges come in a variety of models and price ranges. The least expensive swingspeed device is GRT's StrokeMaxxer, costing less than $25.00 and clipping onto the shaft during a swing to provide the readings. While these are economical, they are not as reliable as more sophisticated devices. A better swingspeed measuring device is the BELtronic Swingmate. This unit, costing in the $90.00 range, is placed on the ground at an angle to the player as he hits balls. It determines club speed and interpolates that into a distance number. It can be used indoors or out. The next level of swingspeed device is some type of computer. Most of these computer-type devices are for indoor use only, but they not only indicate swingspeed, but tempo, face angle, swing path and face impact

SHAFT DEMO PROGRAMS

LOW BUDGET SHAFT PROGRAMS

DSFI Rating	Woods		DSFI Rating	Irons	
	Steel	Graphite		Steel	Graphite
Below 65			below 60		
65 - 70			60 - 65		
70 - 75			65 - 70	Y	
75 - 80	Y		70 - 75	Y	
80 - 85	Y		75 - 80	Y	
85 - 90	Y		80 - 85	Y	
90 - 95	Y		85+	Y	
95 - 100	Y				
100+					

MEDIUM BUDGET SHAFT PROGRAMS

DSFI Rating	Woods		DSFI Rating	Irons	
	Steel	Graphite		Steel	Graphite
Below 65			below 60		
65 - 70			60 - 65		Y
70 - 75		Y	65 - 70	Y	Y
75 - 80	Y	Y	70 - 75	Y	Y
80 - 85	Y	Y	75 - 80	Y	Y
85 - 90	Y	Y	80 - 85	Y	
90 - 95	Y	Y	85+	Y	
95 - 100	Y				
100+	Y				

LARGE BUDGET SHAFT PROGRAMS

DSFI Rating	Woods			DSFI Rating	Irons	
	Steel	Graphite Std.	UL		Steel	Graphite
Below 65		Y		below 60		Y
65 - 70		Y		60 - 65		Y
70 - 75		Y	Y	65 - 70	Y	Y
75 - 80	Y	Y		70 - 75	Y	Y
80 - 85	Y	Y	Y	75 - 80	Y	Y
85 - 90	Y	Y		80 - 85	Y	Y
90 - 95	Y	Y	Y	85+	Y	
95 - 100	Y	Y				
100+	Y	Y	Y			

(Y indicates shafts suggested for demo programs)

Beltronic's SwingMate™

point, among other parameters. The cost of these units may reach several thousands of dollars, but they do provide detailed information related to how a player swings the club.

This GolfTek swing analyzer provides concise data related to swing speeds and tempo of both woods and irons.

DYNAMIC FITTING INDOORS AND OUTDOORS

The Dynacraft Shaft Fitting Index (DSFI)

Beginning more than a decade ago and continuing into this century, Dynacraft constantly updates the golf industry's first quantitative study of golf shafts. The original concept for the testing project was simply to compare the specifications of different shaft models as measured under the same conditions. Almost unbelievably, this had never been done before. Shaft manufacturers had tested their own products "in-house" using their proprietary procedures, but no one had ever brought the shafts of different manufacturers together for "blind" testing.

The Dynacraft Technical Staff felt this was an important project in order to create an "apples to apples" comparison for clubmakers in the field. Previous to this testing, for example, clubmakers had to assume that the torque testing of two different manufacturers were relatively the same. In fact, one shaft manufacturer may suspend the weight 3" from the tip, while another would position the weight 1" from the tip. Given such disparities, clearly there was a need for such standardized testing. Over the eleven-plus years this project has taken, more than 2,500 shafts have been measured.

Additionally, this study also was designed to determine how shafts actually function during the swing and how all the specifications of the shaft are interrelated. Following are some of the major conclusions derived from this study:

1. There is little correlation between one manufacturer's stated flex to another manufacturer's. One company's stiff flex shaft may be equivalent in frequency or deflection to another company's regular, A-flex or even L-flex model. Even within certain manufacturers' lines of shafts, there does not exist uniformity of stiffness.

2. The average deviation in frequency and deflection between each flex designation was not uniform, especially with the L-flex shafts, which appear to be stiffer than for whom they were designed.

3. Due to the differences in testing one manufacturer's stated torque to another's, there does not exist a standardized method of measurement within the industry.

4. The location of bend points and kick points, previously thought to be quite widespread between low, mid and high, tested to within a small of position among the test shafts. Bend points were found to be approximately 40% of the distance from the tip of the shaft; kick points were located at 45% of the shaft length from the tip. At the same time, it was determined the bend point and kick point have only a minor influence on ball flight, but a major effect on feel.

5. A shaft's performance is a combination of several factors including frequency, torque, weight, balance point and bend point, and cannot be properly fit to an individual based only on one of these specifications. All must be considered in unison when fitting a player.

USING DSFI TO FIT GOLF SHAFTS

After analyzing the first set of data gathered from 1989-1991, it quickly became apparent that very little noteworthy revelations about shaft fitting were ready to be made. The one fact we did know was that as torque decreased in a shaft, the stiffer the shaft felt. Using this relationship between shaft stiffness and

shaft torque as a starting point, Dynacraft's Jeff Summitt undertook the monumental task of correlating the results into some type of usable format relating to shaft fitting. After several years of mathematical modeling and experimentation, Summitt determined a formula that approximated the bending and twisting aspect of the shaft and correlated that to a golfer's swing speed. Hence, the Dynacraft Shaft Fitting Index, or DSFI, was born.

In the summer of 1992, the original version of "The Modern Guide to Shaft Fitting" was released which featured the DSFI formula and shared with it the technical data on all the shafts that had been tested. Since then, tens of thousands of golfers have been fit successfully using this method, which eliminates much of the guesswork from shaft fitting. "The Modern Guide to Shaft Fitting" and the accompanying addendum fully detail the "whys" and "wherefores" to modern era shaft fitting. (A reminder: These can be accessed at www.dynacraftgolf.com.) Now that we are familiar with what the DSFI is, let's move on to the practical application of its fitting system.

THE DSFI FITTING PROCEDURE

Step 1 - Examine the golfer's swing speed

It is not only important to measure the swing speed with the Driver and/or #5-iron, but also important to identify how that speed is obtained through the tempo of the swing. For example, if two golfers both have a 100 mph swing speed with their driver, but one has a fast tempo and the other has a slow tempo, the two golfers do not necessarily use the same

FITTING GUIDELINES SWINGSPEED AND DRIVER LOFT	
Swing Speed (mph)	Driver Loft
<50	21°
60	15°
70	13°
80	11°
85	10.5°
90	10°
95	9.5°
100	9°
110+	8° or less

AVERAGE #5-IRON DISTANCE AND SWING SPEED											
mph	distance	mph	distance	mph	distance	mph	distance	mph	distance	mph	distance
40	88 yards	50	110 yards	60	132 yards	70	154 yards	80	177 yards	90+	199+ yards
42	92	52	115	62	137	72	159	82	181		
44	97	54	119	64	141	74	163	84	185		
46	102	56	124	66	146	76	168	86	190		
48	106	58	128	68	150	78	172	88	194		

shaft. We shall make adjustments for tempo after we have obtained the golfer's swing speed.

For accurate clubhead speed recording it is necessary to have the golfer warm up first. After the player hits a few shots, use an accurate swing speed device to obtain the clubhead speed for the Driver and/or #5-iron. To gain a consistent and accurate reading of the golfer's swing speed, have the golfer hit a standard length steel shafted Driver or a #5-

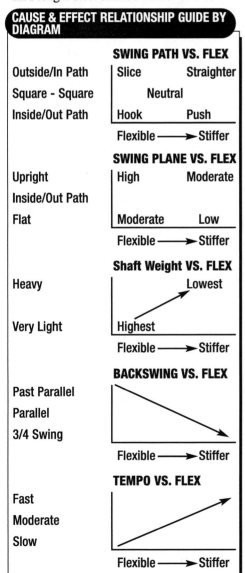

A fitting matrix related to swing characteristics and shaft flex.

iron. Take the average of 10 swings with each club.

The swing speed measurements for DSFI were originally based on the Sportek Swing Analyzer. (This unit is no longer available.) Similar readings can be found using a GolfTek Golfswing Analyzer. Many portable units such as the BEL-tronic SwingMate will yield similar driver swing speeds on average. However, these devices may yield higher #5-iron swing speeds than the Sportek or Golftek analyzers. As a guideline for #5-iron swing speeds, you can also use the chart above based on #5-iron carry distance. (Note: High elevation areas such as the Rocky Mountain region will yield greater distances than in the chart)

Step 2 - Determine the tempo and length of the golfer swing

Tempo is important from an accuracy standpoint when selecting shafts. If the golfer has a smooth tempo, the golfer's swing will look almost effortless. A smooth tempo will allow the golfer to opt for a more flexible shaft as a lesser load is exerted on the shaft during the swing. A golfer with a fast tempo tends to place more stress on shaft. A quick tempo is noted by examining the initial part of the downswing. The reversal from the top of the takeaway to the initial downswing is harder to visualize when compared to the smooth tempo. In a smooth tempo, there is a gradual build up of speed throughout the downswing. The fast tempo has the greatest acceleration at the top of the swing; thus this swing type may need a heavier shaft and stiffer shaft as well. An example of a PGA Tour player with a fast tempo is Nick Price; one with a slow tempo is Ernie Els.

If you cannot distinguish between the smooth and fast tempo swing, this is referred to as a moderate tempo. The moderate swing tempo will most likely need a moderate weight and stiffness shaft.

Length of swing plays a factor as well. Typically, a golfer with a longer

swing will use a more flexible shaft than someone with the same tempo and swing speed, but with a shorter swing. The reason for this is due to the rate of recovery. In a shorter swing (less than parallel) there is less time to allow for the shaft to load and then return to a square position. Thus the stiffer shaft with the shorter swing will yield more accuracy. As golfers get older, they have less flexibility possibly restricting the swing. Even though the swing speed may decrease, it does not necessarily mean that the shaft flex needs to be decreased. Again, Nick Price is an example of a shorter swing, while John Daly has a much longer swing.

The golfer with a short backswing and no wrist cock (all arm swing), may need a much stiffer shaft than you would consider based upon their swing speed. Many newcomers to the game as well as many women golfers have this swing tendency. Not having a wrist cock greatly reduces clubhead speed. But as this golfer develops a wrist cock as a result of taking lessons or through more play, their swing speed will increase; thus it is best to recommend a stiffer shaft for them to grow into.

Step 3 - Adjusted DSFI calculations

Tempo

For a **fast tempo golfer will a full swing**, the DSFI rating of the shaft should be very close to the average swing speed of the golfer. When selecting shafts, multiply the average swing speed by 0.97 and 1.02 to give the DSFI range for possible shaft selections. For example, if the golfer had a 100-mph average swing speed, then look for shafts between 97 and 102 DSFI rating.

In cases of **moderate tempo with a full swing**, the person is not loading the shaft as much as is someone with a quicker tempo. Thus, the person can opt to go to a slightly more flexible shaft. For the moderate tempo range, multiply the average swing speed by 0.92 and 0.97. For

DSFI CONVERSION FOR EXTENDING SHAFTS FROM THE BUTT END ONLY						
Woods	+2" 1.075	+1.5" 1.056	+1" 1.036	+0.5" 1.018	-0.5" 0.983	-1.0" 0.966
Irons			+1" 1.033	+0.5" 1.016	-0.5" 0.984	-1.0" 0.969

To determine proper DSFI ratings of overlength clubs, divide the stated DSFI rating by the conversion factor(s) above.

example, if the golfer has an average swing speed of 100 mph, then the DSFI range of shafts to look for would be between 92 and 97. The 97% would be stiffer and possibly less risk of loss of accuracy than the 92%.

For the **slow tempo golfer with a full swing**, the person barely loads (or deflects) the shaft during the swing. This golfer could benefit from a softer shaft than normally would be suggested of for that swing speed. For example, if the golfer had an average clubhead speed of 100 mph, multiply that amount by 0.87 and 0.92. Thus look for shafts with a DSFI rating between 87 and 92.

If you do not feel comfortable with detecting the tempo of a golfer with a full swing, there is an alternative method. You can choose the higher frequency / higher torque combination for the fast tempo golfer. For the slow tempo golfer opt for the lower frequency / lower torque combination that yields the same DSFI rating.

Golfers who possess a **short back swing, with a wrist cock**, will need a stiffer shaft to compensate for the shorter distance traveled with the clubhead. Multiply their swing speed by 1.02 and 1.07 to find the DSFI range of shafts appropriate for their swing

Golfers who possess a **short back swing, without a wrist cock** will need an even stiffer shaft to compensate for the shorter distance the clubhead travels. Multiply the swing speed by 1.15 and 1.20 to find the DSFI range appropriate for their swing. In some cases, the DFSI rating could be even much high than this range.

Length

With the exception of the ultra-lightweight and 0.865" butt end graphite wood shafts, the men's Driver was tested at 43", the ladies Driver at 42", the men's #5-iron at 37.5" and the ladies #5-iron at 36.5"

for the clubs listed in the DSFI Addendum. The swingweights for the men's club were D-1 and for the ladies they were C-6. Adjustments need to be made if the club(s) to be built is different from these standards used during testing.

If a club is made longer, yet the swingweight remains the same, the club will become stiffer. The longer club will require less head weight to maintain the same swingweight, thus making the shaft stiffer. The shaft being longer should make it more flexible, but if that length is extended on the butt end (which is the stiffest portion of the shaft), the net result will be that the club will be stiffer.

To make adjustments for non-standard DSFI lengths, you need to divide the adjusted DSFI (based on the tempo) by the "length constant" as indicated in the DSFI conversion table at the top of the page. For example, if the golfer needed clubs 1" over length and had a 100 mph average clubhead speed with a fast tempo, then the adjusted DSFI range is 97 - 102. To determine the proper shaft, divide the adjusted DSFI by the listed length constant of 1.036. This new range is now 93.63 - 98.46, which takes in account the length of the club. You will be primarily using this conversion for graphite shafts due to the weights of heads that exist on the market. The same could be true for steel shafts, however the head weights that are currently available tend to make the swingweight heavier than the DSFI test standard.

Swingweight

The men's shafts were tested at D-1 and the ladies shafts were tested at C-6 when obtaining the DSFI figures. In the world of custom clubfitting, all golfers will not play with one specific swingweight. Therefore, conversions must be made to adjust for non-standard DSFI swingweights. If the swingweight of a men's flex shaft is less than D-1 (assuming the grip weight is not decreasing or increasing the swingweight), the shaft becomes stiffer. For example, if the fre-

quency of a shaft were 250 cpm at D-1, then at C-9 the frequency would be 252 cpm. If the swingweight were higher at D-3, the 250 cpm would become 248 cpm. For woods to be built higher than D-1 for the Men's flexes (C-6 for L-flexes) add 0.35 mph per swingweight over the DSFI standard swingweight. For each swingweight under the DSFI standard swingweight subtract 0.35 mph. When fitting irons, the conversion is 0.24 mph per swingweight.

Step 4 - Start looking at the applicable selection of shafts

Study the shafts for a given swing speed range in "Shaft Fitting Addendum", which can be downloaded from Dynacraft's web site. These shafts are labeled either "Driver Shaft Listing by DSFI Swing Speed Ratings", "#5-iron Shaft Listing by DSFI Swing Speed Ratings" or "Ladies Shaft Listing by DSFI Swing Speed Ratings". Examine the data and determine if the shafts are steel, graphite or titanium. There is a legend provided at the end of each section to help you identify the construction of each shaft. (See sample DSFI listing on next page.)

For ultra-lightweight graphite shafts, there is a special section in the DSFI text for these shafts as tested at 2" over standard. Also, there is a section devoted to taper tip shafts as used when replacing or repairing OEM clubs. In each case, these are provided for a quick reference. Both the ultra-lightweight and taper tip shafts also are listed accordingly in the appropriate shaft section as well.

Take note of cost consideration

Naturally, cost is a key contributing factor when fitting a player with a shaft. Determining the best shaft for a player is meaningless if he or she cannot afford the club. Because fitting with DSFI involves considering a wide range of shafts and matching those to a player's swing, there will be times when the shaft of choice ends up being a potentially expensive investment. After all, individual shafts can range from just under $4 to well over $100 or more. Be certain to select the best shaft choice that is within the customer's budget. It may be best to ask the player what his budget may be prior to test fitting shafts. If the player is on a

SAMPLE DSFI LISTING FOR SHAFTS WITH A 90 - 94 MPH RANKING

M

Model	Flex	DSFI	Mat'l
UST ProForce 65	R	90.00	VLG
True Temper EI-70 High Impact	R	90.01	LG
Paragon Syclone	S	90.03	VLG
UST Tour Weight	R	90.03	HG
True Temper Dynamic Gold	R300	90.07	HST
Grafalloy M29 Attack	S	90.17	LG
True Temper Titanium Tour	R	90.26	T
Aldila Tour Grade 70	S	90.27	VLG
Penley Platinum	S	90.32	LG
Harrison Professional	R	90.36	LG
Grafalloy ProLite 35 .370" Tip	R	90.59	VLG
True Temper Dynamic	R	90.67	HST
True Temper Dynamic Gold	R400	90.74	HST
Aldila Tour Grade 90	S	90.76	LG
Rapport Synsor 46" R&S	R	90.93	LG
Aldila Longwood Tour 47"	S	90.98	VLG
Harrison Boron Gold	S	91.01	LG
Apache PM50+	S	91.20	LG
Aldila T.I.P. 350 45"	S	91.26	VLG
T.T. Dynamic Gold w/ SensiCore	S300	91.46	HST
Aldila UL	Tour X	91.53	VLG
Grafalloy SoLite	X	91.56	VLG
Dynacraft Dynatech Standard	S	91.57	LG
True Temper Titanium Low Flex	S	91.63	T
SK Fiber BH30 Augusta	S	91.65	LG
Rapport Cirrus Tour	110	91.66	VLG
Apache PM40+	S	92.34	LG
T.T. Dynamic Gold Graphite	R300	92.40	FW
System Flex KF1	S	92.45	LG
T.T. Dynalite Gold w/ SensiCore	R300	92.51	LST
Rapport Oracle	S	92.67	FW
Apache Micro 58 45"	S	92.72	VLG
SK Fiber SL40 45"	S	92.73	VLG
True Temper EI-70	R	92.82	LG
Grafalloy ProLite 35	R	92.92	VLG
Dynacraft Copperhead	S	93.05	FW
Apollo AP 46	R	93.23	HST
Harrison Professional	S	93.23	LG
True Temper Dynalite	R	93.30	LST
Grafalloy ProLite 45	S	93.39	VLG
Harrison Boron Tour	R	93.60	LG
Rapport Synsor 46"R&S	S	93.68	LG
Grafalloy Attacklite	S	93.84	VLG
SK Fiber SL46 45"	S	93.88	VLG
True Temper EI-70	S	93.92	LG
True Temper TT Lite XL	S	93.96	LST

T - titanium
LG - lightweight graphite
FW - filament wound graphite
HG - heavy weight graphite
HST - heavy weight steel
LST - lightweight steel

(Based on shafts available in 2000)

Take note of compatibility with different head types

Not all shafts listed can be assembled with all clubheads. Do some homework as to what types of heads are compatible with the shafts. For instance, is the shaft designed for through bore, no hosel metal woods or for standard bore metal woods? Is the shaft meant for deep bore wooden or graphite heads or for all head types?

Is the hosel parallel or taper? Does the shaft have ample parallel tip length for the hosel length after tip trimming? Is the shaft weight proper for the head weights and lengths to which you will assemble the clubs? For answers to these questions consult the Dynacraft catalog or the specific shaft manufacturer to determine if the shafts are compatible with the heads that you have chosen for your customers.

Sort shafts by weight and material

Sort shafts by their material(s) - as denoted in the DSFI listing - and weight(s), whether by request from the golfer or through your own fitting recommendations. For example, is graphite a viable choice for the golfer? If so, should it be standard weight, low balance point or very lightweight? Remember the fundamental rules of fitting. Whenever a golfer has a quick tempo, opt for a heavier weight shaft in whatever material you are seeking. For slow tempo golfers, they are candidates for using lighter weight

shafts. Length of swing can also play a role in the selection of proper shaft weight. The longer the golfer's swing, the greater the potential that they could use a lighter weight shaft, while a shorter golf swing may require a heavier weight shaft in order to maintain control of the club.

Sort shafts by bend point description and balance point

Although bend point or kick point are not distinguished by a large measurable range, as stated in Chapter 6 of "The Modern Guide to Shaft Fitting", they do impact a definite "feel" difference. For instance, the True Temper Dynamic steel pattern has a stiffer feel in the tip than does the True Temper Dynalite pattern, but yet has similar DSFI ratings in like flexes. The higher the bend point, the

DRIVER SWING SPEED - DISTANCE CHART

Swing Speed (mph)	Distance (yds.)
50	123
52	128
54	133
56	138
58	143
60	148
62	153
64	158
66	162
68	167
70	172
72	177
74	182
76	187
78	192
80	197
82	202
84	207
86	207
88	217
90	222
92	227
94	231
96	236
98	241
100	246
102	251
104	256
106	261
108	266
110	271

limited budget, it is pointless to show him shafts in the premium price range.

stiffer the shaft tends to feel, while a lower bend point shaft often will provide more head feel according to the player.

The balance point of the completed club may also have some effect on performance. Usually the closer the completed balance point is to the head, the higher the resulting trajectory of the ball. The closer the balance point is to the grip, the lower the trajectory of the ball. These bend/balance point factors may be subtle ones, but they but they do provide potential influences on ball flight.

FINAL CONSIDERATIONS

Dampening: A more recent development in the shaft industry deals with the dampening properties of shaft. In cases of a golfer who has hand, wrist or joint discomfort while hitting golf balls, new technology can provide an assist. Shaft materials such as graphite, aluminum and titanium have been known to dampen shock at impact. Newer steel shafts, such as True Temper's SensiCore line and Royal Precision's FCM Rifle also can dampen shock upon impact.

Multi Material Shafts: True Temper's BiMatrx shaft combines a steel tip section with a main graphite section. This type of design is very tip stable (and thus tip firm). It will provide a firmer feel and lower trajectory.

Color: While not a performance issue, color has some merit when fitting shafts. Does the golfer want a particular color - something flashy or plain? Cosmetically, will the club look "matched" after it is assembled? Even though the shaft may fit the golfer, would a copper colored head match up with a navy blue shaft and a green grip? Be aware of shaft, grip and head colors during a fitting to avoid a potential embarrassment upon delivering the club to the customer.

Geometry: Some customers may ask for specific shafts with unique geometric shapes such as large butts, "bubbles" or straight tapered steel shafts. Identify which shafts in the addendum meet these specifications. Consult the Dynacraft catalog or information from the manufacturers as to these types of shafts.

Brand name loyalty: Certain customers who come into your shop may ask for specific brand names. For companies that offer a full line of shafts, this should pose no problem finding a shaft that meets the swing speed and tempo requirements of the golfer.

Warranty: Some companies offer a lifetime warranty against breakage from normal use. Some companies may offer only limited warranties. Warranties may be a small factor, but one you may deem important.

Example of DSFI Usage

Let's say for example that we have a golfer who is looking for graphite shafts for his irons. He normally carries his #5-iron 170 yards. We have determined that he has a slow tempo. From dynamic fitting a 38.5" #5-iron was best suited to him. Lastly, he felt the clubhead best with a D-3 swingweight using a normal weight grip. Here are the adjustments to find out what range of shafts would work best for him.

After examining the speed vs. distance chart, 170 yards would approximate to a 77 mph swing speed with a #5-iron. Next we adjust for the tempo. With a slow tempo, we multiply the #5-iron swing speed by 0.87 and 0.92. The adjusted DSFI range is now 66.99 and 70.84 respectively.

Next, we want to adjust for the non-standard DSFI length, in this case +1". We will divide by 1.033 which is the factor for +1" irons in the adjustment table. The resultant range would be between 64.85 and 68.58.

Lastly, we will adjust for the non-standard DSFI swingweight of D-1. We will add to the DSFI rating in order to adjust for the additional swingweight of D-3 (or 0.24 mph per swingweight on the irons). The resultant range would now be between 65.33 and 69.06. Now look at the Men's #5-iron Shaft Listings by DSFI Swing Speed Ratings in the Addendum for shaft choices.

DSFI Summary

DSFI shaft fitting follows the same parameters regardless if it is used indoors or outdoors. When using the DSFI system outdoors, the fitter will be able to watch ball flight, and along with the player, will be able to determine which shaft produces the best combination of distance, accuracy and feel. Shaft fitting is one of the key elements in the correct fitting of golf clubs. The vast array of shaft types, designations and styles make matching the correct shaft to the player an incredible challenge for the clubfitter. Through the use of the Dynacraft Shaft Fitting Index, much of the guesswork is taken out of the fitting process. Shafts now can be chosen that will maximize accuracy, distance and feel.

The clubfitter should offer a selection of shafts to allow the customer a choice: steel or graphite, very flexible to very stiff, low torque or high torque, very lightweight or heavy, etc. The golfer will then be able to base his shaft selection on price and feel, as the performance characteristics of the selected shaft range already will be matched to his game.

#5-IRON SWING SPEED - DISTANCE CHART	
Swing Speed (mph)	**Distance (yds.)**
40	88
42	92
44	97
46	102
48	106
50	110
52	115
54	119
56	124
58	128
60	132
62	137
64	141
66	146
68	150
70	154
72	159
74	163
76	168
78	172
80	176
82	181
84	185
86	190
88	194
90	199

STATIC FITTING

It is possible that at some time a situation may arise where you will be required to fit a golf club without having seen the golfer swing or have been able to measure swing speed. Most likely this type of request may come about as a surprise gift for a birthday or Christmas present. In more modern times, it could result from attempting to custom fit a set of clubs via the Internet or on the telephone.

The distance guides (as seen on pages 95 and 96) will help you "zero in" on the average swing speed. These guides should be only when the person being fit is unable to visit you personally. As always, actual dynamic fitting is the recommended practice for Total Clubfitting.

SHAFTS
Summary: Do's and Don'ts of Shaft Fitting

DO'S

DO: Measure the customer's existing clubs for shaft weight and stiffness. This will help understand the cause and effect relationship of why the customer is in your shop and will give you clues to what is a suitable shaft for their game.

DO: Be aware that there is no standardization in golf shafts; thus use the Shaft Fitting Addendum to compare shaft specifications.

DO: Keep in mind that clubhead specifications and shaft specifications go hand in hand. Lighter and more flexible shafts will tend to aid in trajectory, just as loft will.

DO: Whenever possible, not only measure the person's swing speed, but also examine their tempo and length of their back swing when determining the proper shaft weight and flex.

DO: Use demo clubs with shafts that range from very light to very heavy and very flexible to very stiff in order to determine which combinations improve a golfer's accuracy, trajectory, distance and feel.

DON'TS

DON'T: Always assume that one company's R-flex shaft plays similar to another company's R-flex shaft.

DON'T: Assume that low torque will improve accuracy.

DON'T: Assume that bend point or kick point will automatically increase or decrease trajectory.

DON'T: Assume a longer and/or lighter shaft will increase distance.

DON'T: Overlook the fact that feel plays a major role in shaft selection.

Chapter 8
Grips

The grip is the only contact a player has with the golf club. In order for the player to gain the best possible feel and playability, it is important that the grip be not only the correct size for the player, but it be made from a material that is preferred by the player as well. There are grips made from rubber, synthetic materials, leather, or elastomer; the list goes on and on. Grips may be smooth, perforated or lined with cord; they may be round or ribbed, they may be black, gray, yellow or even red. Grips can cost less that a dollar or may approach upwards of $20.00, including installation. The number of grip choices for a player seems limitless; the selection of type and material is a matter of personal preference in most cases. It is up to the clubfitter to make sure the personal tastes of the golfer can be properly sized to fit him for accurate and consistent shotmaking.

A high percentage of golfers simply ignore the grip as being a factor in the performance of the club. At least 50% of all golfers play with grips that are either excessively worn or incorrectly sized. Either of these situations can lead to inaccurate shots. If a grip is worn, the golfer's hands will tend to slip as the club is being swung. There is a tremendous amount of force applied as a club is played. That force, when applied to a slick or worn grip, almost ensures that the golfer's hand position will change at some point during the swing. When this happens, the chances of returning the club to a square impact position are reduced substantially. The same type of situation occurs when a grip is either too large or too small for a golfer. The golfer will attempt to reposition his or her hands during the swing - again, this can lead to nothing but inconsistencies.

A look at grip sizing and how it is measured shows that there are a number of possible methods used to measure the grip. The most common methods are the use of a grip gauge or the use of calipers. A grip gauge has a few openings labeled as to the size of the grip. The gauge is placed on the grip at a point 2" down from the top of the grip. When the correct size if found, the gauge stays in

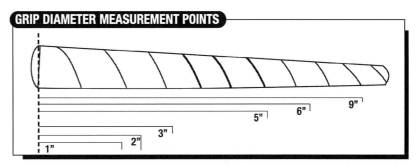

GRIP DIAMETER MEASUREMENT POINTS

A grip's diameter may be measured at various places along the grip.

place. A size too large will cause the gauge to not go onto the grip; too small of a size and the gauge will not stay in place. The major drawback of the gauge is that it lacks a number of size choices. There may only be 3-5 size options on the

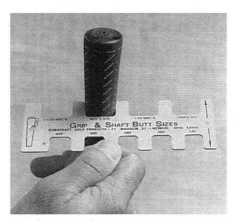

A grip gauge is used to measure certain grip diameters.

gauge; if a grip is not one of these sizes, it cannot be accurately measured. A set of calipers can measure any grip size. At the same point, 2" from the top of the grip, the calipers are positioned on the grip and the dial is read at that point. This decimal reading can be converted to determine if a grip is standard size, oversize or undersize. Any size of grip can be measured with the calipers; the use of them is a recommended method of grip size measurement.

The size of the grip can also be measured at points other than 2" from the top of the grip. These points may be 5" or 6" from the butt end of the grip. These measurements at the lower part of the grip are made in situations in which the player desires the feel of a slightly larger grip

RIGHT HAND GRIP DIMENSION (MEN'S)	
Decimal Reading 5" Below Grip Cap	**Grip Size**
.792"	-1/64" Undersize
.802"	Standard
.822"	+1/64" Oversize
.837"	+1/32" Oversize

than standard under the lower hand. Think about this: A player's two hands are of similar size; most golf grips taper noticeably from top to bottom. It may deserve serious consideration to always check a location under the player's lower hand to ensure accurate grip sizing. More and more grips are being manufactured with larger diameters under the lower hand. The idea of having a larger than standard grip size under the lower hand seems to be a trend, not only among players, but among manufacturers as well.

Standard grip sizing is a fairly simple thing to calculate. It is important to realize there are certain shaft/grip combinations that are able to produce certain sized grips. In other words, not all grips can be made to all sizes, even through the use of buildup tape. As a primer to fitted grip sizes, the most efficient way to create a

STANDARD GRIP SIZES		
Grip Core	**Shaft Butt**	**Grip Size**
M58	.580"	Men's Standard
M60	.600"	Men's Standard
M62	.620"	Men's Standard
L58	.580"	Ladies Standard
L56	.560"	Ladies Standard

Looking at the letter-number designations in the mouth of a grip will show its size.

standard size grip is to use a grip with a core size that matches the butt size of the shaft. For example, to create a standard sized grip using a True Temper Dynamic shaft which has a butt diameter of .600" (You would know this either by measuring the shaft butt using calipers or by referring to technical data related to the shaft as found in the Dynacraft catalog or in the on-line shaft fitting addendum.), a grip with a "60" core size is used. To determine the core size, you may consult a catalog's technical data or you can simply curl the mouth (the open end) of the grip up to reveal a letter/number code. This code will indicate whether the grip is a men's or ladies grip, with either an "M" or an "L", and will give a core size number; for example 56, 58 or 60. Thus, to easily create a standard size men's grip on a Dynamic shaft, a grip that shows M60 in its mouth will be required.

To create grips other than standard size, grip core sizes that do not match shaft butt sizes can sometimes be used. Installing a grip with a smaller core, for example a 58-core grip, on a .600" shaft butt will create a grip that is slightly (+1/64") oversize. This is due to the larger shaft diameter stretching the smaller grip core diameter. Grips may be made slightly smaller by doing the opposite; stretching a 60-core grip down on a .580" shaft will yield a grip slightly smaller than standard. Other methods of achieving larger than standard grips sizes include choosing a grip that is manufactured to a larger diameter. These grips may be 1/32" to 1/8" larger than standard, depending upon type and style; the technical information in a catalog will indicate the core sizes of specific oversize or

midsize grips. Another way to increase grip size is to use masking tape, also called buildup tape, applied to the shaft prior to grip installation. The amount of tape will have a direct effect upon the finished grip size. For example, if an L58 ladies grip is to be installed on a .580", it will create a standard sized ladies grip. The addition of 4 layers of masking tape will create a grip that is @1/32" oversize related to ladies standard. The common way to make a grip smaller is to simply stretch the grip further down the shaft upon installation. Stretching the grip @3/4" will create a grip that is 1/64" undersize. A reminder: The double-sided tape used to hold the grip to the shaft is considered part of all grip sizing. There

OVERSIZE GRIPS

Grip Core	Shaft Butt	Diff.	Grip Size
M58	.600"	.020"	+1/64" Men's Std.
M58	.620"	.040"	+1/32" Men's Std.
M60	.620"	.020"	+1/64" Men's Std.
L56	.600"	.040"	+1/32" Ladies Std.
L56	.620"	.060"	+3/64" Ladies Std.
L58	.600"	.020"	+1/64" Ladies Std.
L58	.620"	.040"	+1/32" Ladies Std.

Air cushion type grips actually have spaces in their walls which create softer feel.

BUILT-UP GRIP SIZING

Fractional Measurement	Men's Decimal Measurement	Ladies Decimal Measurement
-1/32" under	.869	.819
-1/64" under	.885	.835
Standard	.900	.850
+1/64" over	.915	.865
+1/16" over	.931	.881
+1/16" over	.962	.912
+1/8" over	1.087	1.037

*Grip sizes are measured 2" down from edge of grip cap.

Grip Core	Shaft Butt	-1/64"	Std.	+1/64"	+1/32"	+1/16"	+1/8"
M58 +	.580"	*	0	2	4	9	18
M58 +	.600"	X	*	0	2	7	16
M58 +	.620"	X	X	*	0	4	13
M60 +	.580"	0	2	4	7	11	20
M60 +	.600"	*	0	2	4	9	18
M60 +	.620"	X	*	0	2	7	16
M62 +	.580"	2	4	7	9	13	31
M62 +	.600"	0	2	4	7	11	20
M62 +	.620"	*	0	2	4	9	18
L56 +	.560"	*	0	2	4	9	18
L56 +	.580"	X	*	0	2	7	16
L56 +	.600"	X	X	*	0	4	13
L58 +	.560"	0	2	4	7	11	20
L58 +	.580"	*	0	2	4	9	18
L58 +	.600"	X	*	0	2	7	16
L60 +	.560"	2	4	7	9	13	31
L60 +	.580"	0	2	4	7	11	20
L60 +	.600"	*	0	2	4	9	18
L60 +	.620"	X	*	0	2	7	16

*-Grip must be stretched @3/4" longer to reduce outside diameter.
x-not recommended.
Note: Build-up tape is .0035" thick

Layers Of Build-Up Tape Required To Achieve Stated Sizes

GRIP SIZE DIAMETERS	
Decimal Reading 2" Below Grip Cap	**Grip Size**
0.855"	Men's -3/64" Undersize (approximately Ladies Standard)
0.870"	Men's -1/32" Undersize (approximately Ladies +1/64" Oversize)
0.885"	Men's -1/64" Undersize (approximately Ladies +1/32" Oversize)
0.900"	Men's Standard (approximately Ladies +3/64" Oversize)
0.915"	Men's +1/64" Oversize (approximately Ladies +1/16" Oversize)
0.930"	Men's +1/32" Oversize (approximately Ladies +5/64" Oversize)
0.945"	Men's +3/64" Oversize (approximately Ladies +3/32" Oversize)
0.960"	Men's +1/16" Oversize (approximately ladies +7/64 Oversize)
1.025"	Men's +1/8" Oversize

is no need to add any oversizing for this two-way tape.

A possible factor when a player selects a grip in addition to size and feel is whether the grip is round or ribbed. A round grip is just that - the same diameter around its circumference. A ribbed grip, has a ridge, or rib, running straight along the back of the grip, from top to bottom. Some players feel that this rib helps them consistently position their hands on the club or every shot. Others do not like the rib as they claim it inhibits them changing their hand position on the club when playing certain finesse shots. The rib is strictly a matter of personal prefer-

A cut away view shows how a ribbed grip looks inside. The larger area is what creates the rib.

ence, but if fitting a beginning player, ribbed grips might be a good recommendation as these grips may help the player with consistent hand position. The rib fits comfortably in the player's fingers when he takes his normal grip. To determine if a grip is round or ribbed, consult a catalog or look into the mouth of the grip. For example, a Golf Pride grip that is ribbed will have no letter after the core size, for example M60 indicates a grip that has a rib. A round grip will have the letter "R" following the core size. An M60R indicates a men's 60-core grip that is round. Do be aware that not all manufacturers supply both round and ribbed grips in all styles and variations.

A look at grip types shows a wide range of selection for all players. Personal preference plays a larger role in grip selection than perhaps in any other fitting parameter. Feel is a key to grip selection. What feels good to one player may not feel so good to another. As previously stated, the grip is the only place where the player actually contacts the club; it is very important for that contact to fit correctly and feel good. A synopsis of the key features of popular grips types that may be helpful when discussing grip selection with a player are noted as follows. Again, personal preference is the key to selecting a type of grip.

Rubber Grips

There are a number of sizes, both core sizes and finished sizes, of rubber grips. Rubber grips are among the most economical grips. They often have cork mixed in with the rubber for added traction and durability. They will wear well and require a minimum of care. The popular Golf Pride Victory grip is an example.

The Golf Pride victory grip has been the choice of professional golfers for decades.

Cord Grips

Usually made from a rubber base material, cord grips have cord as part of their mold construction. This cord will be visible on the grip. It is designed to provide what some players claim is a superior grip. Others claim cord grips are too harsh-feeling. Cord grips will last longer than rubber grips, but are at least twice as expensive in most cases. Also, the cord in these grips makes creating larger sizes more difficult as the cord will not stretch as much as rubber. The Lamkin Crossline Cord is an example.

Cord grips are preferred by those who seek a firm feel.

Synthetic or Blended Grips

Grips made from a number of polymers have recently become the most popular types of grips. These polymers are touted as being longer-wearing or as providing a better gripping surface than a standard rubber grip. They can easily be sized, are not much more costly than rubber grips and wear will at least as well as rubber grips. Golf Pride's Tour Wrap is

The most popular version of a synthetic grip is Golf Pride's Tour Wrap.

The Softie from Golf Pride is the first example of softer compound, one piece grips.

Elastomer grips, such as this one by Winn, provide among the softest feel of any grip.

in this category.

Air-Cushion Grips

These grips are identified by their "cushiony" feel. When gripped, they can actually be compressed. These grips are designed to provide cushioning for those who prefer a soft feel. They were originally targeted for those players with arthritic conditions due to their vibration absorbing qualities. At only a slightly higher cost than rubber grips, they do offer an alternative for those seeking a

The Chamois grip is the most commonly used "cushion" type of grip.

soft feel, but they wear more quickly than most rubber grips. Avon's Chamois grip is a popular grip of this type.

Soft Compound Grips

The newest in grip material, soft compound grips are aimed at those who like a very soft feel. These grips are available in a range of styles and colors and are priced between the rubber and cord type of grip. Many players claim to

like the soft feel, but there are as many who simply don't care for the lack of firmness. These grips, as with any softer grip, will tend to wear a bit faster than will rubber, synthetic or cord grips. Golf Pride's Sofftie is the first grip of this kind.

Leather Grips

Leather grips, once the only grip material 50 years ago, has been relegated for use mainly on putters, and even then in very limited quantity. Leather grips can cost up to $20.00 installed. While they do provide a tacky feel and do last a long time, they require more cleaning and care than do other types of grips.

Leather grips are rarely seen today due to their high cost and relatively difficult installation.

Elastomer Grips

These new compounds provide a softer feel and are available in a variety of sizes, styles and colors. Originally only available in very soft compounds, elas-

tomer grips are now available in a number of hardness categories, with some treated to be very tacky even in wet conditions. Elastomer grips wear somewhat quicker than do rubber or synthetic grips, but offer a good choice for those who like a soft, wrap-style grip. They cost at least twice as much as most rubber grips. Winn grips are among the most preferred elastomer grips.

EFFECT ON BALL FLIGHT

A grip's effect on ball flight can either help or hinder consistency and accuracy. The more often a player is able to keep his or her hands in the same place on the club during the swing, the more consistent the player's shots will be and the more accurate they will be at the same time. Any hand repositioning during the swing will lead to poor results and may also be a reason a player may complain that the club does not feel just "right" to him.

Consider a grip that is too small for a player. The player will feel that he may have to hold the club very firmly since he cannot get his entire hand(s) on the small grip. As a result, the player may tend to try to hold the grip much more firmly than he should. This will lead to tension in the arms, inhibiting a full release and potentially compromising distance. Plus, if the player actually re-grips the club during the swing, this will change the position of the face relative to the target. On one shot, the face may be open; on the very next it may be closed; in any event, inconsistency is the result. Over the

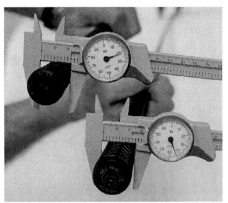
Ladies and jumbo grips show possible extremes in grip sizing.

years, a misconception developed in fitting circles that a grip that was too small for a player caused him to hook the ball or at least hit it left of target as the smaller grip promoted excessive hand action. Unless the grip is several sizes too small (at least in the 1/8" range), this simply will not happen. Unpredictable inconsistency in both directions is a result of a grip that is too small for a player.

What if the grip is too large for the player? He will tend to "fight" to get his hands around the grip. As a result, it may feel to him as if the is swinging a baseball bat. Feel will certainly be compromised, his arm muscles may tighten as he tries to control the club, and distance is compromised. The common misconception involving too large grips is that they will prevent the player from releasing his hands, leading to pushes or slices. Again, this is not the case in actual play. Much in the manner of a grip that is too small, a grip that is oversized for the player will cause misdirected shots in a random pattern. The golf grip must be sized so that the player will not tend to reposition his hands during the swing. It cannot be either too large or too small; in those cases, both distance and accuracy potential potentially suffer.

THE GRIP AND OTHER FITTING PARAMETERS

The grip is the one specification that has a more profound direct impact on feel than on any measured specification of the club. Feel is paramount to the utmost potential performance; thus it is a key part of grip fitting.

WEIGHT

A grip's weight influences other weight parameters of the golf club. A grip that is heavier in weight than standard will add to the total weight of the club. Whatever the grip weighs becomes part of the total weight of the club; a heavier weight grip will add to total weight; a lighter grip will tend to not have as great of an effect on total weight. A heavier grip will alter the swingweight of the club. As a grip's weight increases, the club's swingweight decreases. This is due to the added weight of the grip toward the butt section of the club. For 5 grams that a grip's weight is increased, the club's swingweight will decrease @1 point. Thus, if a fitter recommends a jumbo type of grip for a player, he must be aware of its effect on swingweight. As a jumbo grip may weigh in the neighborhood of 16 grams more than most standard rubber or synthetic grips, a club fitted with a jumbo grip will have a higher total weight (by 16 grams) but a lighter swingweight (by a bit less than 3 points.) Thus anytime a

GRIP WEIGHTS (.600" core unless noted)	
AVON	
Jumbo Chamois	65g
GOLF PRIDE	
Softie	52g
Tour Velvet	50g
Tour Velvet Cord	51g
Tour Wrap	50g
Ladies Tour Wrap (.560")	48g
Victory	50g
Jumbo Victory	69g
Taylor Bubble (.670")	32g
Tour Wrap Ultralite (.865")	28g
LAMKIN	
Crossline	51g
Jumbo Crossline	80g
TACKI MAC	
Arthritic (.580")	81g
WINN	
Wrap (wrap on grip for .865")	14g
Slip on (.595")	39g
XL +1/8" slip on (.595")	45g

jumbo grip is to be fitted to player, swingweight and total weight become a factor.

A similar situation occurs when a lighter weight grip is fitted to a player. Lighter weight grips, in the sub-40 gram range have the effect of reducing the total weight of the club, but increasing its swingweight. Each 5 gram decrease in grip weight will cause a swingweight increase of 1 point. When fitting ultra-light graphite shafts to a player, lighter grips are a method of increasing swingweight; a helpful factor especially when fitting a shorter graphite shaft to a player. The swingweight/total weight relationships apply regardless of whether the club is a wood, iron or putter.

As a reference, a standard grip would weigh in the 50-gram range. A lightweight grip is considered to be in the sub-40 gram range. A "heavy" grip is one that is over 55-60 grams. Just about all grips that are midsize or jumbo will fall at least into this heavier weight class. Also, if grips are made larger, the buildup tape will have an effect of adding weight; the more tape, the more weight. Thus, anytime a grip is larger than standard, there is almost assuredly some effect of swingweight and total weight as a result of the added weight of the larger grip.

BALANCE POINT

A club's balance point will be influenced by grip weight. The heavier the grip, the closer to the grip the balance point of the club will be. Lighter grips move the balance point away from the hands, toward the head. Players preferring a club with more head feel, may benefit from the balance point change a lighter grip causes. On the other side of the coin, if a player prefers a club with not a lot of head feel, heavier grips may help. We previously mentioned swingweight and its relationship with grip weight. The balance point relationship directly correlates with this: Heavier grip, higher balance point; lighter grip, lower balance point.

FACE ANGLE

The club's face angle may be influenced, either intentionally or unintentionally by the grip. If the grip is positioned so that the player will tend to place his hands more clockwise (turned to the right) on the grip then typical, this may have the effect of closing the face of the club at impact as it may encourage more hand action. This could either be done intentionally by the fitter to help counter-act shots to the right or inadvertently during assembly, which may result in a loss of accuracy. This alignment variation will be much more noticeable when working with ribbed grips as compared to round grips since the ribs encourage specific hand positions - in this example a position that encourages face angle position to the left. An opposite situation can occur if a grip is installed so the player positions his hands more to the left (counterclockwise) on the grip. Such a grip alignment/hand position may promote the tendency to hold the face open at impact resulting in shots to the right.

FREQUENCY

The only parameters that affect shaft flex are length and head weight. However, by selecting certain types of grips during the fitting, a change in the shaft's frequency results. This is caused by the softness or firmness of the particular grip selected. A soft compound grip may decrease the frequency of a club as compared to a firm cord type of grip as a result of the clamping pressure of the frequency machine. The frequency reading may change, but the actual stiffness of a club will not change regardless of the type of grip selected.

GRIP DEMO CLUBS

Demo clubs for grips can come in a number of forms. A basic demo would be a club with an undersized grip installed on ot. Gauze tape (available in drug stores) can be added until the proper size is achieved. After fitting, the size can be measured to determine it it is standard, +1/64", etc. A possible demo selection would be a number of grips built to different sizes, installed on shaft butts. The player could hold each grip in his hands to determine which size felt best. Obviously each size would be labeled; each grip size sample would be the same type of grip. The sizes should begin at ladies 1/64" undersize and progress through men's 1/16" oversize, sized in 1/64" increments. A jumbo (+1/8") grip should be included as part of the demo selection as should a junior size grip. Perhaps a few putter samples should be included as well.

An advanced demo selection for grips would include the same (or at least most of the same) sizes listed in the basic program, except at this point, the grips are actually installed on a club, allowing the player to hit test each size. This part of the demo club package becomes somewhat expensive, but it will be an impressive addition to any fitter's collection. Again, each club should be clearly labeled as to test parameter and grip size. Do be certain to keep all grip demos clean; replace them with a new grip of the same

type anytime they show wear. It is advisable to replace all of the demo grips at the same so that they all feel the same; none of the demo grips should feel harder, softer or slicker than any others. As adding size to the grip under the lower hand is becoming commonplace, a few examples of this should be included in the demo selection. A final addition to an advanced grip selection includes putter grips, either installed only on shaft butts or, better yet, actually installed on sample putters.

FITTING GRIPS

DYNAMIC FITTING INDOORS & OUT

Having a player actually hit clubs with various grip sizes is the best route to accurate grip fitting. Suppose the fitter does not have all of the grip sizes on actual clubs to test hit? This is no huge problem. Gauze Tape, found at local drug stores, can be wrapped onto a standard size grip until the player is comfortable with the feel of the grip and both he and the fitter are satisfied with ball flight. The tape can be added or removed as needed; one roll of tape will last several fitting sessions. It is not important to know the size of the grip at this point; it can be measured after hit testing is complete with calipers or a grip gauge.

The fitter will be looking for a couple of key elements. One, does the grip size appear to be comfortable to the player? A grip that is sized correctly will have the middle two fingers of the player's top hand lightly touching the heel pad of that same hand. A grip that may be on the large size will not allow the fingers to touch the hand, while a grip that is too

GRIP DEMO CLUBS		
IRONS & WOODS		
Basic Demo		
Undersize grip plus gauze tape		
Advanced Basic		
Cut shaft butts with these grip sizes installed:	-1/64" ladies	
	standard ladies	
	+1/64" ladies	
	standard men	
	+1/64" men	
	+1/32" men	
	+3/64" men	
	+1/16" men	
	+1/8" men	
Advanced		
Same as Advanced Basic, but installed on actual clubs allowing hit testing		

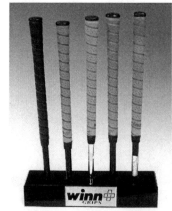

Many grip manufacturers offer displays to showcase their grips.

GRIP SIZE
STD
LADY

As with all demo clubs, labelling grip sizes makes organized fitting easier.

small will be evidenced by the player's fingers digging into the hand. Such an observation will most often closely approximate the correct grip size. Once grip size is approximated in this manner, it is time to get the player's opinion of how it feels. Remember, feel is a key concern when fitting grips. If the player says the grip is too small, try something 1/64" larger; if the player claims the grip is too big, go smaller in 1/64" increments. Follow these patterns until the proper grip size is determined - by feel alone at this point.

Most golfers hold the club primarily in their fingers. In that case, the above approximation of grip sizing works reasonably well. However, there are golfers who prefer to hold the grip primarily in the palms of their hands. Such gripping

style will require a larger grip than would be indicated with the fingers and heel pad test. These players may require not only a larger grip size for their upper hand, but a noticeably larger one for their lower hand as well. Golfers who hold the grip mainly in their palms will most often be best-fit with grips that do not taper a great deal.

The player will now hit balls with the grip size he or she selected from the demo clubs. Both the fitter and the player will observe ball flight when fitting grip sizing outdoors, perhaps trying grip sizes on either side of the initially chosen size to see if there are positive or negative ball flight changes as a result of this "new" grip size. Noticeable inconsistency is a probable sign of incorrect grip size. Further, the fitter will watch the player's hands on the club. The fitter is looking for a grip size for which the player most accurately hits shots while not changing hand position. It is up to the fitter to visually observe whether the player repositions his hands; the best-fit grip is one in which the player does not change hand position, is comfortable with the grip size and hits shots consistently. During indoor grip fitting, the exact same process occurs, with the exception of being able to watch ball flight. What can be observed is the position of where the balls impact the hitting net. Inconsistencies in net impacts often indicate a possible grip size alteration is needed.

STATIC FITTING

Static grip fitting may take a number of forms. It can be as "advanced" as having a player take his grip on test clubs of varying sizes. It can be a bit more basic, having the player hold various sizes of grip samples that have been installed on shaft butts. Or it can be as simplistic as measuring a player's hand on some type of pattern or gauge or asking the player what size glove he wears. Hopefully, the grip fitting will still allow

The finger/hand position on a properly sized grip (top). The grip is too small in the center photo; too large in the lower one.

the player to hold a grip in his hands to determine a good approximation of proper size. In lieu of a number of grip size samples, the gauze tape can be used here as well. As grips are important to a club's feel, fitting them without some type of observation certainly increases the potential for a mis-fit grip size. Even though static fitting of grips is a less than perfect scenario, it is better than simply choosing a standard size grip. Not a great many of us have "standard" swings, why should we have "standard" grips?

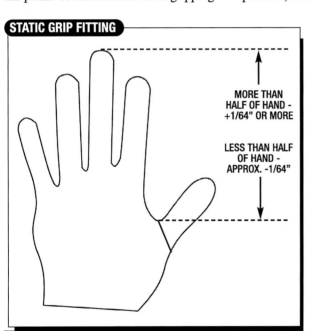

STATIC GRIP FITTING

MORE THAN HALF OF HAND - +1/64" OR MORE

LESS THAN HALF OF HAND - APPROX. -1/64"

* If thumb crease-to-fingertip measurement is more than half of the total hand measurement, grip size should be at least +1/64".

* If thumb crease-to-fingertip measurement is less than half of the total hand measurement, grip size should be @-1/64".

Measuring the length of a player's fingers related to his hand provide a grip size generalization.

PUTTER GRIP FITTING

Just as when fitting woods or irons, the grip is a key element in how a putter feels to a player. The putter grip may actually influence the playability of the putter in similar manners as it does for other clubs. Just about all putter grips have a flat area on the front that allows a player to position his thumbs on this area, promoting a square hand position. This hand position encourages keeping the putter on line during the stroke, leading to added accuracy. Putter grips are available in a number of styles, sizes and weights, allowing a golfer a large selction during fitting. A heavier putter grip will change the swingweight (making it lighter) and the total weight (making it heavier.) The balance point of a putter will change as a result of grip weight. Plus, the size of a grip has a direct effect on the player's stroke. If a player tends to be too "handsy", a larger size grip will tend to eliminate this type of stroke, helping the

Size and shape of a putter grip is somewhat a matter of personal preference.

player to make a smooth stroke. If a smaller putter grip is used, some players claim their feel is enhanced as a result. Two items to remember: If you are assembling "long" putters, they require round grips. Flat front putter grips do not conform to the Rules of Golf when installed on these longer putters. When fitting a chipper, it must be fitted with a round or ribbed grip and not a putter grip. The only club that may have a grip with a flat area is the putter.

NOTE: For a complete look at putter fitting, please refer to Chapter 11.

GRIPS
Summary: Do's and Don'ts of Grip Fitting

DO'S	DON'TS
DO: Know that a proper grip size and preferred grip material is a key to player consistency	**DON'T:** Overlook the importance of player preference when selecting grips
DO: Make certain that grip size is consistent throughout the set	**DON'T:** Look to substantial ball flight differences as a result of small grip size changes
DO: Realize that how a grip feels is very important to club confidence	**DON'T:** Assume that too large of a grip will always produce pushed shots and too small of a grip will yield pulled shots.
DO: Explain cost, performance and durability related to specific grip materials to all players during fitting	**DON'T:** Neglect the effect grip weight may have on swing weight, total weight and club feel.
DO: Use grips of various weights to help achieve specific club weighting requirements	**DON'T:** Fail to remind a player the importance of regripping often for maximum club performance.
DO: Recommend re-gripping a player's clubs every year	

Chapter 9
Weight

The weight of a golf club has a tremendous influence on its feel. As a player picks up a club, one of the first things he or she notices is how "heavy" or "light" the club feels. While each player's perception of what "heavy" or "light" might be, nevertheless, the club's weight is a prime determinant of its feel. Typically, slower swingers, seniors and lady players may prefer clubs that feel lighter, while stronger players seem to prefer heavier clubs. While this is not always the case, heavier clubs seem to "pace" the swings of stronger players, while lighter clubs promote potentially added club head speed for slower swingers.

There are two types of weight that are factors when discussing golf equipment. The more common term related to weight is "swingweight." The second term applied to golf club weight is "total weight." (Total weight may also be labeled as "static weight" or "overall weight".) Swingweight is the measurement of the weight distribution of a golf club. It is the relation between how weight is distributed toward the head end of the club as compared to the grip end of the club. It is measured on a specialized scale, called a swingweight scale, with the club balancing on a 14" fulcrum point nearest the grip end of the club. Any weight that is located at the butt end of the club in relationship to this 14" fulcrum point is considered to be grip weight; any weight away from the fulcrum point toward the sole of the club is classified as head weight.

The more weight there is in the head end of the club as compared to the grip end the higher the swingweight reading. Correspondingly, a club that has a high percentage of weight in its grip will most often have a lower swingweight.

Swingweight is measured in arbitrary alpha-numeric units. The lighter end of the scale begins at "A" and ends at "G". Each of these letter designations contains 10 individual gradations, or "points". Thus a swingweight of A1 indicates a club with a very high concentration of weight towards its grip, while one with a G9 has an unusually large concentration of weight towards its head. Most men's clubs with steel shafts fall within the C9-D3 category at standard length; most ladies' steel shafted club fall between C3 and C7 at standard length. Keep in mind that standards differ from one company to another, so these swingweight numbers may be derived on clubs that may not all use the same standard lengths.

A swingweight point equates very closely to 2 grams in the head of the club. That is, for example, a club that weights D2 with a 257 gram #5 iron head would weigh D3 with a 259 gram head, D4 with a 261 gram head, and so on. If the club's head weight was reduced to 255, the swingweight would be approximately D1. This 2-gram addition or subtraction yielding a 1-swingweight point change applies regardless of whether the club is a man's or ladies model, or whether the club has a steel or graphite shaft. A swingweight point toward the grip end of the club is between 4 and 5 grams. Thus, if a new grip that weighs 5 grams heavier is installed on a club, the swingweight will decrease approximately 1 point. Adding weight to the grip end of the club decreases swingweight; using lighter grips will increase swingweight. The 4-5 gram per swingweight ratio applies on all clubs, regardless of make, model, length, etc.

The reason that the swingweight change is between 4 and 5 grams in the grip end of the club has to do with the length of the grip and the position of the weight. The closer weight is positioned toward the butt end of the grip, the less weight required to cause a 1-swingweight point change. Thus, if a club is counter-balanced using a lead butt weight of 4 grams, the resulting swingweight change would be 1 point. The butt weight is inserted at the very end of the shaft, effectively positioning all of its weight at the point most far from the 14" fulcrum. Normally a grip's weight is positioned along its length and not at its very butt, making 5 grams necessary to cause a 1-swingweight point change in swingweight.

Butt weights that may be placed in the butt end of a shaft will decrease swingweight, but will increase total weight.

Total weight is the measured weight of all of the components of a club in assembled form. That is, it is what the club weighs when placed on a typical weight scale. For instance, if a #5 iron is weighed, an average weight will be somewhere in the 14.8 ounce (@420 gram) range; a typical driver may average 12.9 ounces (@366 grams). These weights are based on the use of a standard weight steel shaft at 37.5" for the #5 iron and 43" for the driver. Anything heavier than these would be considered above average in weight. Anything lighter will be considered to be lightweight. Realizing today's shafts may weigh 50 grams or less, a club assembled with one of these may have a total weight less than 11 ounces (@312 grams) in the driver and 13 ounces (@369 grams) for the #5 iron. The same scale that is used to measure swingweight may also be used to measure a club's total weight. (Note:

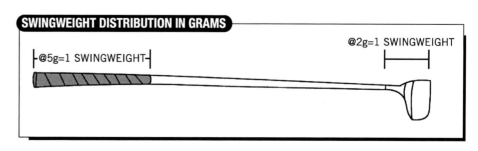

A quality gram scale measures component weights very accurately.

SWINGWEIGHT DISTRIBUTION IN GRAMS

@5g=1 SWINGWEIGHT

@2g=1 SWINGWEIGHT

A swingweight scale measure the weight relationship between head, shaft and grip.

Inexpensive swingweight scales are only equipped to measure swingweight and not total weight.) The club is placed on a holding device at one end of the scale so that it is in balance. Its weight can then be read from the arm of the scale. One side of the arm will show the total weight in ounces, the other side in grams.

Any change in swingweight will result in some change in the total weight of the club. (There is one exception related to changing a club's lie that will be discussed later.) A change in total weight may or may not cause a change in swingweight. This may seem a bit contradictory, but closer examination proves this fact. If a club's swingweight changes, weight either must be removed from the club or must be added to the club. If a club's swingweight is increased, material is either added to the head end of the club or is removed from the grip end of the club. Any time that weight is either added or removed from the club, it is in effect, a change in total weight. If weight is either added or removed, regardless of where it is added or where it is removed from, a total weight change occurs. But, if a club's total weight changes, its swingweight does not necessarily change. For example, let's say a club's total weight is increased by 7 grams. If 5 of those grams are in the grip and 2 are in the head, the swingweight will remain the same, even though the total weight was increased. The swingweight would remain the same as well if 2 grams were removed from the head and 5 from the grip. If the club's head weight was increased by 2 grams and no increase was made to the grip weight, the swingweight will increase by 1 point and the total weight increases by 2 grams. In summary, any change in swingweight, except for lie changes of 3 degrees or more, will yield a total weight change of some type; a change in total weight might cause a change in swingweight.

FACTORS EFFECTING SWINGWEIGHT

Swingweight Change	Increase Factor By	FACTOR	Decrease Factor By	Swingweight Change
+1	2 grams	Headweight	2 grams	-2
+3	1/2"	Club length	1/2"	-3
-1	5 grams	Grip weight	5 grams	+1
+1	@9 grams	Shaft length	@9 grams	-1

There are five key factors that influence the swingweight and total weight of a club. These include length of the club, head weight, grip weight, shaft weight and shaft balance point. Changes in any of these may yield a change in the swingweight or total weight of the club, both the swingweight or total weight of the club or neither the swingweight or total weight of the club.

Club Length A change in the length of a club will cause changes to both swingweight and total weight (unless something is done to make up for the change.) As a club is made longer, its swingweight and total weight both increase. The swingweight increases since the head of the

The longer the club, the higher the swingweight (provided shaft material remains the same).

club is now farther from the fulcrum point of the swingweight scale than it was prior to the length increase. Even though the length may have been in the form of an extension at the butt end of the club, the 14" fulcrum measurement does not change; the length, in essence is to the head side of the swingweight scale. Each 1/2" change in length will cause a swingweight change of @3 points.

This is regardless of shaft material. If a club is lengthened, its swingweight increases; if it is made shorter, its swingweight decreases.

As a club is made longer, its total weight will increase. The amount of increase is equal to the weight of the shaft that was use to extend the club. The total weight increase may be just a couple of grams in the case of ultralight graphite shafts, or it may be higher when steel shafted clubs are used. As a club is shortened, its total weight will decrease by the weight of the shaft that was cut. Both swingweight and total weight increase as a club becomes longer; both decrease as a club becomes shorter.

Should the lie of a club be changed 3 degrees, the swingweight of the club will change as a result. As a club is made flatter, its toe moves away from the butt end of the shaft. This moves weight further from the swingweight scale's fulcrum point. As weight is moved away from the fulcrum point as a result of a lie change of 3 degrees, the swingweight of the club will increase 1 point. Conversely, changing the lie of a club 3 degrees upright will reduce the swingweight of that club by a point. Neither making the club flatter nor more upright will have any effect on its total weight, only on its swingweight. Changing the lie of the club is the only method of altering swingweight without changing total weight in the process.

OVERLENGTH, UNDERLENGTH CLUB HEADWEIGHTS			
Club	Std.	1/2" Longer	1/2" Shorter
#1-wood	198	193	203
#3-wood	208	203	213
#5-wood	218	213	223
#7-wood	228	223	233
#1-iron	230	223	237
#2-iron	237	230	244
#3-iron	244	237	251
#4-iron	251	244	252
#5-iron	265	251	265
#6-iron	272	258	272
#7-iron	279	265	279
#8-iron	286	272	286
#9-iron	299	279	293
PW-iron	230	286	300
SW-iron	300	293	307
UW-iron	302	293	307

Head Weight

A change in a club's head weight has a direct effect upon both swingweight and total weight. If a club's head is made heavier by 2 grams, its swingweight will increase by 1 point. Remember 2 grams is equal to approximately 1 point when added to the head of the club. Any time weight is added - in this instance in the head of the club to increase swingweight - the total weight will also increase. This increase is equal to the amount of weight that is added to the head; in this example, 2 grams. If weight is removed from the head, the club's swingweight decreases one point for every 2 grams that is removed. The total weight of the club will also decrease equal to the amount of weight removed from the head. Keep in mind that any change in the weight of the head of a club will cause some change in the flex of the shaft. For each 2 grams or 1 swingweight addition, expect the shaft to play softer by 1 cpm. For any decrease in head weight, the shaft will play stiffer by a ratio of 1 cpm per 2 gram weight

A two-gram difference in headweight yields an approximate 1 swingweight change.

reduction.

Grip Weight

As the grip weight of a club is changed, there is a corresponding change in swingweight and total weight. If 5 grams is added to the grip end of a club through a grip change, this will add 5 grams to the total weight of the club. But, as more weight is added toward the grip side of the 14" fulcrum scale, the club's swingweight will decrease by 1

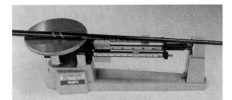

Shaft weight has a noticeable effect on swingweight and total weight.

point. In effect, as a grip becomes heavier, total weight increases, but swingweight decreases. Obviously then the opposite is true as well. If a lighter weight grip is installed on the club (a 40-gram Winn grip as compared to a 50-gram rubber grip), the club's total weight will be reduced by 10 grams, but its swingweight will increase by 2 points.

Shaft Weight: The golf club shaft plays a key role in the swingweight and total weight of the club. The heavier the shaft, the greater both the swingweight and total weight of the club will be. Comparing a 60-gram shaft to a 90-gram shaft, shows that the total weight of the club using the 90-gram will be 30 grams more than the club with the 60-gram shaft. The swingweight of the club with the 90-gram shaft will be approximately 3 1/3 points higher as well. Assuming the balance points of both the 60 and 90-gram shafts are the same, each 9 grams of weight in the shaft equate to a 1-swingweight change. It is very important to note that a shaft's balance point also plays a key role in how shaft weight determines swingweight.

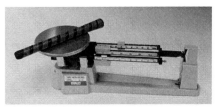

Each 5 grams of weight in a grip may change the swingweight 1 point.

SHAFT WEIGHT CLASSIFICATIONS	
Standard weight	4.25-4.62 oz (120-132g)
Medium lightweight	3.80-4.24 oz (109-120g)
Very lightweight	3.4-3.79 oz (99-109g)
Ultra lightweight	2.0-3.6 oz (57-99g)

SHAFT WEIGHT & SWINGWEIGHT			
Iron	Head Weight	Shaft Weight	Swingweight @Std. Length[1]
2i	236g	4.37 oz.	D-0
2i	236g	4.00 oz.	C-8.5
2i	236g	3.75 oz.	C-7
2i	236g	3.00 oz.	C-2

[1]Standard length = 39" for the #2-iron

The weight of the shaft itself has a direct bearing on the total weight of the club. If the shaft weighs 90-grams, that 90-grams directly is part of the total weight of the club. But, depending upon how that weight is distributed along the length of the shaft, the swingweight may or may not increase as much or as little as expected.

Shaft Balance Point

The balance point of the shaft has an effect on the club's swingweight. It has no effect on its total weight, assuming that the shafts being compared are the same weight. Using two 90 gram shafts as examples, both will have the same effect on the club's total weight - 90 grams being the shaft component of the finished club. If one of the shafts has most of its weight concentrated toward the tip of the shaft and the other has its weight concentrated toward the shaft butt, there will be a noticeable difference in the swingweights of the two clubs that use

An easy method by which to determine as shaft's balance point is to rest it on a piece of angle iron.

these shafts. As more weight is concentrated toward the tip, the swingweight of the club will increase; if a high percentage of weight is concentrated toward the shaft butt, the swingweight will be reduced. There is no one-to-one correspondence of how much the swingweight will be influenced by balance point - it will vary from shaft to shaft - but it is a certainty that shaft balance point will have a quantifiable effect on the swingweight of the club.

EFFECT ON BALL FLIGHT

The weight of a club has the potential to have both positive and negative influences on the swing. If a club's weight matches a players' swing, the result will be more consistent impacts. This will translate into more accurate shots and potentially lower scores. On the other hand, a club that is either too heavy or too light will often result in inconsistent shots. In instances when the club is too heavy, the player often tends to feel that he has to put extra effort into swinging the club. This often results in the player losing balance, leading to inconsistent shots. In most instances of the club being too light, the player will not be able to "feel" where the club is during the swing, again leading to inconsistent shots. Do not assume that a light club is always better for a player; face impacts must be observed in order to determine which club weight will yield the most consistent results at impact.

The inconsistencies that result from a club being either too heavy or too light will potentially vary from player to player. Clubs that are too heavy may cause a player to tire toward the end of the round. Increases in shaft, head or grip weights, even by a few grams, are noticeable at as a round progresses. Fatigue may lead to inconsistencies and pushing the ball as well as to lower trajectories. In situations where clubs may be too light for a given player, loss of distance control may be evident. A lighter club has the potential to be swung faster, leading to the potential for longer shots. However, lighter clubs may be more difficult to return squarely to impact, possibly causing directional problems. When light clubs are returned to impact in a square position, added distance is realized - often even more distance than anticipated. When light clubs are not in a square impact position, distance, accuracy and feel suffer. Random shot patterns are a result; also light clubs may tend to possibly produce shots that are higher than desired. If a club is too light for a player, it may become more difficult to swing faster; not all lighter clubs will produce higher swingspeeds - there is a point of diminishing returns that will vary from player to player.

WEIGHT AND OTHER FITTING PARAMETERS

SHAFT FLEX

As the head of a club is made heavier or the grip end of the club is made lighter, the swingweight of the club changes. A change in swingweight will elicit a corresponding change in the flex of the shaft. For each swingweight the club becomes heavier, the frequency of the shaft will decrease by one cycle, or approximately 1/10 of a flex. While 1 cycle is virtually imperceptible, changes of 3 or more swingweights will not only noticeably change the feel for the club, they will change the frequency as well. This 1-cycle per swingweight relationship is true regardless of whether the club is made longer or shorter.

SHAFT BALANCE POINT

If a club's swingweight is increased, its balance point will move toward the head end of the club. This will make the club feel more "head heavy" in most cases due, not only to the balance point change, but to any swingweight change as just discussed. The further the balance point is from the player's hands, the more difficult it is to get the club in motion, a situation that potentially may result in the face being open at impact. Balance points closer to the hands add to the ease of clearing the hands through at impact, leading to more accurate impacts. In some cases, a heavier grip and/or weight under the grip (counterbalancing) have been known to improve swingspeed, accuracy and distance. Counterbalancing, while it will add total weight to the club and decrease the club's swingweight, has the effect of slowing the hands at the top of the swing, eliminating casting the club from the top and delaying the release later in the swing, potentially helping with shot control and distance. Perhaps the most famous example of counterbalancing involves Jack Nicklaus. Nearly every driver Nicklaus used in his prime was counterbalanced helping to slow his hands through impact, virtually eliminating unwanted hooked shots. The balance point becomes lower with the addition of head weight and higher with the reduction of head weight. Balance point will also change along with grip weight; lighter grips create a lower balance point, while heavy grips lead to higher balance points.

FEEL

While feel may be an intangible that varies from one golfer to another, suffice it to say that if a player likes how a club feels to him, the chances he will hit it well are increased. Such a club will instill confidence when he addresses the ball and waggles the club. This should carry on into improved ball contact. Feel is among the first impressions of a golf club. If it is positive, player success may be enhanced. If the first thought a player has when picking up a club is that it doesn't "feel right", the odds of him hitting it well are vastly decreased.

Feel not only occurs at address, but at

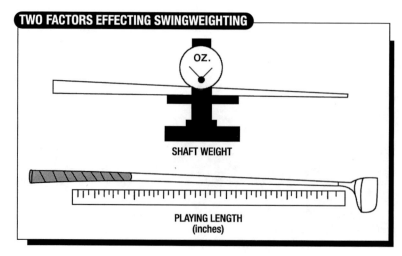

TWO FACTORS EFFECTING SWINGWEIGHTING

OZ.

SHAFT WEIGHT

PLAYING LENGTH
(inches)

impact as well. The way a club feels to the player as he swings it makes it either a club that is a good choice or one that is not. Impact feel is a combination of things (flex, length, head design, etc.), but weight certainly plays a key role. Virtually all components of a club combine to produce its feel, but one of the most obvious of those components to a golfer of any ability, is how heavy or light the club feels to the player.

WEIGHT DEMO CLUBS

A basic weight demo selection requires only a few clubs and some lead tape. The basic setup includes two clubs, a mid-iron and a driver, both made a light as possible, both in swingweight and total weight. The fitter allows the player to hit each club, adding lead tape to the club until it feels "good" and yields consistent results. The amount of tape added is not important during the hit testing as the fitter can simply weigh the club afterwards and ascertain its swingweight and total weight. There is little worry that a player will choose a weight that is out of the "normal" weight range. Modern day components are designed to perform within certain weight ranges; anything outside of these weight ranges does not feel good, nor does it produce consistent shotmaking results.

It may seem logical for an advanced demo selection to include demo clubs such as a number of mid irons swing-weighted in 3 point increments. Three points is chosen as the incremental unit as most players can discern between three points, but not between one or two. The demos could start at a light weight, C8 for example in a man's club and C2 in a ladies. These would be followed by D1 and D4 as well as C5 and C8, respectively. If units closer than three points is desired, lead tape (4 1/2" of 1/2" wide tape equals 1 swingweight) can be added to fine-tune the club's feel. The same could be done with drivers. Added demo clubs could include a graphite shafted mid-iron and driver, commencing a few points lower than the steel demos related to swingweight. But, in all honesty, as the shaft and length of the club are the prime determinants of its weight, money devoted to demos such as these is not wisely spent. Weight demo clubs, either in a basic or advanced setting may be best

left to using clubs that have the same type and length of shaft that will be used in the player's actual clubs. Lead tape can fine tune the clubs for final weight determination.

Perhaps a couple of demos could be added that approximate total weight differences as well. A few irons and drivers weighing in the D2 range, but with heavy and light total weights may help a male golfer determine if he prefers a heavy or light feel. The same type of demos, but in the C8 range will offer the same comparison to female players. Perhaps even having a demo driver that weighs a few pounds but swingweights at D2 will help players learn the difference between swingweight and total weight. This type of driver can be made by filling the shaft (and perhaps the head) with lead powder or lead shot. It is important that this driver be used for feel testing only; such a club should never be used to hit balls! A counterbalanced demo may be added to help benefit those who may have fast hands through impact; such a club may improve directional control for "handsy" players.

Another interesting demo that can be done to show how swingweight changes (or doesn't change) feel is that of using coins to approximate swingweight. If a player wants to know how much a single swingweight point feels, tape a dime to the back of a club. The dime weighs 2

grams and will add approximately 1 swingweight point to the club. In nearly all instances, the player will not be able to pick out the club with the dime added when compared to a similar club with no dime added. Next, do the same test with a quarter. The quarter weighs approximately 6 grams and will cause a 3-swing-weight point increase on the club. Most players will be able to select the heavier club now that there is a 3-swingweight point difference. This simple demo may help players who mistakenly believe that there is a great difference between increments of one swingweight.

FITTING WEIGHT

Dynamic weight fitting best utilizes the shaft and length option as determined during previous fitting steps. Shaft demo clubs can be utilized, along with lead tape, to optimize both swingspeed and accuracy. As shaft weights will vary more than head weights or grip weights, using the shaft that best fits the player is a wise starting point in weight fitting. If the player claims he club is too light, add a strip or two of lead tape to the club to determine if a heavier club feels and performs better. Keep in mind that in most cases, the club will not be able to be made lighter due to the weight of the components used. Making a club heavier may improve its feel, making it lighter is usually not an option.

SWINGWEIGHT TO PLAYING LENGTH RECOMMENDATIONS (FOR PRELIMINARY FITTING GUIDELINES ONLY)		
	Swingweight	
Men's Length	**A,R,S and X** **Steel Shafts**	**A,R,S and X** **Graphite Shafts**
-1" under Std.	C6 to C8	C4 to C6
-1/2" under Std.	C8 to D0	C6 to C8
Standard	D0 to D2	C9 to D1
+1/2" over Std.	D0 to D3	D0 to D2
+1 1/2" over	D6 to D9	D3 to D6
+2" over Std.	D9 to E2	D5 to D8
	Swingweight	
Ladies Length	**L-Flex** **Steel Shafts**	**L-Flex** **Graphite Shafts**
-1" under Std.	C0 to C3	B8 to C1
-1/2" under Std.	C2 to C5	C0 to C3
Standard	C4 to C7	C2 to C5
+1/2" over Std.	C6 to C9	C4 to C7
+1 1/2" over	C8 to D1	C6 to C9

During the dynamic fitting of weight using a club with the shaft that fits the player or by using demo clubs and lead tape, the player will make comments as to what weight feels best to him. This is the weight that will most likely provide the best consistency and shotmaking potential as well. Weight fitting, to some degree, takes care of itself. Based upon the length of the club as well as the weight of the components (head, shaft and grip), total weight and swingweight are basically determined. The fitter can change the weight a few points heavier if the player desires this feel, but very often cannot remove weight to make the clubs lighter in either swingweight or total weight. Through the use of lead tape, perhaps a best-fit feel can be determined. In the case of static fitting for weight, norms must be used when making the weight choice. Steel-shafted, standard-length clubs will be fitted at D1, an average swingweight for a male and at C6 as an average for a female. Graphite shafted clubs will be matched correspondingly lighter. Typically, more aggressive swingers are better matched to heavier shafts and head weights as these will tend to help slow the swing, improving accuracy in the process.

Fitting weight is very much like fitting feel. What one player may prefer another may not. A key consideration, not mentioned until this point, involves that fact that the weight of the components used to build a player's clubs are the defining factor in the weight of those clubs. For example, a player who is best fit in the initial fit testing for a length of 1" over standard and swings a steel shaft more consistently than graphite, will have clubs that are higher in total weight as well as in swingweight. The components dictate that the weights will be in the mid-high D range; the clubs simply cannot be made lighter. (Of course, counterbalancing to achieve a specific swingweight is possible, but this will create a club heavier in total weight.) In most cases, these clubs will probably not feel too heavy for the player as during previous hit testing he hit the longer (and heavier) clubs most consistently as shown by impact label tests.

As a contrast, if the player was tested and hit ultralight graphite better than any other shaft, the total weight of this person's clubs is likely to be on the lighter side of average. If this same player was fitted to a 45" long driver, the swingweight might not be too unusual - it might actually be higher than expected - but the total weight will be light as a result of the shaft's weight. Trying to achieve a heavier total weight will defeat the purpose and effectiveness of the ultralight shaft. The components dictate the weight of the club. The fitter can fine tune that weight a couple of points one way or the other, but is limited as to the ability to make big changes in the weight of the club.

The fitter should take into account the idea that all of the clubs in the set should be similarly weighted. That is, once the weight of the clubs that feels best to the golfer is established, all clubs with like shafts should be weighted to the same swingweight and should follow a progression of total weight from lightest in the longest club to heaviest in the shortest. Thus if a player is fitted to a set of steel shafted irons, and D2 is the swingweight he prefers, all of the irons should be made the same swingweight. (The wedges, as their heads are heavier are likely to swingweight higher.) But, if

Clubhead Head	Weight	Raw Shaft Weight	Grip Weight	Club Length	Swingweight
SWINGWEIGHT AS DETERMINED FROM STANDARD COMPONENT SPECIFICATIONS FOR HEADWEIGHT, SHAFT WEIGHT, CLUB LENGTH AND GRIP WEIGHT					
1 wood	198 grams	125 grams[1]	52 grams	43"	D-0
3 wood	208 grams	125 grams[1]	52 grams	42"	D-0
4 wood	213 grams	125 grams[1]	52 grams	41 1/2"	D-0
5 wood	218 grams	125 grams[1]	52 grams	41"	D-0
7 wood	228 grams	125 grams[1]	52 grams	40"	D-0
1 iron	230 grams	125 grams[1]	52 grams	39 1/2"	D-0
2 iron	237 grams	125 grams[1]	52 grams	39"	D-0
3 iron	244 grams	125 grams[1]	52 grams	38 1/2"	D-0
4 iron	251 grams	125 grams[1]	52 grams	38"	D-0
5 iron	258 grams	125 grams[1]	52 grams	37 1/2"	D-0
6 iron	265 grams	125 grams[1]	52 grams	37"	D-0
7 iron	272 grams	125 grams[1]	52 grams	36 1/2"	D-0
8 iron	279 grams	125 grams[1]	52 grams	36"	D-0
9 iron	286 grams	125 grams[1]	52 grams	35 1/2"	D-0
PW[2]	293 grams	125 grams[1]	52 grams	35 1/2"	D-3
SW[2]	300 grams	125 grams[1]	52 grams	35 1/2"	D-6

[1] Raw shaft weight is based on a 45" UDWS (parallel tip Dynamic S-flex for woods) and a 39" UDIS (parallel tip Dynamic S-flex for irons). Under proper trimming and installation, each shaft's weight will drop slightly through the set.

[2] Traditionally, the pitching wedge and sand wedge are designed to be played at slightly to significantly higher swingweights than the #1-9 irons.

that same player is fitted to a set of 1-3-5 graphite-shafted woods and likes the feel of a C9 swingweight for those, the irons (or woods) should not be changed to match. The woods are "like-shafted" and are a specific swingweight; the irons are shafted with a different type of shaft and are a specific swingweight themselves.

Some weight guidelines that may assist when establishing a swingweight/total weight that best matches a player include:

1. A club made shorter will most often have lighter total weights and lower swingweights

2. A club made longer will have higher total weights and heavier swingweights

3. Clubs with lighter shafts will have lower swingweights and total weights than will similar clubs with heavier shafts

4. Clubs with heavier shafts will have higher swingweights and total weights than will those with lighter shafts

5. Clubs with heavier heads will have higher swingweights and total weights than will those with lighter heads.

6. Clubs with lighter heads will have lower swingweights and total weights than will those with heavier heads

7. Clubs with lighter grips will have higher swingweights, but lower total weights than will those with heavier grips

8. Clubs with heavier grips will have lighter swingweights but heavier total weights than will those with lighter grips.

9. Clubs with lower balance point shafts will have higher swingweights; clubs with higher balance point shafts will have lower swingweights.

WEIGHT
Summary: Do's and Don'ts of Weight Fitting
DO'S

DO: Realize the importance of feel when fitting weight.

DO: Keep in mind any change in any club component will cause some type of weight change.

DO: Know wedges are usually the heaviest clubs in a set-both in swingweight and total weight.

DO: Familiarize yourself with the factors that influence swingweight including length, grip weight, head weight, shaft weight, balance point and club lie.

DO: Always pre-calculate swingweight prior to fitting or building a club.

DO: Remember the interrelationship of total weight and swingweight.

DON'TS

DON'T: Assume strong players need heavy clubs and weaker players should have lighter clubs.

DON'T: Assume D2 (or some other standard) should be used for all clubs.

DON'T: Forget the effects that a club's weight has on its other parameters such as flex, feel, etc.

DON'T: Overlook the fact that not all clubs can be built to all swingweights. That is, a 45" steel shafted driver cannot normally be built to D2.

DON'T: Fail to weigh all components used in assembly and fitting.

Chapter 10
Wedges

Well over 50% of a player's shots (not counting putts) are taken within 110 yards of the green. Based upon this statistical fact, hard evidence shows the need for the accurate fitting of clubs used close to the green. Through the proper fitting of wedges, distance and accuracy can be improved, leading to the chance for more one-putts, and thus lower scores. Most players hit their wedges straighter than any other club in the bag. This is due to their shorter lengths and higher lofts. This is not to say that all players hit the wedges in the direction of the green every time, but generally direction is not the biggest problem. What does pose the most problem related to wedges is distance. Many players only carry two wedges - a pitching wedge and a sand wedge. These may have lofts of 50 and 55° respectively. A full swing with the PW may produce a shot of 120 yards, for example, while the full SW is closer to 90 yards. The dilemma becomes how hard to hit either wedge as the player gets closer to the green.

It is much easier to control the distance of a full shot as compared to a half or 3/4 shot. This is why, when pros lay up on par 5's, they lay up to a distance that provides them a full shot. This distance will vary depending on the loft characteristics of their wedge(s). Most pros add at least one more wedge to their bag, usually some type of higher-lofted model, known as a lob wedge. This allows them to hit full shots closer to the green as the LW has a loft in the 60° range. There are a number of pros that also add a 64 or 65° club, further refining their distance control. By having a variety of wedges that permit the accuracy of full shots, the problem of distance control is reduced. Now a player can hit the scoring shots both straight and to the correct distances.

DYNAMIC WEDGE FITTING AND SPECIFICATIONS

LENGTH The length of most wedges is in the 34 1/2" to 35 1/2" range. As wedges are considered scoring clubs in

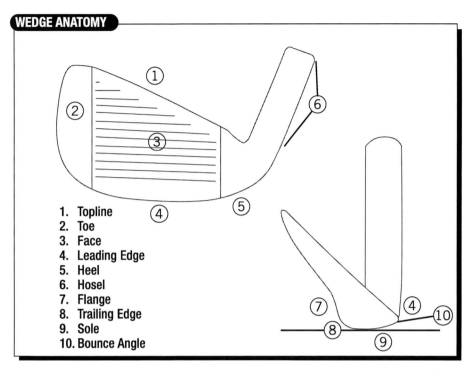

WEDGE ANATOMY

1. Topline
2. Toe
3. Face
4. Leading Edge
5. Heel
6. Hosel
7. Flange
8. Trailing Edge
9. Sole
10. Bounce Angle

much the same manner as are putters, there will be proponents of making all of the wedges the same length. There are also short game experts, among them Dave Pelz, who advocate a slightly different length for each wedge. Length will have an effect on the wedge's weight as well as on the length of the arc on which it is swung. Hitting a wedge a long distance is not the goal; hitting it a specific distance is. By testing a number of wedges at different lengths, the one that feels and performs best can be determined. In all reality, there will not be a noticeable performance difference between a wedge that is 35" and one that is 35 1/2" in length, except perhaps in the hands of the best players in the world.

LIE The lie of a wedge deserves consideration. Club lie will effect ball direction; a club that is too upright will tilt the face plane of a club to the left, resulting in pulled shots. The opposite is true as well; a flat lie results in pushed shots due to the face plane tilt to the right. But as wedges are the most lofted clubs in a set, they will produce the most backspin. This backspin may help to counteract and sidespin produced by a lie that is not

correct for the player. Also for consideration is the fact that many player will not sole the wedges in the same manner all of the time (for example, when choking down on the club), making the effective lie of the club change depending upon a player's hand position. This is not to say that lie is not an important factor in wedge fitting; but it is to say that if the lie of a wedge does not match by 1-2 degrees, there probably will not be noticeable accuracy effects, especially with more lofted wedges on less than full shots. The lie of a pitching wedge is more critical than the lie of a sand wedge for example.

When it comes to adjusting the lie angle of a wedge, the same parameters

TYPICAL WEDGE SPECS

	G	S	LW	LW2*
loft	50	55	60	64
lie	64	64	64	64
weight	300	300	300	300
sole width	19	19	21	22
face height	58	59	59.5	60
offset	1	1	0	0
bounce	6	12	3	4

*LW is a common designation for any wedge that has 60° or more of loft.

PELZ WEDGE RECOMMENDATIONS
(from Dave Pelz *Short Game Bible*, 1999)

Wedge Type	Loft Angle (degrees)	Lie Angle (degrees)	Shaft Length (inches)	Bounce Amount (inches)	Bounce Depth (inches)	Shaft Flex Code Letters (frequency)
PW	50-51	61-63	35-36	.20-.40	.30-.50	R (6.0)
SW	55-56	61.5-63.5	34.5-35.5	.45-.75	.45-.90	R (5.5)
LW	60-61	62-64	34-35	.20-.55	.20-.40	R (5.0)
XW	62.5-64	62.5-65	33.5-34.5	.20-.40	.35-.60	L (4.5)

Note: Royal Precision rates the flexes softer than those mentioned.

apply as when bending irons. Wedges are bendable up to a couple of degrees. These include wedges that are made of either stainless steel, or carbon steel. Beryllium copper wedges are best left alone when it comes to alteration as beryllium tends to fracture more easily than stainless or carbon steel. Also, the finish on melonite or other black finish wedges tends to crack as the club is bent; this has no effect on playability, only on the cosmetic look of the club. A 1-2 degree alteration in lie is fine for most cast or forged wedges; more than this may cosmetically damage or fracture the head

LOFT

Wedges are available in any number of lofts. Pitching wedges are available with a little as 45° of loft, utility wedges can have loft up to 65°. There are just about all lofts in between as well. If the fitter looked long enough, he could probably find, in addition to the two lofts already listed, a 46°, 47°, and so on, all the way up to the 65°. Wedge fitting becomes a matter of matching the loft to the player's needs. These needs are most often a direct byproduct of the course the player most often plays. If, for example, the course has deep grass bunkers around elevated greens, a higher-lofted utility

wedge may be helpful. If the course is flat with few bunkers, such a wedge would be limited in its use. A goal of the fitter is to select three or four wedge lofts that will accommodate the vast majority of a golfer's shots within the 100 yard range when used with a full swing.

BOUNCE AND SOLE ANGLE

Sole angle is a most important consideration when matching a wedge to a player. Also called bounce, it is the measurement in degrees, from the leading edge of the wedge to the ground. The more the leading edge is off the ground when the wedge is soled facing the target, the higher the bounce measurement. The soles of wedges may be flat, they may radius from heel to toe or from front to back, or they may feature four-way radius, which is radius both from front to back and heel to toe. Each wedge's sole design will have a direct

relationship with its bounce. Typically pitching wedges have less bounce than do most sand wedges; utility wedges may have either more or less.

The purpose of bounce is to help the club travel through sand or tall grass more easily. The more bounce a wedge possesses, the more its sole will tend to get "under" the sand or grass and help to get the ball up and out quickly. A club with no bounce used in the same situation will tend to stick in the sand or ground, making it difficult to get the ball airborne. Clubs with less bounce are better suited to use from fairways or "tight" lies since their soles do not dig into the ground. Also, the more bounce a wedge has, the higher its leading edge is off the ground, making it "look" as if it will be more dif-

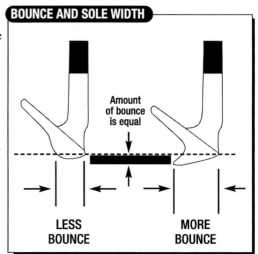

BOUNCE AND SOLE WIDTH

Amount of bounce is equal

LESS BOUNCE   MORE BOUNCE

ficult to hit. A higher bounce wedge will often lead to thin shots from close lies as its leading edge is well off the ground. Thus there are specific uses for each design of wedge.

The amount of bounce on a wedge, particularly a sand wedge, allows it to be matched closely to course conditions. A SW with little bounce will be better suited to a course where the sand is firm and tightly packed or where the grass around the green is not very deep or coarse. The club does not have to go as deeply into the sand in order to get the ball

COMMON WEDGE SPECS

	Loft	Lie	Weight	Bounce
PW	50-54	64-65	290-295	5-7
SW	55-60	64-65	304-310	10-12
LW	60-65	64-65	295-305	0-5

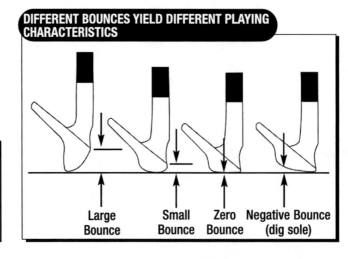

DIFFERENT BOUNCES YIELD DIFFERENT PLAYING CHARACTERISTICS

Large Bounce   Small Bounce   Zero Bounce   Negative Bounce (dig sole)

WEDGES: PRIMARY USAGE/AVERAGE SPECIFICATIONS				
Loft/Name	Bounce	Lie	Weight	Recommended Use
50 PW	4	64	292	Standard PW use, fairways, long approach shots
52 PW	7	64	294	Strong PW, deeper path at impact, long grass, rough
54 SW	10	64	304	SW, hard sand, standard bunker/fringe shots
56 SW	12	64	304	SW, softer sand, fringe shots out of longer grass
58 LW, UW	3	64	298	Hard pan, shots that need quick height
60 LW, UW	6	64	298	Longer grass, sand shots requiring quick height
64 LW, UW	4	64	300	Highest loft, deep bunkers, mounded greens

out. A low-bounce sand wedge would have less than 8 degrees of bounce. If the course the golfer played most often had loose, fluffy sand or had high, coarse grass surrounding the greens, a higher bounce wedge will be helpful as the club will tend to bury itself in the sand, something more bounce helps to prevent. For fluffy sand, wedges of over 12 degrees make good choices. Obviously there are limitations to either very low or very high bounce sand wedges; that is why most SW's fall into the 10-12 degree range, making them useful from both types of sand conditions.

Utility wedges or lob wedges may have bounce as low as zero or as high as 18. The zero bounce wedges are strictly designed with fairway use in mind. They will hit high, soft shots from closely mown grass. But, they will not be nearly as effective in California's kikuyu grasses as they will not cut through the coarse grass efficiently. For such situations, higher bounce UW's or LW's are more effective for the same reason that added bounce helps a sand wedge goes through sand. As an average, most wedges in this category feature a bounce of approximately 5 degrees. The majority of the very high lofted wedges - those of 64+ degrees - have wide soles and low bounce (under 5 degrees.) These clubs are typically designed to get the ball up very quickly, usually from grassy conditions. By matching the bounces of a player's sand wedge, utility wedge and high-lofted wedge to a specific course condition, shots hit closer to the pin are easier to achieve, regardless of the player's ability.

Do be aware that as a player may open the face of a wedge to play any number of finesse shots, the sole angle of the wedge will change. As a club is "opened", typically (although not always) its bounce angle will increase. As a club is placed in more of a de-lofted position, its effective bounce will decrease. It may be wise during wedge fitting to have the player position the wedge(s) in various open and de-lofted position in order to familiarize himself with various bounce angles created by these positions.

Any alteration of the loft of a wedge will have a direct effect on its sole angle. If a wedge is made stronger, its sole angle will change; the bounce will be reduced. The amount of reduction in bounce is roughly equivalent to the number of degrees the wedge's loft was strengthened. Thus a 2-degree loft change causes a 2 degree bounce change. If a wedge is made weaker, its bounce increases. The offset of a wedge will change slightly if its loft is altered. As a wedge is strengthened, the offset will increase slightly; the opposite is true when loft is added to the wedge. For specific player applications, soles of wedges may be ground in order

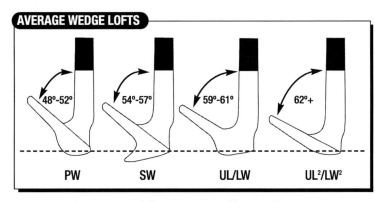

AVERAGE WEDGE LOFTS

48°-52°	54°-57°	59°-61°	62°+
PW	SW	UL/LW	UL²/LW²

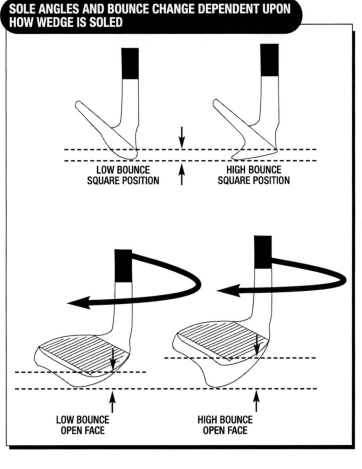

SOLE ANGLES AND BOUNCE CHANGE DEPENDENT UPON HOW WEDGE IS SOLED

LOW BOUNCE SQUARE POSITION

HIGH BOUNCE SQUARE POSITION

LOW BOUNCE OPEN FACE

HIGH BOUNCE OPEN FACE

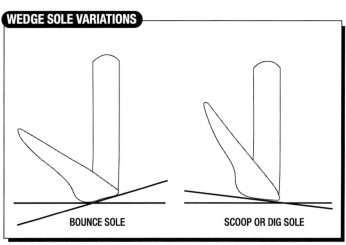

WEDGE SOLE VARIATIONS

BOUNCE SOLE

SCOOP OR DIG SOLE

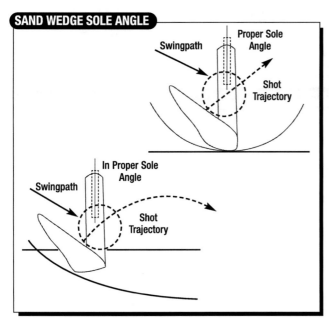

SAND WEDGE SOLE ANGLE

A sand wedge with the proper sole angle (top) goes through sand easily. A wedge with too little bounce tends to dig into the sand (bottom).

to create precise bounce or sole angles. If a player or fitter chooses to grind any material from the sole toward either the leading edge of the club or the trailing edge of the club, a change in bounce will result. Grinding for the purpose of reducing bounce should be done toward the trailing edge; to increase bounce, the leading edge is ground. Keep in mind that sole grinding very often will change the cosmetics and weight of the club; make the player aware of this prior to any sole grinding.

Wider sole wedges are generally better from softer sand; narrow soled wedges perform better from firmer sand.

SOLE WIDTH

Sand wedges have the widest soles of any irons in the set. This helps them to go through sand easily. It is also the key reason wedges have more bounce than any other clubs. The wide soles cause the leading edge of the club to be off the ground; the wider the sole, the more the bounce. Pitching wedges do not generally have wide soles as they are primarily hit from the shorter grasses. Wider soled wedges will have lower centers of gravity as well, further making them useful in going through sand or high grass and getting the ball airborne easily. The width of the sole of a sand wedge is a good indication of the loft and purpose of the wedge. Wider soles are typically coupled with higher lofts and are designed to get the ball airborne quickly. Thin soles usually indicate lower lofts for longer approach shots to the green.

A note here concerning the measurement of a wedge's specifications: As the soles of certain wedges are shaped differently running from heel to toe, often they will not tend to sole in the same manner as a typical iron club. As a result, when placing these wedges in a specifications gauge, it may require a bit more practice to sole them correctly. If you place a wide-soled wedge in the specs gauge and the gauge provides an "unexpected" reading, try to

BOUNCE VS. APPLICATION

Depth of Bounce

Amount of Bounce		SHALLOW .10-.40"	MEDIUM .40-.70"	DEEP .70-1.0"
Low .0"- .3"		Hardpan Tight Fairways Fringes Hard Sand	Fairways Light Rough Firm Sand	Plush Fairways Light Rough Moist Sand
Mid .3"- .6"		Fairways Firm Sand Moist Sand	Light Rough Plush Fairways Medium Sand	Medium Rough Soft Sand
High .7"-1.2"		Medium Rough Soft Sand	Heavy Rough Very Soft Sand	Very Heavy Rough Fine, Soft Sand
Very High 1.2"		Heavy Rough Very Soft Sand	Very Heavy Rough Fine-Soft Sand	Super-Deep Rough Finest Sand Pine Needles

align the club's scoring lines with the groundline. This will often help to ensure that the wedges will be measured correctly in the gauge. Any club who sole is wide may exhibit this property. Also, many wedge manufacturers purposely make the heel of the wedge's sole thinner than the toe area in order that the club may be positioned "open" to help get the ball airborne more quickly. Clubs with these sole grinds will require more care in measuring when using the specs gauge.

WEIGHT

The wedges are the heaviest clubs in the set. Think about how they are used. They are designed to go through high grass and sand. The added weight of these clubs makes that a more efficient process. The added weight of a wedge tends to help the player pace his swing as well, leading to more accuracy and better feel. Plus, wedges are the shortest clubs in the set; they must be heavier to maintain feel and balance at the shorter lengths. A light sand wedge is difficult to control, especially when hit from coarse sand. Added weight adds a measure of control. It is not uncommon that the pitching wedge be at least 1-2 swing-weight points heavier than the other clubs in the set. Sand wedges and certain utility wedges may be as many as 10 points higher than the other clubs. Without this weight, the function of the club is compromised; if the player likes the look, feel and performance of a certain wedge, do not worry that is heavier than expected; it is designed to be that way.

SHAFTS

As the wedge is the shortest club in the set, most often its shaft will be the stiffest as a result. The fact that the wedge head is heavy will make this stiffer shaft feel not quite so stiff and perhaps will enhance the club's feel. The type of shaft in a wedge will have almost no effect on playability, but may have an effect on feel. If a player likes a heavy wedge, choose a standard weight steel shaft; for a lighter feel, go with a light-weight steel shaft or maybe even a graphite shaft. If the player wants more head feel, perhaps going to a softer flex will help (see Pelz chart, page 116). Most OEM wedges are fitted with stiff shafts, but any shaft can be installed in the club

to create a certain feel. The fitter may also use the practice of putting a softer shaft in the shortest wedges, a slightly stiffer one in the next longest wedge, and so on, in an effort to equalize feel.

MATERIAL AND MANUFACTURE

Wedges are primarily made from one of three materials, stainless steel, carbon steel or beryllium copper. There is virtually no playability difference between these materials. There will be some players who like the cosmetic look of one material over another, or who may claim that one material feels softer or better than another and that is fine. That would be the wedge material that should be chosen for the player; as a factual matter, the hardness differences between wedge materials is incomprehensible to all but the very, very best players in the world.

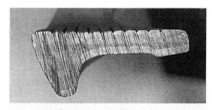

V-grooves (top) and U-grooves do not have a great effect related to wedge performance.

One of the most common inquiries made about wedges concerns the grove type of the club. Many players have been led to believe that grooves that are square-shaped (also called "U" or "box" grooves) will spin the ball more than grooves that are "V" shaped. Here again, for all but the best players in the world, there will be little difference from dry conditions. But, as USGA tests have shown, in wet conditions, the square grooves may offer a bit more spin due to their wider surface area. From a playability point of view this means that the square grooves may stop the ball quicker when the ball hits the green. As long as the player realizes this and can hit the ball just a bit farther to allow for less roll,

Black chrome is a surface plating for cosmetics only; it will have no playability effect.

there is no problem. But doing so requires much skill on the part of the player, something most average players do not possess. For all practical purposes, groove type will not have a huge effect on performance, but may have an effect on ball wear. Square grooves tend to scuff balls more than do "V" grooves; something worth mentioning to a player during wedge selection.

Face treatments have become popular on wedges in recent years. The idea of these treatments is to provide more friction between the ball and the club, thus adding spin. These treatments, which are long wearing, tend to offer the possibility of more spin, but as they have rougher surfaces, they may tend to be a bit hard on golf balls. Tests have shown that these coatings do make the ball stop more quickly; if the player is seeking the utmost in spin, face treatments are the way to go. The USGA does have a rule concerning surface roughness. A face cannot be so rough that it unduly influences ball flight in the eyes of the USGA. Nearly all face treated wedges on the

Wedges with no grooves do exist as in the milled-face sample.

Wedge Fitting Form

1. Wedge Type
Player Preferences

_____ Pitching Wedge

_____ Sand Wedge

_____ Utility or Lob Wedge

_____ High Loft wedge

Current Type of Wedges: _____

Bounces: _____

---

2. Wedge Lengths

_____ PW

_____ SW

_____ UW, LW

_____ High Loft Model

Other:

3. Wedge Lies

_____ PW

_____ SW

_____ UW, LW

_____ High Loft Model

4. Wedge Lofts

_____ PW

_____ SW

_____ UW, LW

_____ High Loft Model

---

5. Grip Type & Size

Player Preference - Grip Type

Model _____

Size _____

6. Shaft Flex & Type

PW _____

SW _____

UW, LW _____

High Loft _____

Other:

An example of a face coating is this "Black Ice" material designed to improve spin and wear.

market fall within this surface roughness requirement.

Yet another wedge trend is toward unplated models. These wedges, either cast or forged from carbon steel, will rust through normal use. The Cobra Rusty, produced in the 1980's, was the first of this type of wedge. Now, many companies offer unplated wedges designed to rust. The theory behind these wedges is two-fold. One, as they are unplated, they will feel softer due to having no plating applied to them. Secondly, as they rust, the rust will create roughness, potentially enhancing spin. Just how much spin is debatable, but many touring pros use these types of wedges, helping to add to the growing popularity of such models.

WEDGE FITTING

The best opportunity toward successful wedge fitting is to listen to the player describe what course conditions he plays most often as well as what shots from 110 yards-in he has trouble executing. These discussions will put the fitter well on the right track toward proper wedge selection. Unless the player asks otherwise, the specifications of a wedge (shaft, grip, length, etc.) should fall in line with the rest of the set. But, as wedge play does have a high feel element, there may be specification changes requested. The other key to wedge fitting involves how many wedges the player should have. If the player wants four wedges, set makeup will have to be studied in order to see what club(s) will be deleted from the set. Having a number of wedges can improve playability near the green; it is up to the fitter to make certain that the addition of extra wedges does not compromise player performance in any other category. Wedge fitting involves a combination of the following: How many wedges does the player need? What head design and material does the player prefer? What loft and bounce best meet the player's requirements best? What is the proper length, weight and lie of the wedges? By combining these factors, accurate wedge fitting is accomplished.

WEDGE DEMO CLUBS

A wedge demo selection, in all reality, could be limitless. Offering a test wedge with each of these characteristics will be helpful: wide and narrow sole; low and high bounce; soft and stiff shaft; rusty and high-friction face; beryllium, stainless and carbon steel heads. By having a player look at and hit a number of wedges, fitting is best accomplished. The player may ask to take some samples to the course for testing; this is perfectly acceptable and highly recommend. Testing various products under actual playing conditions is a great way to determine the playability of the wedge(s).

Many players prefer the look and playability of a heavier, mallet style chipping club.

CHIPPERS

While not necessarily in the wedge class, chipper use is primarily around the green and deserves mention. A chipper is not truly an iron, wood or putter, but may be a combination of all three. Chippers may look very much like irons cosmetically, they may look like mallet putters or they may be "wood-like" with a putter hosel. All types of variations exist in chipper design. The idea behind a chipper typically is to provide the player with confidence when hitting shots around the green.

Most chippers, though not all, share some common traits. Most chippers have loft between 20 and 35 degrees. This is a fairly wide variation, making some chippers more of a run-up club and others more like a chipping club. If an average chipper loft existed, it would be in the #6 iron range. Most chippers have upright lies, usually 70 degrees or more. Most are fairly heavy, weighing at least 300 grams. The vast majority of chippers are made to a putter length, in the 35"-36" range. Most have offset hosels or are fitted with curved shafts that create offset. Chippers seem to be much more popular with senior players, perhaps due to accuracy or confidence factors.

Why choose a chipper for a given player? If the player is having trouble with chipping from the fringe or light grass around the green, perhaps the weight and length of a chipper will improve accuracy. As the club is swung much like a putter (and putters are the shortest clubs), accuracy may be improved. Plus, the heavier weight may help keep the club on line more easily than a lighter weight iron. The offset hosel of some chippers may help to further keep the club on the correct path. Chippers are not used often from high grass or for distances over 10 yards in most instances, although there may be exceptions. Keep in mind that if a player wants a chipper, it will be somewhat specialized (limited) in its usage and will require that another club in the set be removed to be in accordance with USGA Rules that limit the number of clubs a player may carry to fourteen. Also keep in mind that chippers must not utilize putter grips to be in accordance with USGA Rules.

This 2-way chipper does not conform to USGA Rules as it has two striking surfaces.

CONCLUSION

Wedge fitting is a key element in a player's short game success. By matching the specifications of loft, lie, length, weight and bounce to the player's course conditions and playing preferences, lower scores are virtually assured. As the highest percentage of any player's strokes occur within 110 yards of the green, matching wedges to appropriate distances permits much more accurate shotmaking. While most players carry two wedges; it makes more sense for most to have three; even four wedges deserve consideration for some. Additional wedges eliminate distance gaps for most golfers - the fitter and player should work together to determine which clubs and specifications are best - matched to each individual. Be certain to include wedge fitting as a key element in a Total Clubfitting situation.

Chapter 11
Putters

Putting potentially comprises 50% of a golfer's strokes. It is said to be the most individual part of the game; each player has his or her own style. Take a look at the pros; you see 50" putters on the Senior PGA Tour, you have seen American pro Ken Green putting with a 24" model on the PGA Tour; putting with the butt of the putter is against the "belly" has been popular; you see mallets, blades and everything in between... It should follow that since putting may be the most individualized part of the game, it would be the most important to custom fit. Regretfully, the vast majority of golfers and fitters ignore the putter when it comes time to look at matching clubs to a player. All too often, a player seeks a new set of woods and/or irons during a fitting, but the most-used club in the set - the putter - is seldom examined.

Many times when a golfer looks to buy new clubs, they think only of a new driver or perhaps a set of irons. While certainly there is merit in having irons and woods matched to his or her game, think about where most of a player's strokes occur. In a typical round of golf, a player, regardless of his or her ability, uses a putter much more than any single club in the bag. Why not begin (or at least include) a search for new clubs with a look at the putter? The typical amateur golf carries a handicap of 19 shots; that same player most likely averages well over 30 putts per round. One of the quickest ways to improve scores is to examine putting, not only related to technique, but to equipment as well.

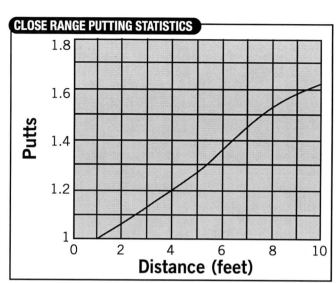

A low handicap (10 handicap or under) player's average number of putts from close range.

DYNAMIC PUTTER FITTING AND SPECIFICATIONS

LENGTH

Perhaps one of the very first things a player notices when he picks up a putter is its length. The ideal fitting putter fitting scenario will have the player's eyes positioned directly over the ball at address and throughout the stroke. A putter that is too short will tend to position the golfer's eyes outside the target line; too long of a putter will usually result in the eyes being on the body-side of the putter. Either of these cases will provide the player with a skewed picture of how the putter is actually aligned at address. In an attempt to make a putter of incorrect length feel bet-

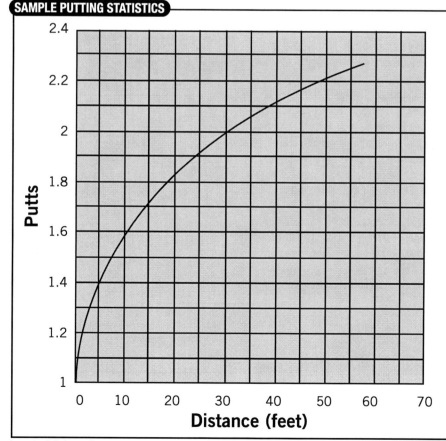

A sub-10 handicap player's average number of putts from specific distance.

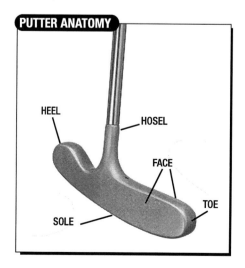

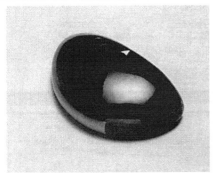  

From left to right: Mallet style, heel-toe-balanced and cavity back blade.

ter, the player may actually position his head/eyes in various positions at various times, definitely creating inconsistencies. By having the player address the ball using a number of putter lengths, it can be determined which putter feels most comfortable, while at the same time determining which one best positions his eyes directly over the ball. A CD disk placed under the ball works well when determing if a player's eyes are indeed over the ball.

The most common type of putter in the game today is a heel-toe weighted model.

LIE

The lie of a putter deserves consideration. Although the lie - if incorrect for the player - will not have as noticeable an effect as it would on middle or short irons, proper lie will help the player sole the putter on the ground consistently at address. Here is where file cards can be used to determine lie. By placing file cards under the heel and toe of the putter as the golfer holds it in address position, the proper lie can be found. When the cards are equidistant from the center of the face, the lie is correct. If the cards go under the head farther toward the heel, the putter needs to be flatter; the opposite is true as well. Just about all good putters will have putters that tend to sole flat on

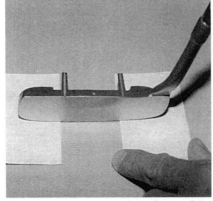

File cards may be used to determine a proper lie for a player's putter.

the ground at address; perhaps the most notable exception is Senior PGA Tour player Isao Aoki who holds the toe of his Bullseye type of putter at least 1" off the ground at address.

When it comes to adjusting the lie angle of a putter, the same parameters apply as when bending irons. Certain putters are bendable up to a couple of degrees. These include putters that have hosels and whose heads are made of either stainless steel, carbon steel, brass or manganese bronze. These putters will be bent using a loft/lie machine specially fitted with a putter-bending jig. Some models of putters with curved shafts may be adjusted as well. To bend these putters, the curvature of the shafts will be changed through the use of a tool that will re-bend the shaft without damaging it.

SOLE ANGLE

Sole angle is another consideration when matching a putter to a player. The soles of putters may be flat, they may radius from heel to toe or from front to back, or they may feature four-way radius, which is radius both from front to back and heel to toe. The more radiused a putter's sole may be, the less it will tend

to "catch" any grass on the backswing or follow through. Thus if a player tends to drag the putter back along the ground, a sole radius of either four-way or from front to back will help. A player who "lifts" the putter quickly away from the ball at the start of the backswing will not need to be concerned nearly as much with sole radius from a playability point of view.

Yet another important consideration related to putter sole angle involves the player's address position. If the player tends to forward press his hands, he will change the manufactured sole angle. The forward press will reduce the sole angle (as well as the loft), potentially creating what is known as a dig or scoop sole. Such a sole configuration may actually cause the player to contact the ground behind the ball, leading to "scuffed" putts and directional problems. A player who positions his hands behind the ball at address will create the opposite type of sole angle. A bounce sole is one in which the leading edge of the club is noticeably of the ground at address. Such a sole angle will result in the ball being contacted with the leading edge of the putter, often causing the ball to bounce as a result - obviously leading to both distance and accuracy deficiencies. It is important that the fitter analyze the player's hand position related to how the putter soles on the green. If the putter does not sole with its leading edge in the proper position, less than perfect results are bound to happen.

WEIGHT

The weight of a putter will play a key role in its performance. A heavier putter may help the player with a fast stroke to slow that stroke down for more consistency. Further, if a player has trouble maintaining a smooth stroke, often a heavier putter will help. If a player has trouble getting the ball to the hole, a heavier putter might help him to better judge distance correctly. If a player plays on greens that are not closely mown, the heavier putter may help to get the ball rolling closer to the hole related to distance. Lighter putters may have the opposite effects; they may provide more feel to some, especially on fast greens. If the player's tendency is to hit putts way past the hole, a lighter putter model may help to solve this distance problem. In all actuality, the weight of the putter is a key element in the player's overall perception of that putter. Players will waggle the putter; the weight becomes obvious at that point. As feel and weight, when related to putters, have a strong relationship, weight should be one of the key concerns early in the putter fitting session.

LOFT

Next take a look at how true the player's ball rolls on the green as you putt. If the ball bounces, this could be an indication that the loft of the putter does not match the stroke. Loft is designed to assist in getting the ball rolling on top of the grass as quickly as possible. As far as loft is concerned, most putters have between 2 and 6 degrees of loft. More loft tends to get the ball rolling better on greens that are not so closely mown, where less loft may be better on "tournament" type greens. If the player forward presses his hands a great deal, then a putter with more measured loft might be a good choice. This is because the forward press effectively reduces the loft of the putter. Try to match the player's stroke with a loft that gets the ball rolling as quickly as possible. There will actually be a point, immediately after impact, in which the ball is airborne. Minimizing this distance will help produce a truer roll and will best approximate the proper loft for a given player.

GRIP

Not all golfers have the same size hands. Hand position must be consistent and comfortable to the golfer; grip size also potentially affects the performance of a putter. The larger the grip, the less chance there may be for excessive wrist action. If the player's hands are too active or he seems too "wristy", it may be

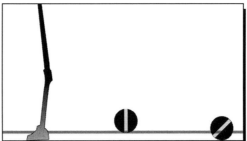

This illustration demonstrates how the ball is lifted by the loft on a putter prior to beginning its roll toward the hole. The ball is actually airborne for a time.

a good idea to build up the size of the putter grip. One of the easiest and most economical methods through which to do this is with gauze tape. Gauze tape is a thin medically used tape available at most drug stores. The tape is self-adhesive and can be wrapped on the grip of the putter to see how a larger size feels. If the larger grip feels good, either leave the tape on the club or select a larger grip for the club. A possible concern when using a larger grip is that of weight and balance. Larger putter grips can weigh over 100 grams. (70-75 grams is an average putter grip weight.) The addition of such a grip will move the balance point of the putter away from the head and more toward the grip; some players like this, others may not. Obviously, the heavier grip will add to the total weight of the putter; again some players are happy with this, others are not. A fitting/USGA Rules note: If a player is being fitted with a 50" long or similar length putter that has two grips as part of its design, be certain that both of those grips are circular in cross section. In other words, standard flat-front putter grips on overlength putters do not conform to the Rules of Golf.

Measuring the loft of a putter on a specifications gauge.

SHAFTS

The shaft type and material of a putter has an effect on the feel of the club. Some of the older pencil-shafted putters transmitted tremendous feel to a player's hands. Some golfers, though, said these shafts were not stiff enough; they would actually flex during the stroke. If you tend to like more feel or is a "handsy" type putter, you might want to suggest a softer-shafted putter for the golfer. On the other side of the coin, if the golfer uses a quick, "pop" type of stroke, it may be best to suggest a stiffer shaft. A note here, perhaps the player should experiment with different shaft materials also. Feel can be changed dramatically when comparing a steel, aluminum or graphite shaft in a putter. As successful putting is quite dependent on feel, having the player try as many putters as possible may help make final selection of the best one more accurate.

Oversize putter grips tend to help players whose stroke includes excessive wrist action.

HEAD SIZE

What about putter size; bigger is the trend in irons and woods, what about for putters? The size of putter heads vary from manufacturer to manufacturer. The idea that a large head is better stems from the fact that it may be better balanced on off-center hits since its weight is farther from the hitting point. To some degree the same applies to putters. A larger putter that may be heel and toe weighted will twist less on less than perfect impacts. But do keep in mind that while a driver is being swung at upwards of 100 miles per hour, you strike a putter in the 3-5 mile

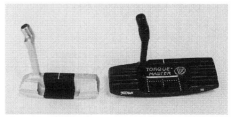

An example of a very large putter head (right) as compared to one of standard size.

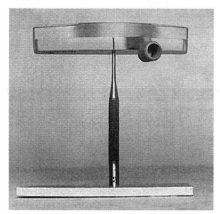

Balancing a putter on a punch shows its static balance point.

per hour range. It's a lot easier to mis-hit the driver than the putter. Another factor to be aware of is the visual effect of an extremely large putter; many players feel such a club looks unwieldy. Typically putters nearly match the size of the hole (4.5") from heel to toe; often anything larger will not be accepted visually. From a fitting point of view, if a player seems to be having difficulty striking the ball in the same location consistently on the putter face, a larger head might be a good recommendation. The larger head may not twist as much on off-center hits and may help the inconsistent putter with some directional improvement on these less-than-perfect hits.

HOSEL CONFIGURATION

Regardless of the size of a putter, it has a hosel or socket into or onto which the shaft fits. The hosel can either be straight, where the shaft goes into the approximate center of the putter (Bullseye type), or it can be offset, where the shaft enters the head in front of the face (Ping Anser type). If a player tends to prefer his hand position naturally forward, then an offset model might be a good choice. If, on the other hand, a golfer prefers to align the hands directly over the ball, a non-offset Bullseye type is best. As most teaching professionals encourage a player's hands to be ahead of the ball, an offset model will be a better choice for most players. Be aware that it doesn't matter if that offset is created in the design of the club itself or if the shaft helps to create the offset. In either case the hands will be positioned ahead of the ball.

A putter can be heel-shafted, face-balanced or somewhere in-between. A heel-shafted putter has a hosel at the rear-

ward part of the putter head. This type of putter, when balanced a your finger will very often tend to hang with the toe of the putter pointing more or less directly toward the ground. If a putter is face-balanced, its face will be parallel to the ground when the shaft is balanced on your finger. This is because the putter design specifically positions the shaft in line with the center of the face of the putter. (most face-balanced putters have either curved shafts or unusual hosel

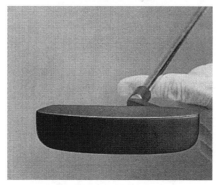

A putter is face balanced when its face is parallel to the ground when balanced.

designs to accomplish the face-balancing.) There are a number of putters that will balance somewhere in-between the heel-shafted and face-balanced models. Most of the putters whose hosel is not directly at the heel or whose shaft is not in line with the center of the putter face fall into this category. A player who has a noticeable "in to in" stroke by which he takes the club back inside the target line, returns it to square at impact and then goes inside again on the follow through, will benefit by the balance of a heel shafted putter. PGA pros Ben Crenshaw and Phil Mickleson putt in this manner. A player with a straight back and through stroke will benefit from a face-balanced

Non-face balanced putters "hang" in a manner similar to this when balanced on a person's finger.

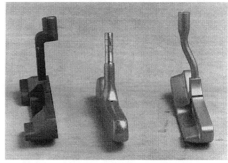

Offset, neutral and onset putter hosels.

putter. Face-balanced putters encourage the player to move the putter directly up and down the target line. If the player's stroke and putter type are not well-matched, the player will tend to say the

Face balanced mallet putters encourage a straight back-straight through stroke.

putter doesn't feel good or that it tends to "fight" his natural stroke. Feel is a key element of putting - be aware of how a player says a certain putter or putter specification feels and take this under great

A heel shafted putter is best suited to a inside-square-inside stroke.

Putters milled from one piece of carbon steel are favorites among players of all levels.

Face inserts, usually made from softer materials, are popular on many putters today

advisement when making fitting recommendations.

MATERIAL AND MANUFACTURE

Putter material is often a matter of personal preference. Putters may be made from any number of materials, among them being stainless steel, carbon steel, brass, aluminum, glass, and literally hundreds of other possibilities. As far as a

direct effect on performance, there may not be a great deal of difference between one material and another. What can be accurately stated is that softer metals such as brass or zinc or putters with face inserts will create a softer feel on the greens. This is especially true when a player uses a solid ball; the softer putter will make the ball feel more responsive and easier to control. If enhanced feel can be equated with better performance, softer metals may help, but there is no 100% consensus about materials related to performance.

Putters with face inserts deserve consideration during fitting. Certain insert materials, be they balata, rubber, plastic or any number of polymers, will allow the ball to have a "different" feel as it is struck. The manufacturers of face insert putters may claim that the inserts promote smoother roll or more accurate roll, but the general perception of face inserts is that they have a much greater effect on feel than on actual ball roll. That said, as feel is a key element of putting, face inserts are thus an important element of putter selection. Odyssey putters, with their proprietary Stronomic inserts, Titleists with their Terrylium inserts or Pixl golf with their pixilated faces, are examples of popular face insert putters. Some players will also claim that inserts help them "frame" the ball at address for better alignment.

Somewhat related to putter material is a process used on putters made from softer metals. The process, known as face milling, ensures a flat, consistent putter face. CNC (Computer Numerically Controlled) milling creates the entire putter from a single block of material, making a very precise model, typically at a

Extremes in putter length at 50" and less than 24".

substantially higher price. But does this create a better putter? It's hard to say, but it is a fact that either face-only milling or total CNC milling, will give a flatter, more consistent face to the putter. If we all putted on a billiard table, this may be critical. But we putt on grass greens that have been stepped on by all who play before us, not to mention that every blade of grass is not identical. Milled putters more often than not feel softer to a player since, in order to be able to be milled, the putter must be made of a soft metal. It's safe to say, milling helps consistency of the face for sure, as to less putts per round as a result, that's debatable.

RULES

There are a number of USGA Rules to keep in mind during putter fitting. In addition to the previously mentioned grip rule related to long putters, keep in mind that putters are the only club in the set that may have a grip with a flat side on it. While putters do not have to have flat-sided grip, most do, as the flat area of the grip helps the player consistently position his hands on the putter in a similar manner every time. The grip cannot have a bulge or waist; it must either be the same diameter along its length or must taper (either up or down) uniformly along that

The first hand position lends itself to an offset head design; the second to a neutral design and the third to an onset design.

Putter Fitting Form

1. Putter Style
a. Player Preferences - PUTTERS

Putter Configuration   Hosel Type

_____ Blade   _____ Offset

_____ Cavity Back   _____ Non-Offset

_____ Mallet   _____ No Preferences

Current Type of Wedges: _____

Recommendations:_____

---

2.   Putter Length   ## 3. Putter Lie

_____ 34"   _____ Recommended Putter Lie

_____ 35"   ## 4. Putter Loft

_____ 36"   _____ Recommended Putter Loft

_____ Recommended Putter Length

---

5.   Grip Type & Size   ## 6. Shaft Flex & Type

Player Preference - Grip Type   _____

_____ Pistol

_____ Paddle

_____ Other

Grip Recommendation (size): _____

---

length. Also, the grip must not be larger than 45mm (1.75 inches) in cross section.

USGA rules also govern specific lie and shaft configurations for putters. A putter, while it may have a curved shaft, cannot have any bend or curve in that shaft higher than 5" from the groundline. In other words, if the putter has a curved shaft, the shaft must be curved close to the club head and not near the grip.   The lie angle of a putter must not exceed 80 degrees. This rule perhaps comes into play when fitting "long" putters. The hosel cannot be pointing straight up at 90 degrees; the putter must deviate from vertical by at least 10 degrees. Another factor when fitting long putters is their shaft length. While there is no rule governing how long a club may be, there are some longer putters that may have two-piece shafts. These shafts conform to the Rules so long as they are not easily adjustable. That is, they simply cannot screw together. They must be held by a set screw or some other type of locking mechanism in order to conform. An added note: Any club, including a putter, must be at least 18 inches long to be conforming to the USGA Rules.

STATIC PUTTER FITTING

Trying to match a player to a putter without either seeing the player putt or without actually getting his feedback from the testing of sample putters, is, in all honesty, next to impossible. A couple of hints that may help would be to ask the player if he bends over or stand erect during putting. A crouched player will need a shorter putter. Ask if the player normally plays on low cut or shaggy greens; the lower the grass, the lower the loft or the recommended putter. Ask if the player has seen or putted with any designs he remembers liking. This may help in the selection of head style. Ask if player thinks he putts straight back and through or in-to-in. While he may not know for sure, if he does, the straight path will be better matched to a face-balanced putter. Question and answer information may help to better match the putter to the player in cases of not being able to see the player actually roll the ball.

PUTTER DEMO CLUBS

As putting is perhaps the most individual part of the game of golf, having enough demo clubs to satisfy every player's wants and needs will be impossible. A good demo assortment of putters might include three heel-toe (Ping Anser type) models assembled to various lengths, for example 33", 35" and 37". A mid length

model at 40" and a 50" "long" putter will complete the length demo selection. The demo selection might include two of the above models, one with a very firm shaft, one with a soft shaft. A couple of putters of distinctly different weights will be an asset to your demo choices. A good addition to your selection would be two more of the same type putters at 35"; one with a larger grip, one with a smaller grip. In order to help a golfer determine which head design works best for him, have at least one of each of the following putters: center-shafted, heel-shafted, face-balanced, blade-style, mallet style and insert putter . By having the player try a number of demo clubs, his or her likes and dislikes will become obvious. At that point, you can combine the desired cos-

metics along with the actual fitting session for a best-fit putter.

SUMMARY

Statistically, 43% of a golfer's strokes are putts. Putter fitting must be part of a competent fitter's plan of attack for any player. By using length, lie, loft, weight and cosmetics, a golfer's scores can quickly be reduced. Over the past twenty years on the PGA Tour, scoring average has decreased just about one stroke per round. Not surprisingly putts per round have decreased a like amount. Putting has a proven correlation to scoring. Don't ignore it when fitting any customer.

Glossary

Allen Screw: Threaded screw found in certain metal and wooden woods that leads to a weight port for swingweighting. May also be known as a hex or set screw.

Allen Wrench: Type of wrench used to remove or install Allen screws. Also called a hex wrench.

Alloy: Any combination of metals used to produce a club head or shaft. Alloys may contain aluminum, steel, beryllium, nickel, copper, titanium, or any number of other metals in varying combinations.

Aluminum Wood Head: A type of metal wood head constructed primarily from aluminum alloys through a die casting process. Aluminum woods are generally utilized by beginning players due to their lower price. They typically are not as durable as stainless steel woods. They may also be known as aluminum alloy heads.

Aluminum Shafts: Golf shafts formed from aluminum tubing, used primarily in the 1960's and early 70's. They did not gain popularity due to their softer feel and due to them being less durable than steel shafts. Today, they are used primarly in putters.

Anti-Shank: General term given to irons that have large bends or offsets in their hosels to eliminate shanked shots. Common in pre-1950 clubs.

Appendix II (Design of Clubs): United States Golf Association (USGA) Rule Book section dealing specifically with regulations for the design of golf clubs.

Ascending Weight Technology: The concept of utilizing lighter shafts in the long irons of a set for added club head speed and distance, while using heavier shafts in the shorter irons to promote control.

Autoclave: A pressurized heating device used for shaft construction. The autoclave is a heat treating chamber which applies pressure and high temperature to a material in order to cure it.

Back Weight: A weight, usually brass or aluminum attached to the back of a wooden, graphite or titanium wood head. Powerbilt popularized the use of back weights on their woods in the 1960's and 70's. The back weight is designed to move the center of gravity rearward to assist in getting the ball airborne.

Backscrew: Steel pin or screw used to help secure a steel shaft to a wooden wood head. The backscrew is located on the back of the heel approximately 3/4" from the sole of the club.

Backspin: The backward rotation of a golf ball in flight around a horizontal axis as caused by the club hitting the ball. Typically the more loft on a club, the more backspin will be imparted to the ball.

Balance Point: The point at which a shaft achieves equilibrium; the point at which a shaft's weight is evenly distributed in both directions when rested on a single fulcrum point.

Balata: A natural or synthetic compound used as a cover material for balls. Characterized by a soft feel and high spin rate. Generally preferred by better players. Balata balls are less durable than other types of balls.

Ball Size: The size of a USGA conforming ball must not be smaller than 1.680" (42.67mm.)

Ball Weight: The weight of a USGA conforming ball must not be greater than 1.620 ounces avoirdupois (45.93 grams.)

Beltronics (Beltronics Swingmate): Device (approximately 4" X 6") used for measuring swingspeed and ball distance. Placed on the ground at an angle to the swing, the Beltronics is an economical way to measure swingspeed either indoors or out.

Bend Point: The point of maximum bending on a shaft as measured by a compression test of the shaft on both the tip and butt ends.

Beryllium Copper (BeCu): An alloy used to produce club heads, typically irons. The alloy is more dense than stainless and is claimed to provide a softer feel by some players. Beryllium heads are easily identified by their copper coloration.

Beryllium Nickel (BeNi): An alloy comprised of beryllium and nickel typically used to produce iron heads. This alloy is considered softer than stainless steel and is identified by a bronze-type of coloration.

Beta-Titanium: An alloy of Titanium that is stronger and lighter than typical titanium allowing the walls of the head to be made thinner due to the higher strenth of beta-titanium.

Big Butt Shaft: Any shaft with a butt size over .620" is classed as a big (or large) butt shaft.

Big Butt Grip Installation Tool: An expandable plastic tool that helps to start the big butt grip over the butt of the over .620" shaft. Grip installation on such shafts is very difficult without this tool.

Big Tip Shaft: A shaft that fits into an aoversize hosel club. A shaft larger than .335" in a wood or .370" in an iron is considered a big tip shaft.

BiMatrx™: A shaft made by True Temper™ comprised of a graphite and steel tip section.

Bi-Metal: A club head constructed from two different materials. A common example is a stainless steel club head with a brass sole insert or brass sole rails.

Black Ice™: A proprietary face coating applied to the face of a club in order to increase spin. Primarily used on wedges, but can be applied to woods, irons and putters also.

Blade: The general term given to the striking face of any iron head.

Blade Style Head: The class of irons identified by their equal weight distribution. Blades are identified by their relatively smooth back shape. Blade style irons are popular among better players due to the increased feel and feedback they may provide. Blades are also known as muscle-back irons due to a possible concentration of weight directly behind the center of the club face.

Blade Length: The measurement of an iron head from the radius of the crotch of the head to the farthest point of the toe.

Blade Height: The measurement of an iron head at the center of the face from the ground line to the top line.

Blind Bore: A bore configuration of metal woods in which the shaft penetrates the bore a standard depth of 1/2" from the sole of the club head.

Bore-Through: A hosel type in which the shaft penetrates through the sole of the club. Callaway™ clubs are the most common examples of bore-through heads.

Boring: (Hosel Boring): The process, using a drill or drill press, of enlarging the hosel size (bore) of a wood, iron or putter.

Boron: A high strength element added to some graphite shafts to increase tip strength. It is a very expensive material, thus shafts containing boron tend to be more expensive.

Bounce: The measurement from the leading edge of the club face to the groundline. Wedges typically have the most bounce in a set of clubs. Bounce helps these clubs go through sand and high grass easily.

Bounce Sole Iron: A iron in which the trailing edge is lower than the leading edge. Visually, it may appear that the leading edge is off the ground at address in this type of iron.

Bubble™ Shaft: A composite shaft, proprietary to TaylorMade™, that is designed to stabilize the club head at impact. It features a recessed section just below the grip. It is also unique in that the butt diameter of the shaft is .810", requiring a special grip.

Bubble™ Grip: The specialized type of grip that must be used on a Bubble shaft.

Build-Up Tape: Masking tape applied to the butt section of the shaft to increase grip size. Two layers of masking tape (.038" thick) will increase grip size @ 1/64."

Bulge: The curvature of the face of a wood or metal wood from heel to toe. Bulge aids in imparting corrective spin to shots hit on the toe or heel of the wood face.

Bushing Ferrule: A type of ferrule used to reduce the size of an oversize metal wood or iron hosel to a .335" (wood) or .370" (iron) diameter. The bushing ferrule is epoxied into the hosel; the shaft is then epoxied in place as in a normal shaft installation.

Butt (Shaft Butt): The large end of the shaft onto which the grip is installed.

Butt Cap: The end of the grip of a club. Also the plastic or rubber cap used in certain leather or Winn or leather grip applications. (See also "End Cap.")

Butt Diameter: The measure of the larger end of a shaft, typically expressed in thousandths (.580" or .600" for example.)

Butt Heavy: A type of shaft construction in which the butt section of the shaft is heavier than an equal length of the tip section. Most graphite shafts and parallel tip shafts are considered to be butt heavy shafts.

Butt Section: The parallel portion of the butt end of a shaft down to the first step on steel shafts.

Butt Size: The measure of the larger end of a shaft, typically expressed in thousandths (.580" or .600" for example.)

Butt Trim: Term applied when cutting a shaft from its butt end.

Butt Weight: The process of adding weight to the butt end of a shaft, either by wrapping it with lead tape or by installing a lead plug in the shaft. The "Butt Weight" is also the term given to the plug that may be placed into the shaft.

Caliper: Measuring device used to accurately measure the diameters of shaft tips and butts as well as finished grip sizes.

Camber: The radius measurement of the sole of a club. A sole can be cambered from toe to heel, or from front to back, or both.

Carpenter Steel™: Variety of steel, made by the Carpenter Steel Company, used in oversize metal wood heads and certain iron models.

Casting: See Lost Wax Investment casting

Cavity Back: The design of an iron head in which the weight is distributed toward the perimeter of the head. Cavity backs are easily identified as having a recessed area on the back of the head.

Center of Gravity (CG): The point in a club head at which all of the points of balance intersect. CG is often mistakenly referred to as the "sweet spot."

Center-Shafted: A type of hosel configuration, common in putters, in which the shaft enters the head toward the center. Bullseye-type putters are the best known examples of center-shafted putters.

Ceramic Fiber: A series of man-made ceramic materials that may be used in shaft or head manufacture. Ceramic is a mid-modulus material that has better compression properties than graphite, but not as good as boron.

Chamfer: Generic term used to describe the process of using a special tool to "countersink", "radius" or "cone" the inside of a hosel of a club in order to help reduce a shear point between a shaft (particularly graphite) and head.

Chrome Plated Finish: Type of finish electrostatically applied to forged or cast carbon steel irons. Identified by its high lustrous appearance.

Coefficient of Restitution (COR): The amount of energy put into a golf ball as compared to the amount of energy at (after) impact. The COR is the relation between rebound velocity and initial velocity. Putty would have a COR of 0. A perfectly elastic material has a COR of 1. Any golf club with a COR exceeding .83 does not conform to the Rules of Golf.

Component: Any of the parts used to assemble golf clubs, be they heads, shafts or grips. Most typically, a component is thought of as the club head more so than the shaft or grip.

Compression: The deflection a ball undergoes under a compressive load. Loosely defined as the hardness of a ball. Identified by a number; a higher number indicates a ball that requires more force to compress it. Lower compression balls will flatten more when struck.

Compression Molded: A manufacturing method for graphite heads and face inserts in which layers of graphite are placed upon one another and heat cured to create the clubhead or insert.

CNC (Computer Numerically Controlled) Milling: A production method, usually used for putters, in which the entire head is milled from a soft block of metal. A computer controls the milling machine.

Conforming Ball: Any golf ball that is permitted for tournament use under the USGA Rules of Golf as detailed in Rule Book Appendix III.

Conforming Club: Any golf club that is permitted for tournatment use under the USGA Rules of Golf as detailed in Rule Book Appendix III.

Constant Weight: A shafting concept in which all of the shafts in a given set weigh the same. The idea is to promote consistent feel through this concept.

Core (Ball): Any one of various material used inside the golf ball. A solid core ball utilizes a hard material inside the cover; a wound core ball typically has softer core covered by a series of windings and the cover.

Core (Grip): The inside diameter measurement of a grip. Typically core sizes match shaft butt sizes. For example, an M60 grip core will match with a .600" shaft butt size and produce a standard size grip.

Counter Balance: The process of adding weight in the butt end of a shaft to achieve a specific swingweight and/or feel. Counter balancing will increase the overall weight of the club and is not a widely recommended procedure.

Countersink: Generic term used to describe the process of using a special tool to "chamfer", "radius" or "cone" the inside of a hosel of a club in order to help reduce a shear point between a shaft (particularly graphite) and head. Also, the term given to the process of creating the countersink.

Cover: Outside surface of a golf ball. The cover may be one of any number of materials, Surlyn™ and balata being most common.

Crown: The upper portion of the head of a wood or metal wood. It is the portion of the head most visible to the player at address.

Cryogenics: Branch of science dealing with the freezing of an object to alter its physical properties. Used to treat club heads, cryogenics aligns the molecules in the head material for a harder, more durable product. Balls may also be cryogenically treated.

Cubic Centimeters (cc's): The units used to measure the volume of a wood head. The measurement is generally made as a water displacement test whereby a wood head is immersed in water and the amount of water displaced equals the head's volume.

Curved Shaft: A shaft, usually steel or aluminum, designed for use in no-hosel putters, that features a bend or bends no more than 5" from the shaft tip. The curved shaft tends to create offset and/or lie and possibly face balancing on putters with no hosels.

Cycles Per Minute (CPM): The common measurement units when discussing the frequency of a shaft.

Deflection: The comparative measure of the relative stiffness of a shaft as measured by securing a weight toward the tip of a shaft (club) and relating this to a known stiffness scale.

Deep Face: A club face that measures higher than average from the sole of the club to the crown. This is a relative measure; no specific measurement dimension is applied to the term deep face. Deep face clubs tend to have a higher CG and thus may launch the ball on a lower trajectory.

Demo Clubs: Clubs of known specifications used as part of the fitting process.

Diamond Face: Popularized by the Purespin™ Golf Company, a face coating utilizing fine diamond crystals to produce more backspin and a longer wearing face surface.

Die-Cast: Process of club head production (primarily used with zinc or aluminum) in which heads are formed through the injection of material into a pre-formed die. This process is generally used on lower-priced heads.

Dimple: Depression on the cover of a ball providing lift, leading to distance and/or accuracy. Deeper dimples generally cause a lower ball flight; while shallow dimples add to trajectory. Large diameter dimples tend to make the ball stay in the air longer than do smaller diameter dimples.

Dimple Pattern: Arrangement of dimples on a ball. Various dimple patterns provide added lift, accuracy and/or distance. Patterns vary greatly from one manufacture to another.

Discrete Flex: A shaft having a specific flex designation. For example, True Temper's Dynamic Gold™ S300 is a discrete flex shaft, while the company's parallel tipped Dynamic™ shaft is not.

Distance Standard: USGA parameter for conforming balls that limits their overall carry and roll to 280 yards or less (+/-6%).

Dot Punch: A series of circular indentations or dots on the face of an iron head in place of lines. Dot Punch patterns may be arranged much like lines or may be in a more circular pattern. They are most common on wedges.

Double-Cover Ball: A ball with a large central core surrounded by two thinner materials, one of them being the cover. The purpose of the additional cover is to add spin on shorter shots for control and to reduce spin on longer shots for distance.

Double-Sided Tape: Also known as "Two-Way" or "Grip" tape, a type of tape, with adhesive on both sides that is used along with a solvent to secure grips in place.

Drag: Wind resistance as a golf ball flies, or resistance caused when a club contacts the ground or goes through grass.

Driver: Term given to the club that is typically used to hit the ball for the first shot on a par 4 or par 5 hole. It is the longest hitting club in the set.

Driving Iron: General term given to an iron club with little loft; typically the name for a #1 iron.

Droop (Shaft Droop): The movement of a club head, toe down, as caused by the club being swung and the shaft bending perpendicular to the ground line.

DSFI (Dynacraft Shaft Fitting Index): The industry's first "apples-to-apples" method of shaft classification. The DSFI is a comparison of shaft characteristics under exacting conditions in an effort to describe the particular playing characteristics of the shaft. A DSFI "number" is given to each shaft tested in order to best match the shaft to a given player. Developed by Jeff Summitt of Dynacraft Golf Products, Inc. Newark, Ohio.

Dynamic Fitting: The preferred method of fitting in which the golfer undertakes a series of fitting tests while actually hitting balls.

18-8 Stainless Steel: A type of stainless steel sometimes used in the manufacture of iron and putter heads. Its composition is no more than 0.08% carbon, 18-20% chromium, 8-11% nickel, with the remainder being iron and a few trace elements. As 18-8 cannot be treated to make it harder, it is best used only on non-offset iron heads with thicker hosels.

Elastomer™: Material used in the formation of golf balls, particularly by Titleist™. Also, a variety of material used in the manufacture of Winn™ grips.

Elastomer™ Ring: A piece of polymer material used to surround the inner cavity of certain models of irons, notably Lynx Black Cat™ models. The ring is used for cosmetic and acoustic purposes according to Lynx.

End Cap: The end of the grip of a club. Also the plastic or rubber cap used in certain leather or Winn™ grip applications. (See also "Butt Cap.")

Extension: A piece of material inserted into the shaft butt to make the shaft longer. The extension, with a maximum of 1 1/2", may be made of wood, steel, aluminum or graphite.

Face Angle: The position of the club face relative to the intended line of ball flight. A square face angle aligns directly at the target, an open face aligns to the right, while a closed face aligns left. (Assuming right handed golfers.)

Face Balanced: A putter that, when balanced toward the shaft tip, will exhibit the property of the putter face being parallel to the groundline. Face balanced putters tend to be favored by players who employ a straight back-straight through putting stroke.

Face Centerline: An imaginary line intersecting the center of a club face.

Face Insert: The center portion of the face on a wooden, composite, or metal head, typically constructed from epoxy, graphite or some type of fibrous material. Effective with a 1992 USGA ruling, all types of woods, irons and putters may have face inserts.

Face Progression: The measurement from a shaft's centerline to the leading edge of the club face.

Fancy Face: Generic term given to antique wooden woods whose faces featured unusual designs, usually constructed from different materials (dowels, pins, etc.)

Fat Shaft™: A shaft, designed by Wilson, that utilizes an oversive tip, over-hosel design in an attempt to provide head/shaft stabilization on off-center hits.

Ferrule: The decorative trim ring, usually black (It may have additional trim colors.), that is found directly on top of the hosel on many woods and irons.

Fiber (Fibre): Material, usually comprised of layers of a paper or phenolic material used to make inserts for wooden woods.

15-5 Stainless: A stronger lighter alloy of stainless as compared to 17-4 stainless. 15-5 is commonly used in oversize (250+ cc) driver head. It is composed of @75% iron, 5% nickel and 15% Chromium.

Filament Winding: A method of composite shaft manufacture in which a continuous strands of material (typically graphite fiber) is wrapped around a mandrel to create a shaft. Filament wound shafts are often a bit more consistent than sheet wrapped models.

First Step: The step on a steel shaft closest to the tip of the shaft.

Fit-Chip: A computerized device that attaches to a shaft used to determine the proper frequency of a shaft for a player. Information downloads into a computer program for definitive shaft fitting.

Flange: The part of the club head protruding rearward from the head. Mainly a term used when discussing putters, a "flange" is the part of the putter from behind the face to the very back of the head.

Flare™ Tip Shaft: A composite shaft characterized by a tip diameter of +/- .440" at the point it enters the hosel. Originally designed by Unifiber for the Lynx Black Cat™ golf club, the design theory behind this shaft is head stabilization at impact.

Flat Lie: The term given to an iron or a wood having a lie flatter than specification. For example, if the spec is 60 degrees, a 2 degree flat club would have a lie angle of 58 degrees.

Flat Line Frequency: A method of frequency matching in which all of the woods or irons in the set maintain the same frequency. When plotted on a graph, the frequencies appear as a straight line.

Flex: The common term given to the relative bending properties of a golf club shaft. Flex is usually identified by a letter: L for Ladies, A for Amateur, R for regular, S for Stiff and X for Extra Stiff.

Flow Weighting: A method of head design in which the positioning of the weight in the head moves across the head from one club to the next. For example, a #1 iron may have more weight concentrated on its toe, a #2 iron slightly less, and so on.

431 Stainless Steel: A type of stainless steel used in iron and putter head construction. In composition, it is not more than 20% carbon, 15-17% chromium, and 1.25-2.5% nickel, with the remainder being iron and a few trace elements.

Forged Titanium: A method of wood head manufacture in which the body and sole of the head is formed (forged) from 100% (pure) titanium. The face and hosels of such woods are typically produced from 6-4 ti. Forged titanium woods are less costly due to their ease of forming as well as their lower raw material cost.

Forging: The process of producing a golf club in which the head is made from a series of forging dies stamping the head to final shape. Forged heads are typically made of softer metals than are cast heads and require laborious hand finishing and chrome plating in order to produce a finished product.

Four Piece Ball: A golf ball constructed from four specific materials. There will be a central core surrounded by windings covered by a harder secondary cover (for distance) and a softer outer cover (for spin and feel.)

Four Way Radius: The sole design of an iron or wood in which there is a measurable radius of the sole both from heel to toe and from trailing edge to leading edge.

Frequency: The number of oscillations of a golf shaft in a given time as seen when the tip is pulled down and the shaft vibrates in a specialized machine. Frequency is measured in cycles per minute (cpm's.)

Frequency Analyzer: Specialized machine used to measure the frequencies of golf clubs and shafts.

Frequency Matching: The process of ensuring that all of the clubs in a given set are matched in some manner by their shaft frequency. Frequency matched clubs are said to be more consistent in both feel and performance.

Frequency Slope: The graph line formed when plotting the frequencies of the shafts in a set of clubs. A well-matched set will have a consistent slope; a mis-matched set will show shafts that vary several cycles from their expected range.

Gear Effect: The effect, caused by face bulge, that tends to cause a ball hit toward the toe or heel side of face center to curve back to the intended target line.

GolfTek™: Popular computer used to fit clubs. Generally details swing dynamics such as speed, tempo, face angle, path, etc.

Graphite: A synthetic material used for shaft and head production. It is produced through a series of heating steps to make soft, black carbon graphite filaments. Graphite fibers may differ greatly in strength and modulus.

Gooseneck: A general term given to a putter (or iron) that has an extremely offset hosel.

Grip Collar: Plastic collar used to secure the bottom of a leather or Winn™ style grip.

Grip Core: The internal diameter of a grip as measured in thousandths. For example, a men's grip with a .600" core is labeled as M60.

Grip Gauge: Aluminum or plastic tool used to determine a shaft butt or grip diameter. It sees limited use in most shops as it has only a few specifically sized openings for identification.

Grip Mouth: The opening at the small end of the grip. The mouth will contain a code (i.e. M58) indicating the size and type of grip (men's grip to fit .580" shaft.)

Grip Tape: Also known as "Two-Way" or "Double-Sided" tape, a type of tape with adhesive on both sides to be used along with a solvent to secure grips in place.

Ground Line: The term given to the flat surface on which a club head is placed to measure its specifications. It is the line running from the club face to back, perpendicular to the shaft centerline. Ground line may be loosely interpreted to mean the position the club is placed in on the ground as the player address a shot on the course as well.

Gunmetal: Black oxide type of finish applied to irons, most typically to wedges.

Hard-Stepping: Assembly process of placing a shaft that has a shorter than normal tip section into a given club. For example, placing a #4 iron shaft into a #3 iron is hard stepping. The #3 will then play stiffer than expected.

Heel-Toe Weighting: A type of club head design in which weight is positioned toward the heel and toe of the clubhead in an attempt to stabilize the clubhead (and produce straighter shots) on off-center impacts.

High-Modulus Graphite: A shaft material stiffer than standard graphite. The higher the modulus of graphite, the lower its compression strength.

High Polish Finish: Shiny (mirror) finish applied to stainless steel iron heads through a series of polishing belt operations.

High Spin Ball: Any one of a number of golf balls designed for maximum spin and control. High spin balls are generally soft feeling and are preferred by better players.

Hook Face: A wood that has a face angle that is closed. Hook face woods may help players who slice to hit the ball straighter.

Horizontal Flow Weighting: A manner of distributing weight from club to club in a set of irons in which the highest concentration of weight moves from the toe of the longer irons to the heel of the shorter irons or vise versa.

Hosel: The entry point of the shaft into the head on any golf club.

Hump Shaft™: Developed by Apollo Golf (no longer in business effective January 2000) to move the balance point of the shaft toward the tip. This shaft is identified by a noticeably enlarged area directly above the hosel, extending approximately 5" up the shaft. The shaft was available in both steel and graphite.

Hybrid: Generic term given to any club designed from characteristics of a wood and an iron. The Rescue™ from TaylorMade™ popularized this type of club also known as an "Iron/Wood."

In-Hosel: The common shaft-to-head installation in which the shaft penetrates into the hosel. Used on woods, irons and putters.

Injection Molding: A method of manufacture (typically involving wood heads and face inserts) in which the material (ABS, epoxy, graphite, etc.) comprising the head is heated to a liquid state and injected under pressure into a mold. When the material hardens, it takes the shape of the mold into which it was injected.

Inset Hosel: A club design that moves the position of the hosel toward the center of the club face in an attempt to reduce head twisting. The United States Golf Association (USGA) Rule lists a maximum inset of 0.625" or 16 millimeters above the horizontal plane on which the club is resting in its normal address position.

Iron/Wood: See Hybrid.

Jumbo Wood Head: A metal or wooden wood head having a volume of 250cc or more.

Keel Sole: The sole of a wooden or metal wood that is "V" shaped and designed to lower the club's center of gravity to assist in getting the ball airborne from a less than perfect lie.

Kevlar: A synthetic fiber manufactured by DuPont™ used in shaft and head production. It is known for its high energy absorbing characteristics, but is a lower modulus material and has limited compression properties.

Kick Point: The point of maximum bending of a shaft as measured by deflecting the tip end while the butt remains stationary.

Knurling: Decorative cosmetic engraving on the hosel of an iron or putter. Knurling commonly consists of a series of lines or "X's" near the top of the hosel. It is more often found on clubs from the 1960's and prior.

Laminated Wood: A type of wooden wood head manufactured by gluing and compressing thin pieces of maple together and forming them into the shape of the head.

Large Butt Shaft: Any shaft with a butt size over .620" is classed as a large (or big) butt shaft.

Launch Angle: The angle of a ball's flight immediately after it leaves the club face.

Launch Monitor: Specialized fitting device that measures the launch angle and ball spin at impact and just after impact. Results from Launch Monitor testing seek to determine the optimal loft for a player's club.

Lead Powder: Common swingweighting material used in either a wood's weight port or in a steel shaft tip to achieve a given club weight.

Lead Tip Pin (Tip Weight): A short piece of lead that is epoxied into a shaft from the tip end prior to shaft installation. Tip pins are more commonly used in graphite weighting applications.

Leading Edge: The forward most point of the club face.

Lie: The angle between the shaft and the ground line when the club is measured in normal playing position.

Lift: Upward force on a golf ball as it flies.

Light Weight Shaft: A weight classification of shaft that falls within 3.80-4.24 ounces in steel or alloy shafts and within 2.50-3.17 ounces related to composite shafts.

Line Scored: On the face of an iron or wood club, the pattern of lines or grooves on the face. Typically the lines are parallel to the ground line, but may be positioned in a variety of ways dependent upon the design of the club.

Liquid Center: Term generically given to three-piece balls as most have a center filled with some type of liquid.

Lithium: Element added to the core of a certain balls to promote feel and/or durability. The covers of these balls may be labeled as "lithium surlyn" or "lithium balata."

Liquidmetal™: A proprietary combination of metals designed by the Liquidmetal™ Golf Company. The special alloy is designed to feel soft, yet have a high coefficient of restitution.

Loading (Shaft Loading): The energy buildup or deflection in a shaft as it is swung.

Loft: The angle created as measured from the center of the club face in relation to the hosel bore. More simply, it is the angle of the club face as related to the shaft position.

Lorythmic Swingweight Scale: A type of swingweight scale that measures swingweight at a point 14" down from the butt end of the club and displays those measurements in letter/number designations (D-1, D-2, etc.)

Lost Wax Investment Casting: The investment casting process used to produce irons, putters, and metal woods that initially involves making a master model of the club head. A mold is then made from this master. Wax is injected into these molds, forming a duplicate of the club head. A ceramic material is then used to coat the waxes. The ceramic is heated after hardening, causing the wax to be removed. Metal is then poured into the now empty ceramic pieces to form the actual investment cast club head.

Low Balance Point (LBP): A shaft that has a high percentage of its weight toward the tip. Such shafts are designed to assist in positioning more mass toward or behind the hitting area of the club. LBP shafts will tend to create clubs with higher than normal swingweights.

Low Profile Head: An iron or wood head that is smaller from topline to soleline than typical.

Low Spin Ball: Any of a variety of balls designed for less spin. Reduced spin generally yields more distance. Low spin balls may feel harder and are preferred by players in search of maximum distance.

M1 Bore: The bore type in a metal wood in which there is 1 1/2" from the ground line to the point at which the shaft bottoms out in the hosel. May also be called "standard bore" or "metal wood bore."

M2 Bore: Type of metal wood bore in which the shaft bottoms out in the hosel 1" from the groundline.

Mallet: A type of putter head identified by its broad appearance from front to back when positioned at address. The Ram Zebra™ was one of the first popular mallet style putters.

Mandrel: A tapered steel rod around which composite materials are wrapped when making a shaft.

Maraging Steel: An alloy or family of steels with unique properties. Typically maraging steels are harder than are non-maraging steels such as 17-4 and 15-5. Maraging steel is commonly used in club face applications, rather than in entire club heads.

Master: The exact replica (typically made from brass or aluminum) of a wood, iron or putter head from which all heads will be duplicated.

Medallion: Any number of mylar and urethane type units which are affixed commonly in the cavities of woods or putters, but may also appear on metal woods. The units are designed for cosmetic purposes, enhancing the attractiveness of the club heads.

Melonite™: A quenching process applied to heads that is designed to prevent corrosion. The process gives the heads a black appearance.

Metal Matrix Composite (MMC): Any of a number of alloys used to produce either a golf club head or a shaft.

Metal Wood Bore: The bore configuration of a type of metal wood head in which the standard distance form the groundline to the bottom of the bore is 1" or greater.

Milled Face: A club face, usually on a putter, that has, on a specialized machine, its face milled to .001" for flatness. The concept that a flatter face will promote smother roll is embraced by a majority of golfers.

Midsize Wood: Any wood that approximates a 185cc size.

Mirror Finish: See High Polish Finish.

Modulus: The measure of a fiber's stiffness or resistance to bending. The higher the modulus, the stiffer the material.

Moment of Inertia (MOI): The resistance to twisting of any golf club head when that head is impacted off-center.

Multi-Layer Ball: Design of a ball in which a large core comprises most of the ball. The core is then surrounded by one or two outer layers of material, with one of those being the cover.

Muscleback Iron: See Blade Style Iron.

Non-Conforming Ball: Any ball that does not meet the requirements as set forth in Appendix III of the USGA Rules of Golf.

Non-Conforming Club: Any ball that does not meet the requirements as set forth in Appendix II of the USGA Rules of Golf.

OEM (Original Equipment Manufacturer): A golf club company that, as its main concern, sells completed clubs either on the wholesale level or to the general public.

Official Swingweight Scale: A type of swingweight scale that uses a 12" fulcrum as its measuring point, providing balance in ounces and total weight in ounces or grams. Not typically used in many shops.

Offset: The distance from the forward most point of the hosel to the leading edge of the blade. Offset will help a player who slices to align the club face with the target, thus reducing the slice.

Onset (Negative Offset): The design of a head in which the leading edge of the blade or face is forward of the leading edge of the hosel.

Overall Weight: See Total Weight.

Over-Hosel: Type of shaft-to-head assembly in which the shaft fits over a post protruding from the head. Not nearly as common as in-hosel assemblies, over-hosel applications are used on irons and putters only.

Oversize Iron Head: The generic name given to any number of iron heads larger than standard. An oversize iron has a blade height of approximately 47+ millimeters and a blade length of 80+ mm.

Oversize Shaft Tip: An iron shaft with a tip larger than .370" or a wood with a tip larger than .335". Certain manufacturers claim that larger tip diameter shafts will assist in the stabilization of club heads, especially on off-center impacts.

Oversize Wood Head: A wood head having a volume between 200 and 250 cc's

Parallel Tip Shaft: The type of shaft construction in which the shaft has one constant diameter in its tip section. .370" is a common tip size for parallel tip iron shafts, while .335" is common for wood shafts. Parallel tip shafts can often be used in any club in a set; the same shaft can be used to assemble a #1 iron or an SW. Parallel tip shafts are favored by clubmakers, although a number of OEM's use them as well.

Perimeter Weighting: The design concept of redistributing the weight on the head to the heel and toe in an attempt to stabilize the club on all types of impacts.

Persimmon: A material with which to manufacture wooden woods. Woods made from persimmon are made from one solid block of wood. Persimmon woods, while once very popular in the 1960's and before, have lost favor to metal woods. Persimmon woods are considered to be the "best" type of wooden woods produced and demand a premium price as a result. Persimmon is still being manufactured today, most notably by Louisville Golf in Louisville, Kentucky.

Pixel: A face insert section (metal or polymer) or part that is designed to produce a specific type of roll or spin on a golf ball. Proprietary to Pixl™ Golf.

Pole: The upper and lower areas of the ball, much like the poles on the globe.

Progressive Flexibility: A shafting concept in which longer irons are fitted with more flexible shafts to promote feel and aid in getting the ball airborne and shorter irons utilize stiffer shafts for added control.

Progressive Offset: Iron head design feature in which longer irons have more offset and shorter irons have less. The offset progresses in somewhat uniform increments through the set. More offset is featured in long irons as offset tends to eliminate slicing and helps to get the ball airborne, qualities that help most players hit the ball straighter.

Proprietary: Any feature of a golf club that is unique to a particular manufacturer. For example, each manufacturer's head or shaft designs are proprietary to that manufacturer. Proprietary designs, logos, etc. are often patented by the company developing them in order to secure their exclusive use for a given time period.

Prorythmic Swingweight Scale: A type of swingweight scale that bases its measurements on a 14" fulcrum system, additionally providing weights in ounces or grams.

Rails: Found on the soles of metal woods, rails function to lower the center of gravity of the club and to provide less resistance as the club travels through the turf.

Ram Rod: Long steel rod used to force a cork down a steel shaft when using lead powder as a method of swingweighting.

Relative Stiffness: The stiffness of a shaft when compared to another shaft or shafts.

Ribbed Grip: A grip that has a noticeable ridge along its backside to assist in hand positioning. This type of grip may also be known as a reminder grip.

Rifle™ Shaft: Manufactured by Royal Precision Golf™, the Rifle™ shaft is a steel shaft that is characterized by its lack of steps. Royal Precision™ claims the shaft combines the consistency of steel with the dampening properties of graphite.

Rocker Sole: See Camber Sole.

Rockwell Hardness: One possible scale used to determine the hardness of golf iron heads. Typically 1030 stainless steel has a Rockwell Hardness of B80, 18-8 steel rates B90, 431 tests at C18, while 17-4 has a hardness of C35 and cobalt is hardest at C45.

Roll: The measure of face curvature from crown to sole on woods.

Roll Face™ Putter: Patented by Teardrop Golf™, Roll Face™ putters feature a uniformly curving face from top to sole. Such a face, according to the company, promotes a smoother roll of the ball on the green.

Round Grip: A grip that tapers uniformly the entire distance along its length and has no discernible ribs.

Rusty: Generic term given to any wedge that is made from carbon steel and is not plated. These types of clubs will rust through normal use as a result of oxidation .

Sandblast: The finish applied to the faces of many iron heads. It is slightly rough in texture. It is also the term given to the gray color applied to certain metal wood heads.

Satin Finish: Type of finish applied to stainless steel iron heads and metal wood soles through a series of finishing belts. Appears as a brushed aluminum type of finish.

Scoop (Dig) Sole: An iron whose leading edge is lower than its trailing edge is determined to have a scoop sole.

Scoring: Any marking on a club face, primarily for decorative or alignment purposes. Examples include, but are not limited to, lines, dots, circles and/or triangles.

Sensicore™: A vibration dampening core, developed by True Temper™, and inserted into the shaft to reduce vibration. Sensicores™ are used in both wood and irons shafts, steel and graphite.

17-4 Stainless Steel: A type of stainless steel used in iron head and all metal wood head construction. In composition, 17-4 is no more than 0.07% carbon, between 15 and 17% chromium, 4% nickel, 2.75% copper, and 75% iron and trace elements.

6-4 Titanium: A grade of titanium used in wood head manufacture. Its technical formula is 6Al-4V, indicating that its composition is 90% titanium, 6% aluminum and 4% vanadium. Its high strength to weight ratio allows it to be used to manufacture heads 300+ cubic centimeters in volume.

Shaft Extension: A piece of material inserted into the shaft butt to make the shaft longer. The extension, with a maximum of 1 1/2", may be made of wood, steel, aluminum or graphite.

Shaft Identification (ID) Gauge: Rectangular aluminum gauge (@3" X 5") used to measure various shaft tip sizes.

Shaft Lab™: Computerized system of shaft fitting developed by True Temper™ that places a high emphasis on how a player "loads" a shaft during the swing. Shaft Lab™ provides computer readouts and graphics as part of its fitting recommendations.

Shaft Pattern: The design of a particular shaft, indicating the distribution of flexibility about the shaft. Pattern is also the term used to designate a particular model of shaft, e.g., Dynamic™, TT Lite™, FCM™, etc.

Shallow Face: Any wood or iron having a face height less than the norm. Shallow face clubs typically have lower CG's, thus making them easier to get airborne.

Sheet Wrapping: The process of making a graphite shaft in which sheets of graphite and epoxy resin are wrapped around a mandrel to produce a shaft. It may also be known as "Table Rolling."

Shot Peen Finish: Type of finish applied to stainless steel iron heads that leaves the appearance of a "silvery, semi-rough" surface.

Silkscreen: A method of identification found on most shafts. On steel shafts, it typically encircles the shaft approximately 1/4" of the shaft length from the tip end. Related to graphite shafts, it is much more colorful and noticeable and is found toward the middle of the shaft length.

Slope Frequency: The graph line formed when plotting the frequencies of the shafts in a set of clubs. A well-matched set will have a consistent slope; a mis-matched set will show shafts that vary several cycles from their expected range.

Soft-Stepping: A process of assembly in which a shaft with a longer tip section is put into a club that would normally require a shorter tip section in order that the club play to a softer flex. Installing a #2 iron shaft into a #3 iron to gain more flexibility is an example of this process.

Sole: The underside portion of any type of golf club. It is the area where the club rests on the ground in playing position.

Sole Width: The measure of a club's sole from its leading edge to its trailing edge.

Sole Weighted Iron: The design of an iron had in which the majority of its weight is concentrated toward the sole of the club. This produces a lower center of gravity making it easier to get the ball airborne.

Solid Ball: Also known as a two-piece ball, a solid ball is characterized as one with a cover (usually of a durable material) molded over a central core. Solid balls are considered to have a harder feel and may tend to go farther than other types of balls.

Spherical Symmetry: USGA rule parameter that states a ball must have flight patterns of a spherically symmetrical ball. In other words, regardless of how a ball is positioned at address or struck at impact, the ball must perform the same in respect to ball flight versus ball orientation.

Spin Rate: The amount of spin on a golf ball. A high-spin ball will carry longer and roll less than a low spin shaft. High spin balls will also react to side spin more than do low spin shaft, and are said to be easier to draw or fade as a result. Low spin balls will fly lower and roll farther; their overall distance may be greater.

Spine: The point of a shaft in which it exhibits uniform bending properties in relation to the target.

Spine-Aligning: The process, patented by Mr. Dick Weiss, that allows shafts to be positioned in a club or set of clubs with the spine aligned in either a 3:00 o'clock or 9:00 o'clock position as per a ruling from the USGA.

Spoon: Antique wooden club identification equal to modern #3 wood.

Spring-Like Effect: A general term given to the faces of metal woods elated to how much the face compresses and decompresses (springs back) upon ball impact. The USGA recently established standards for this effect, based upon their assumption that if a face springs more, overall ball distance may be increased, making some of today's courses obsolete. Also known as the "Trampoline Effect."

Square (Box, "U") Grooves: Face lines (or grooves) pressed, cut or cast in a rectangular shape during manufacture.

Standard Size Iron Head: Generic term given to an iron with a size of approximately 44 mm in blade height and 77 mm in blade length.

Standard Size Wood: Any wood head that approximates a volume of 150-185cc.

Standard Weight Shaft: A steel shaft weight classification that falls within the range of 4.25-4.62 ounces or a graphite shaft at 3.17 ounces or greater

Static Fitting: The process of fitting an individual without actually watching him or her hit balls. Examples of static fitting include mailed in fitting forms, and telephone fitting.

Static Weight: Also known as overall weight or total weight, static weight is the weight of the entire assembled club as expressed in ounces or grams.

Steel Center: Term given to three-piece balls having a small center made of steel.

Step: Location on a steel shaft where the diameter of the shaft changes or "steps up" to a larger diameter. The average steel shaft has numerous steps which help identify its playing characteristics and/or manufacturer.

Stepless: A shaft that does not have any steps. Nearly all graphite shafts are stepless. The most popular stepless steel shaft today is the Rifle™ from Royal Precision™.

Strong Loft: The loft of any club, particularly an iron, that is less than the standard specification for that club. Stronger lofted clubs tend to hit the ball lower and longer than standard lofts, but may sacrifice some control.

Stronomic™: Proprietary face insert material from Odyssey™ Golf that helped to first popularize face insert putter designs.

Super-Steel: A term given to any number of alloys of steel that are stronger and often lighter than the 17-4 type of steel used commonly in metal woods.

Surlyn™: A thermoplastic resin (ionomer) cover, invented by DuPont in the late 1970's, Surlyn™ is a very common material in durable cover balls.

Sweet Spot: The position on the club face at which maximum energy and feel will be transferred.

Swing Computer: Device used in club fitting to accurately define swing characteristics such as swing path, speed, tempo, face angle, etc. Typically used indoors only, swing computers will cost several thousands of dollars and will graphically display a golfer's swing, aiding in the fitting process.

Swingweight: A club's weight distribution around a fixed fulcrum point. The fulcrum point is typically 14" from the butt of the club. Swingweight is commonly referred to as the relationship between the weight of the grip end of the club and head end. It is measured in alpha-numeric units such as D-1, D-2, and so on with higher letter-number units indicating more weight in the head relative to the grip.

Swingweight Scale: A measuring scale specific to golf clubs that utilizes a balance system to determine the swingweight and possibly the total weight of a golf club.

Taper Tip Shaft: One of a number of shafts manufactured with a tip section that varies in length and thickness below the first step. This type of shaft requires that a specific length, known as a discrete length, shaft be made for each club in a set. Taper tip shafts are more commonly used by OEM's as compared to custom clubmakers.

1030 Carbon Steel: A softer form of steel typically used in iron forgings. It is more malleable than other stainless steels used in golf clubs making it easier to hand work during forging. 8620 is another common example of carbon steel.

Tensile Strength: Resistance of a material (i.e., epoxy) to being stretched or elongated.

Teryllium™: Proprietary insert material used by Titleist™ in many of their Scotty Cameron™ putters. The material is a mix of many alloys producing a softer feeling insert for putters.

Thermoplastic Hosel: Type of hosel found on Ping Tisi™ drivers allowing the company to produce these clubs with a variety of face angle and lie options. This is unique in the industry as of 2001.

Thermoplastic Shaft: A type of shaft material that once formed may be re-shaped or re-formed. The Phoenixx TPC Company™, formerly Quadrax™, is the only producer of this type of shaft.

Thermoset: An epoxy based material that, once formed, cannot be re-shaped or re-formed.

Three-Piece: Generic term given to a ball with a center core, rubber windings and a cover. A three-piece ball may also have a center and two "cover" materials, eliminating the windings.

Ti-Alloy: A metallic alloy used for wood heads that contains some titanium. Typically ti-alloy heads are comprised mostly of aluminum and are considered to be of lesser quality than other head materials.

Tipping (or Tip Trimming): The process of trimming a shaft from the tip to increase its stiffness.

Tip Stiff: Design of shafts (typically graphite shafts) which feature a firmer tip section as compared to the remaining portion of the shaft.

Titanium: Club head material utilized primarily for woods and irons, it has a higher strength-to-weight ratio than most steel alloys. See also Beat-Titanium, Forged Titanium and 6-4 Titanium. Titanium is also used in shaft production

Titanium Ball: The general term given to a ball that has either a titanium based core or that contains titanium as part of its cover material.

Topline: The uppermost part of an iron blade, running from heel to toe. It is the part of the iron head that a player typically looks down upon when addressing the ball.

Torque: The resistance of a shaft to twisting is its torque. Lower torque shafts twist less than do higher torque shafts and, as a result, may be recommended for stronger players.

Total Weight: Also known as overall weight or static weight, total weight is the weight of the entire assembled club as expressed in ounces or grams.

Tour Weighted: The somewhat generic term applied to composite shafts that weigh approximately the same as standard weight steel shafts (@125 grams.)

Trajectory: The shape and height of a shot in relation to its direction.

Trailing Edge: The most rearward part of a club's sole.

Trampoline Effect: See Spring-Like Effect.

Tri-Metal: A club head comprised of three separate materials. Popularized by Orlimar™, a tri-metal type head may contain 17-4 stainless steel body, a maraging steel face and a copper alloy in sole rails.

Tumble Finish: Type of finish applied to iron and metal wood heads via a specialized tumbling machine containing various tumbling media. Finish is characterized by its dull, durable look.

Tungsten: A heavy metallic compound used to add weight to a club head, either as a swingweighting material in the shaft or as a defined weight attached somewhere in/on the head.

Two-Piece: Type of ball characterized by a center core surrounded by a cover, usually made of a durable material.

Two-Way Tape: Also known as "Double-Sided" or "Grip" tape, a type of tape, with adhesive on both sides that is used along with a solvent to secure grips in place.

Ultralight Shaft: A class of composite shafts that weigh less than 2.50 ounces or 70 grams.

Underlisting: The rubber or paper material onto which a leather or Winn™ grip is wrapped.

Unitized: A shaft in which one model can be used to build an entire set of irons or a full set of woods through successive trimming of the shaft tip section.

Unloading (Shaft Unloading): The energy release as a shaft is swung or as the shaft straightens out from its deflected state.

Upright Lie: A club's lie that is more upright than the standard specification for that particular head. For example, a 62 degree head would be 2 degrees upright if the stated specification was originally 60 degrees.

Very Lightweight Shaft: A weight classification of shafts that falls within 3.40-3.79 ounce weight range for steel or alloy shafts and 2.50-3.17 ounces for composite shafts.

"V" Grooves: Face lines (or grooves) pressed, cut or cast into a triangular (or "V") shape during club manufacture.

Velocity: The speed of a golf ball. Also known as initial velocity, the USGA limits conforming balls to velocities of no more than 250 feet per second (76.2m/s) as measured on USGA test equipment. A 2% tolerance is allowed at a test temperature of 23 degrees Celsius +/-1.

Vertical Flow Weighting: The method of flow weighting in which the weight moves vertically from a concentration of weight toward the sole of long irons to more traditional weighting on short irons.

Viscoelastic Material: A proprietary material used by the Cleveland Golf Company™ to assist in providing vibration absorption in their patented VAS™ clubs.

Volume: A numerical designation given to the size of a wood head as measured by liquid displacement.

Warbird™ Sole: Bi-concave sole deigned patented by Callaway™ Golf for use on their Big Bertha™ line of woods.

Weight-Sorted: Club components that are weighed prior to assembly in an attempt to ensure consistent specification of the finished golf club.

Whipping: Black, thread-like covering applied over the neck of a wooden wood to prevent the neck from splitting during play.

Windings: The elastic rubber material tightly wrapped around the core of some three-piece balls. Typically 35 yards of material will be stretched to over 250 yards in a single ball.

Wood/Iron: Generic term given to any club designed from characteristics of a wood and an iron. The Rescue™ from TaylorMade™ popularized this type of club also known as an "Iron/Wood."

Wound Ball: Type of ball characterized by a cover over a matrix of rubber windings that cover a central core. Wound balls often have a softer feel and higher spin rate than other ball types. They may also be called three-piece balls.

X-Out: General term given to less than perfect balls. Usually top grade balls with a slight cosmetic or manufacturing defect, X-outs are identified by a row of "X's" somewhere on the cover. X-outs are substantially less costly than first-quality balls.

Zinc Iron Heads: Iron heads die cast from an alloy of zinc. These heads typically are considered less expensive and less durable than their stainless counterparts and thus are designated primarily for beginner sets. Zinc heads can be identified by their non-magnetic properties as well as by their typically larger diameter than normal hosels.

Appendices

SUGGESTED FITTING STEPS FOR TOTAL CLUBFITTING

CLUBHEADS
• Determine the design that fits a player's game •

LENGTH
• Establishes comfortable address and consistent shotmaking •

LIE
• A key to directional control for irons •

FACE ANGLE
• A critical element in wood shot direction •

LOFT
• A vital component of trajectory and distance •

SHAFTS
• The critical element in feel and performance •

GRIP
• Proper fit promotes feel and consistency •

WEIGHT
• Swingweight and total weight establish overall club feel •

CURRENT SET MAKEUP

CUSTOMER _____

DATE _____

SPECIFICATION	WOODS					IRONS								
	1	3	5	7	X	1	2	3	4	5	6	7	8	9
Manufacturer														
Model														
Length														
Loft														
Lie														
Face angle														
Swingweight														
Total Weight														
Shaft Type														
Shaft Flex														
Grip Type														
Grip Size														

SPECIFICATION	WEDGES					PUTTER		OTHER	
	PW	SW	UW	AW					
Manufacturer									
Model									
Length									
Loft									
Lie									
Swingweight									
Total Weight									
Shaft Type									
Shaft Flex									
Grip Type									
Grip Size									

Personal Interview Form

Player Information

Name _____

Address _____

_____

Phone (H) _____ (W) _____

Player Profile

Height _____   Weight _____   Age _____   RH/LH _____

Frequency of play _____   Handicap/Average Score _____

Number of times per week of practice _____

Average Putts Per Round _____   Are you getting better, worse or the same? _____

Physical Considerations _____

Rank the following, excellent, good, fair or poor:

Driver _____   Fairway Woods _____   Long Irons _____

Mid Irons _____   Short Irons _____   Full Wedge _____

Chipping _____   Bunker Play _____   Putter _____

Favorite Club _____   Least Favorite Club _____

Where do your mishits tend to go? (slice, push, hook, pull, high, low, short or long?)

Driver _____   Fairway Woods _____   Long Irons _____

Mid Irons _____   Short Irons _____   Full Wedge _____

Chipping _____   Bunker Play _____   Putter _____

PUSH   FADE   SLICE

PULL   DRAW   HOOK

Custom Golf Club Fitting Form

Player Information

Name _____

Address _____

_____

Phone (H) _____ (W) _____

Player Profile

Height _____ Weight _____ Age _____ RH/LH _____

Number of rounds played per week _____

Number of times per week of practice _____

Handicap/Average Score _____

Average Putts Per Round _____

Physical Considerations _____

Player Goals

To Hit Ball:

_____ Higher

_____ Lower

_____ Longer

_____ Straighter

_____ More Solidly

_____ With Better Feel

_____ More Consistency

To Stop:

_____ Slicing

_____ Hooking

_____ Skying

_____ Topping

_____ Pulling

_____ Pushing

Fitting Procedures

1. Set Makeup
A. Player preferences - IRONS

Blade Configuration	Hosel Type	Head Size
_____ Muscleback	_____ Offset	_____ Standard
_____ Cavity Back	_____ Non-Offset	_____ Oversize
_____ No Preference	_____ No Preference	_____ No Preference

Current Irons _____

Recommendations _____

B. Player Preferences - WOODS

Hosel Type	Head Size	Face Angle
_____ Offset	_____ Standard	_____ Open
_____ Non-Offset	_____ Midsize	_____ Closed
_____ No Preference	_____ Jumbo	_____ Square

Current Type of Woods _____

Recommendations _____

_____

2. Loft

Current Driver Ball Flight	Current 5 Iron Ball Flight
_____ Very High	_____ Offset
_____ High	_____ Non-Offset
_____ Acceptable	_____ No Preference
_____ Low	_____ Low
_____ Very Low	_____ Very Low
Recommended Driver Loft _____	Recommended 5 Iron Loft _____

3. Shaft

Player Preference

_____ Steel	Average Driver Distance _____
_____ Graphite	Average Driver Distance _____
_____ No Preference	Clubhead Speed: Driver _____ 5 Iron _____

Shaft Recommendations: Driver _____   5 Iron _____

4. Length

_____ Height   _____ Finger Tip To Floor Measurement

<u>IMPACT FEEL CONSISTENCY TEST RESULTS</u>

5 Iron		Driver	
36 1/2"	_____	43"	_____
37"	_____	43 1/2"	_____
37 1/2"	_____	44"	_____
38"	_____	44 1/2"	_____

Recommended Driver Length _____   Recommended 5 Iron Length _____

5. Lie

Finger Tip To Floor Measurement _____

Sole Impact Test 5 Iron _____

Recommended Lie _____   Driver _____   5 Iron _____

6. Grip

Players Glove Size _____

Players Hand Measurement   A. _____   B. _____

<u>PLAYER FEEL PREFERENCES</u>   <u>GRIP TYPE PREFERENCES</u>

- 1/64"   _____   _____ Rubber
Standard _____   _____ Cord
+ 1/64"   _____   _____ Synthetic
+ 1/32"   _____   _____ Other (specify)
+ 1/64"   _____   _____ No Preferences
Jumbo   _____

Recommended Grip Size _____   Grip Type Selection _____

7. Weight

Recommended Swingweights: Driver _____   5 Iron _____

8. Miscellaneous Notes

_____

_____

_____

_____

_____

_____

_____

_____

_____

_____

_____

_____

_____

STATIC FITTING FORM

First Name _____

Last Name _____

Address _____

City _____

State/Province _____

Postal Code _____

Country _____

Email Address _____

Phone _____

I play golf: _____ RH _____ LH

I am _____ Male _____ Female

I am _____ feet, _____ inches tall

I weigh _____ pounds

I am _____ years old.

I've played golf for _____ years.

My handicap is _____ (Enter a "?" if you don't know)

My average score is _____.

Do you take golf lessons? _____ Yes _____ No

Woods I play now _____

Irons I play now _____

Shaft type (woods) _____

Shaft type (irons) _____

Shaft flex (woods) _____

Shaft flex (irons) _____

Swingweight driver _____

Swingweight 5 iron _____

Driver length _____

5 iron length _____

STATIC FITTING FORM (continued)

Grip type _____   Grip size _____

What's your glove size? _____

Distance from knuckles to the ground _____ inches

Distance from top of shoulder to fingertips _____ inches

Distance from grip cap to the ground _____ inches

How man yards is your average tee shot? _____

I push _____ % of the time

I fade _____ % of the time

I slice _____ % of the time

I pull _____ % of the time

I draw _____ % of the time

I hook _____ % of the time

I hit straight _____ % of the time

I hit my driver _____ yards

I hit my irons _____ yards

APPENDIX VI

ROCKWELL HARDNESS SCALE		
MATERIAL	**HARDNESS**	**PRIMARY USE**
Aluminum	B50-60 **Softest**	Woods, Putters
Carbon Steel	B60-70	Irons, Putters
304 Stainless	B75	Irons only
Beryllium Copper	B70-80	Irons, Putters
431 Stainless	C18-25	Irons, Putters
100% Titanium	C24-28	Woods
6-4 Titanium	C32-36	Woods, Faces
17-4 Stainless	C34-38	Woods, Irons, Putters
450 Steel (Supersteel)	C36-40	Woods, Irons
15-5 Stainless	C36-44	Woods
Beta Titanium	C40+	Woods
Maraging Steel	C45-55 **Hardest**	Woods, Faces

INDUSTRY AVERAGE GOLF CLUB LENGTHS THROUGH THE YEARS

	1950's & 60's	1970's & 80's	1990's	2000's
WOODS				
Driver	43"	43.5"	44"	45"
3	42"	42"	43"	44"
5	41"	41"	42"	43"
7	N/A	40.5"	41"	42"
9	N/A	N/A	40.5"	41.5"

N/A indicates clubs were not produced during those years

Notes:
1) During 1990-2000's, Titanium drivers were 45" and beyond depending upon manufacturer."
2) Graphite shafted clubs in the 1970's and 1980's were at least ½" longer than the above standards.
3) Ladies lengths are typically 1" less than the above standards.

IRONS				
1	39"	39.5"	40"	
2	38.5"	39"	39.5"	
3	38"	38.5"	39"	
4	37.5"	38"	38.5"	
5	37"	37.5"	38"	
6	36.5"	37"	37.5"	
7	36"	36.5"	37"	
8	35.5"	36"	36.5"	
9	35"	35.5"	36"	
PW	35"	35.5"	35.5"	
SW	35"	35.5"	35.5"	
UW	N/A	35"	35.5"	
AW	N/A	N/A	35.5"	

N/A indicates clubs were not produced during those years

Notes:
1) Irons with graphite shafts produced in the 1970's through the present are at least 1/2" longer than the above standards.
2) Ladies lengths are typically 1" less than the above standards."

APPENDIX VIII

COMPONENT WEIGHTING VERSUS SWINGWEIGHTING

Clubhead Head	Weight	Raw Shaft Weight	Grip Weight	Club Length	Swingweight
1 wood	198 grams	125 grams[1]	52 grams[2]	43"	D-0
3 wood	208 grams	125 grams	52 grams	42"	D-0
4 wood	213 grams	125 grams	52 grams	41.5"	D-0
5 wood	218 grams	125 grams	52 grams	41"	D-0
7 wood	228 grams	125 grams	52 grams	40"	D-0
1 iron	230 grams	125 grams[1]	52 grams	39.5"	D-0
2 iron	237 grams	125 grams	52 grams	39"	D-0
3 iron	244 grams	125 grams	52 grams	38.5"	D-0
4 iron	251 grams	125 grams	52 grams	38"	D-0
5 iron	258 grams	125 grams	52 grams	37.5"	D-0
6 iron	265 grams	125 grams	52 grams	37"	D-0
7 iron	272 grams	125 grams	52 grams	36.5"	D-0
8 iron	279 grams	125 grams	52 grams	36"	D-0
9 iron	286 grams	125 grams	52 grams	35.5"	D-0
PW[3]	293 grams	125 grams	52 grams	35.5"	D-3
SW[3]	300 grams	125 grams	52 grams	35.5"	D-6

NOTES

[1] Raw shaft weight is based on a 45" UDWS (parallel tip Dynamic S-flex for woods) and a 39" UDIS (parallel tip Dynamic S-flex for irons). Under proper trimming and installation, each shaft's weight will drop slightly through the set.

[2] Grip weight is based on an average weight of an M58 Men's Victory or Tour Wrap rubber grip.

[3] Traditionally, the pitching wedge and sand wedge are designed to be played at slightly to significantly higher swingweights that the #1-9 irons.

APPENDIX IX

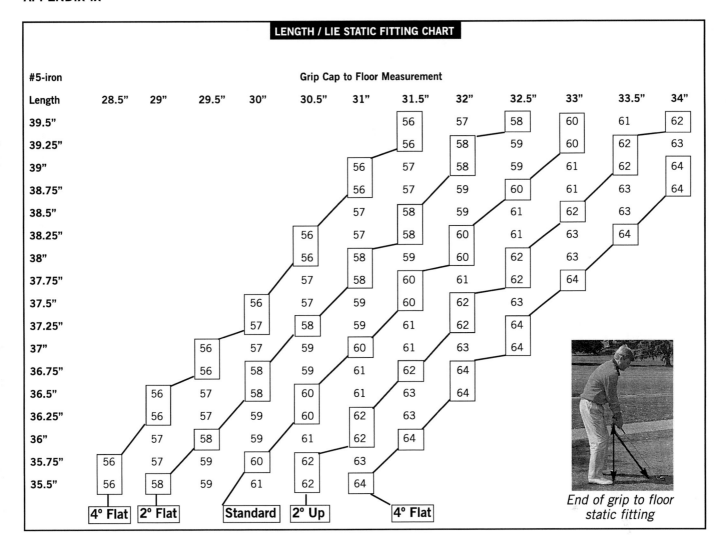

LENGTH / LIE STATIC FITTING CHART

#5-iron — Grip Cap to Floor Measurement

Length	28.5"	29"	29.5"	30"	30.5"	31"	31.5"	32"	32.5"	33"	33.5"	34"
39.5"							56	57	58	60	61	62
39.25"							56	58	59	60	62	63
39"						56	57	58	59	61	62	64
38.75"						56	57	59	60	61	63	64
38.5"						57	58	59	61	62	63	
38.25"					56	57	58	60	61	63	64	
38"					56	58	59	60	62	63		
37.75"					57	58	60	61	62	64		
37.5"				56	57	59	60	62	63			
37.25"				57	58	59	61	62	64			
37"			56	57	59	60	61	63	64			
36.75"			56	58	59	61	62	64				
36.5"		56	57	58	60	61	63	64				
36.25"		56	57	59	60	62	63					
36"		57	58	59	61	62	64					
35.75"	56	57	59	60	62	63						
35.5"	56	58	59	61	62	64						

4° Flat | **2° Flat** | **Standard** | **2° Up** | **4° Flat**

End of grip to floor static fitting

APPENDIX X

JUNIOR HEIGHT BASED FITTING CHART								
Height	(Inches)	Driver	3-wood	3-iron	5-iron	7-iron	9-iron & Wedge	Putter
3'-0"	36"	27.5-28.5"	6.5-27.5"	23-24"	22-23"	21-22"	20-21"	19.5-20.5"
3'-2"	38"	28.5-29.5"	27.5-28.5"	24-25"	23-24"	22-23"	21-22"	20.5-21.5"
3'-4"	40"	29.5-30.5"	28.5-29.5"	25-26"	24-25"	23-24"	22-23"	21.5-22.5"
3'-6"	42"	30.5-31.5"	29.5-30.5"	26-27"	25-26"	24-25"	23-24"	22.5-23.5"
3'-8"	44"	31.5-32.5"	30.5-31.5"	27-28"	26-27"	25-26"	24-25"	23.5-24.5"
3'-10"	46"	32.5-33.5"	31.5-32.5"	28-29"	27-28"	26-2""	25-26"	24.5-25.5"
4'-0"	48"	33.5-34.5"	32.5-33.5"	29-30"	28-29"	27-28"	26-27"	25.5-26.5"
4'-2"	50"	34.5-35.5"	33.5-34.5"	30-31"	29-30"	28-29"	27-28"	26.5-27.5"
4'-4"	52"	35.5-36.5"	34.5-35.5"	31-32"	30-31"	29-30""	28-29"	27.5-28.5"
4'-6"	54"	36.5-37.5"	35.5-36.5"	32-33"	31-32"	30-31"	29-30"	28.5-29.5"
4'-8"	56"	37.5-38.5"	36.5-37.5"	33-34"	32-33"	31-32"	30-31"	29.5-30.5"
4'-10"	58"	38.5-39.5"	37.5-38.5"	34-35"	33-34"	32-33"	31-32"	30.5-31.5"
5'-0"	60"	39.5-40.5"	38.5-39.5"	35-36"	34-35"	33-34"	32-33"	31.5-32.5"
5'-2"	62"	40.5-41.5"	39.5-40.5"	36-37"	35-36"	34-35"	33-34"	32.5-33.5"
5'-4"	64"	41.5-42.5"	40.5-41.5"	37-38"	36-37"	35-36"	34-35"	33.5-34.5"

APPENDIX XI

INDUSTRY AVERAGE GOLF CLUB LIES THROUGH THE YEARS			
	1950's & 60's	1970's & 80's	1990's & 2000's
WOODS			
Driver	55	55	56
3	56	56	58
5	57	57	59
7	N/A	58	60
9	N/A	N/A	61
IRONS			
1	55	56	59
2	56	57	59.5
3	57	58	60
4	58	59	60.5
5	59	60	61
6	60	61	62
7	61	62	63
8	62	63	63.5
9	63	64	64
PW	63	64	64
SW	63	64	64
UW	N/A	64	64
AW	N/A	N/A	64

N/A indicates clubs were not produced during those years
Notes:
1) All numbers are measured in degrees
2) Ladies lies are typically 1° flatter than the above standards

APPENDIX XII

INDUSTRY AVERAGE GOLF CLUB LOFTS THROUGH THE YEARS			
	1950's & 60's	1970's & 80's	1990's & 2000's
WOODS			
Driver	11°	10°	9.5°
3	16°	15°	14°
5	22°	21°	18°
7	N/A	27°	21°
9	N/A	N/A	25°
IRONS			
1	17°	16°	15°
2	20°	19°	18°
3	24°	22°	20°
4	28°	25°	23°
5	32°	28°	26°
6	36°	32°	30°
7	40°	36°	34°
8	44°	40°	38°
9	48°	44°	42°
PW	52°	49°	46°
SW	56°	55°	55°
UW	N/A	60°	60°
AW	N/A	N/A	50° & 52°

N/A indicates clubs were not produced during those years

SHAFT DEMO PROGRAMS

LOW BUDGET SHAFT PROGRAMS

Woods			Irons		
DSFI Rating	Steel	Graphite	DSFI Rating	Steel	Graphite
Below 65			below 60		
65 - 70			60 - 65		
70 - 75			65 - 70	Y	
75 - 80	Y		70 - 75	Y	
80 - 85	Y		75 - 80	Y	
85 - 90	Y		80 - 85	Y	
90 - 95	Y		85+	Y	
95 - 100	Y				
100+					

MEDIUM BUDGET SHAFT PROGRAMS

Woods			Irons		
DSFI Rating	Steel	Graphite	DSFI Rating	Steel	Graphite
Below 65			below 60		
65 - 70			60 - 65		Y
70 - 75		Y	65 - 70	Y	Y
75 - 80	Y	Y	70 - 75	Y	Y
80 - 85	Y	Y	75 - 80	Y	Y
85 - 90	Y	Y	80 - 85	Y	
90 - 95	Y	Y	85+	Y	
95 - 100	Y				
100+	Y				

LARGE BUDGET SHAFT PROGRAMS

Woods				Irons		
DSFI Rating	Steel	Graphite Std.	UL	DSFI Rating	Steel	Graphite
Below 65		Y		below 60		Y
65 - 70		Y		60 - 65		Y
70 - 75		Y	Y	65 - 70	Y	Y
75 - 80	Y	Y		70 - 75	Y	Y
80 - 85	Y	Y	Y	75 - 80	Y	Y
85 - 90	Y	Y		80 - 85	Y	Y
90 - 95	Y	Y	Y	85+	Y	
95 - 100	Y	Y				
100+	Y	Y	Y			

(Y indicates shafts suggested for demo programs)

APPENDIX XIV

DRIVER SWING SPEED - DISTANCE CHART	
Swing Speed (mph)	Distance (yds.)
50	123
52	128
54	133
56	138
58	143
60	148
62	153
64	158
66	162
68	167
70	172
72	177
74	182
76	187
78	192
80	197
82	202
84	207
86	207
88	217
90	222
92	227
94	231
96	236
98	241
100	246
102	251
104	256
106	261
108	266
110	271

#5-IRON SWING SPEED - DISTANCE CHART	
Swing Speed (mph)	Distance (yds.)
40	88
42	92
44	97
46	102
48	106
50	110
52	115
54	119
56	124
58	128
60	132
62	137
64	141
66	146
68	150
70	154
72	159
74	163
76	168
78	172
80	176
82	181
84	185
86	190
88	194
90	199

BUILT-UP GRIP SIZING

Fractional Measurement	Men's Decimal Measurement	Ladies Decimal Measurement
-1/32" under	.869	.819
-1/64" under	.885	.835
Standard	.900	.850
+1/64" over	.915	.865
+1/16" over	.931	.881
+1/16" over	.962	.912
+1/8" over	1.087	1.037

*Grip sizes are measured 2" down from edge of grip cap.

Grip Core		Shaft Butt	Layers Of Build-Up Tape Required To Achieve Stated Sizes					
			-1/64"	Std.	+1/64"	+1/32"	+1/16"	+1/8"
M58	+	.580"	*	0	2	4	9	18
M58	+	.600"	X	*	0	2	7	16
M58	+	.620"	X	X	*	0	4	13
M60	+	.580"	0	2	4	7	11	20
M60	+	.600"	*	0	2	4	9	18
M60	+	.620"	X	*	0	2	7	16
M62	+	.580"	2	4	7	9	13	31
M62	+	.600"	0	2	4	7	11	20
M62	+	.620"	*	0	2	4	9	18
L56	+	.560"	*	0	2	4	9	18
L56	+	.580"	X	*	0	2	7	16
L56	+	.600"	X	X	*	0	4	13
L58	+	.560"	0	2	4	7	11	20
L58	+	.580"	*	0	2	4	9	18
L58	+	.600"	X	*	0	2	7	16
L60	+	.560"	2	4	7	9	13	31
L60	+	.580"	0	2	4	7	11	20
L60	+	.600"	*	0	2	4	9	18
L60	+	.620"	X	*	0	2	7	16

*-Grip must be stretched @3/4" longer to reduce outside diameter.
x-not recommended.
Note: Build-up tape is .0035" thick

Wedge Fitting Form

1. Wedge Type
Player Preferences

_____ Pitching Wedge

_____ Sand Wedge

_____ Utility or Lob Wedge

_____ High Loft wedge

Current Type of Wedges: _____

Bounces: _____

2. Wedge Lengths	**3. Wedge Lies**	**4. Wedge Lofts**
_____ PW	_____ PW	_____ PW
_____ SW	_____ SW	_____ SW
_____ UW, LW	_____ UW, LW	_____ UW, LW
_____ High Loft Model	_____ High Loft Model	_____ High Loft Model

Other:

5. Grip Type & Size

Player Preference - Grip Type

Model _____

Size _____

6. Shaft Flex & Type

PW _____

SW _____

UW, LW _____

High Loft _____

Other:

APPENDIX XVII

Putter Fitting Form

1. Putter Style
a. Player Preferences - PUTTERS

Putter Configuration   Hosel Type

_____ Blade   _____ Offset

_____ Cavity Back   _____ Non-Offset

_____ Mallet   _____ No Preferences

Current Type of Wedges: _____

Recommendations:_____

---

2. Putter Length   ### 3. Putter Lie

_____ 34"   _____ Recommended Putter Lie

_____ 35"   ### 4. Putter Loft

_____ 36"   _____ Recommended Putter Loft

_____ Recommended Putter Length

---

5. Grip Type & Size   ### 6. Shaft Flex & Type

Player Preference - Grip Type   _____

_____ Pistol

_____ Paddle

_____ Other

Grip Recommendation (size): _____

Loft and Lie Alteration
Information About Bending
Release Form

Golf clubs are cast or forged from a variety of metals. Clubs may be cast from stainless steel known by their composition names of 431, 17-4 or 15-5. These numbers refer to the hardness of each metal. Forged clubs are produced from a softer metal known as carbon steel. Clubs may also be made from more exotic metals such as beryllium copper, nickel or similar types of material.

Each indiviudal club may have its own unique properties even though it will be cast from one of the above matierals. Because of this, as a golf club is altered for loft and/or lie, there is a chance that the head may break unexpectedly. This may happen regardless of the type of machine being used or the experience of the rperson doing the bending. As a result, there can be no warranty stated or implied that a golf club being bent will be guaranteed against breakage.

The person bending the clubs will practice common and tested bending preactices at all times. The amount of bending to be done will be clearly stated. But, in the event of metal failure from the golf club, the facility and person altering the clubs cannot be held liable and responsible for any head breakage. No remuneration to the club owner or replacement of club head(s) is implied due to breakage. This is strictly due to the nature of the golf head manufacturing process and is no reflection upon the skills of the person bending the clubs.

I have read the above and understand the nature of golf club bending. I release the facility and the person performing the loft and lie alteration from any responsibility should damage occur to any heads during the bending process.

Signed,

Date: _____

APPENDIX XIX

Appendix II
Design of Clubs

A player in doubt as to the conformity of a club should consult the United States Golf Association.

A manufacturer should submit to the United States Golf Association a sample of a club which is to be manufactured for a ruling as to whether the club conforms with the Rules. If a manufacturer fails to submit a sample before manufacturing and/or marketing the club, the manufacturer assumes the risk of a ruling that the club does not conform with the Rules. Any sample submitted to the United States Golf Association will become its property for reference purposes.

The following paragraphs prescribe general regulations for the design of clubs, together with specifications and interpretations.

Where a club, or part of a club, is required to have some specific property, this means that it must be designed and manufactured with the intention of having that property. The finished club or part must have that property within manufacturing tolerances appropriate to the material used.

1) Clubs
a) General
A club is an implement designed to be used for striking the ball and generally comes in three forms: woods, irons and putters distinguished by shape and intended use. A putter is a club with a loft not exceeding ten degrees designed primarily for use on the putting green.

The club shall not be substantially different from the traditional and customary form and make. The club shall be composed of a shaft and a head. All parts of the club shall be fixed so that the club is one unit, and it shall have no external attachments except as otherwise permitted by the Rules.

b)Adjustability
Woods and irons shall not be designed to be adjustable except for weight. Putters may be designed to be adjustable for weight and some other forms of adjustability are also permitted. All methods of adjustment permitted by the Rules require that:

(i) the adjustment cannot be readily made;
(ii) all adjustable parts are firmly fixed and there is no reasonable likelihood of them working loose during a round;
  and
(iii) all configurations of adjustment conform with the Rules.

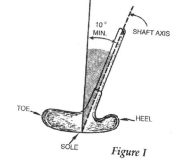

Figure I

The disqualification penalty for purposely changing the playing characteristics of a club during a stipulated round (Rule 4-2a) applies to all clubs including a putter.

c) Length
The overall length of the club shall be at least 18 inches (457.2mm) measured from the top of the grip along the axis of the shaft or a straight line extension of it to the sole of the club.

d) Alignment
When the club is in its normal address position the shaft shall be so aligned that:
(i) the projection of the straight part of the shaft on to the vertical plane through the toe and heel shall diverge from the vertical by at least 10 degrees (see Fig I);
(ii) the projection of the straight part of the shaft on to the vertical plane along the intended line of play shall not diverge from the vertical by more than 20 degrees (see Fig. II).

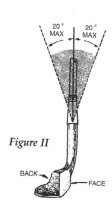

Figure II

Except for putters, all of the heel portion of the club shall lie within 0.625 inches (15.88mm) of the plane containing the axis of the straight part of the shaft and the intended (horizontal) line of play (see Fig. III).

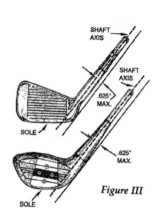

Figure III

2) Shaft
a) Straightness
The shaft shall be straight from the top of the grip to a point not more than 5 inches (127 mm) above the sole, measured from the point where the shaft ceases to be straight along the axis of the bent part of the shaft and the neck and/or socket (see Fig. IV).

b) Bending and Twisting properties
At any point along its length, the shaft shall:
(i) bend in such a way that the deflection is the same regardless of how the shaft is rotated about its longitudinal axis; and
(ii) twist the same amount in both directions.

c) Attachment to Clubhead
The shaft shall be attached to the clubhead at the heel either directly or through a sing plain neck and/or socket. The length from the top of the neck and/or socket to the sole of the club shall not exceed 5 inches (127mm), measured along the axis of, and following any bend in, the neck and/or socket (see Fig. V).

Exception for Putters: The shaft or neck or socket of a putter may be fixed at any point in the head.

3) Grip (see Fig. VI)
The grip consists of material added to the shaft to enable the player to obtain a firm hold. The grip shall be straight and lain in form, shall extend to the end of the shaft and shall not be molded for any part of the hands. If no material is added, that portion of the shaft designed to be held by the player shall be considered the grip.
(i) For clubs other than putters the grip must be circular in cross-section, except that a continuous, straight, slightly raised rib may be incorporated along the full length of the grip, and a slightly indented spiral is permit ted on a wrapped grip or a replica of one.
(ii) A putter grip may have a non-circular cross-section, provided the cross-section has no concavity, is symmetrical and remains generally similar throughout the length of the grip. (See Clause (v) below).
(iii) The grip may be tapered but must not have any bulge or waist. Its cross-sectional dimension measured in any direction must not exceed 1.75 inches (44.45mm).
(iv) For clubs other than putters the axis of the grip must coincide with the axis of the shaft.
(v) A putter may have two grips provided each is circular in cross-section, the axis of each coincides with the axis of the shaft, and the are separated by at least 1.5 inches (38.1mm).

4) Clubhead
a) Plain in Shape
The clubhead shall be generally plain in shape. All parts shall be rigid, structural in nature and functional . It is not practicable to define plain in shape precisely and comprehensively but features which are deemed to be in breach of this requirement and are therefore not permitted include:
(i) holes through the head,
(ii) transparent material added for other than decorative or structural purposes.
(iii) Appendages to the main body of the head such as knobs, plates, rods or fins, for the purpose of meeting dimensional specifications, for aiming or for any other

purpose. Exceptions may be made for putters.

Any furrows in or runners on the sole shall not extend into the face.

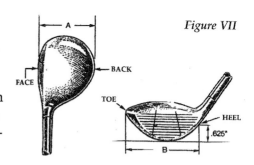
Figure VII

b) Dimensions

The distance from the heel to the toe of the clubhead shall be greater than the distance from the face to the back. These dimensions are measured, with the clubhead in its normal address position, on horizontal lines between vertical projections of the outermost points of (i) the heel and the toe and (ii) the face and the back (see Fig. VII, dimension A). If the outermost point of the heel is not clearly defined, it is deemed to be 0.625 inches (15.88mm) above the horizontal plane on which the club is resting in its normal address position (see Fig. VII, dimension B).

c) Striking Faces

The clubhead shall have only one striking face, except that a putter may have two such faces if their characteristics are the same, and they are opposite each other.

5) Club Face
a)General

The material and construction of, or any treatment to, the face or clubhead shall not have the effect at impact of a spring (test on file), or impart significantly more spin to the ball than a standard steel face, or have any other effect which would unduly influence the movement of the ball.

The face of the club shall be hard and rigid (some exceptions may be made for putters) and, except for such markings listed below, shall be smooth and shall not have any degree of concavity.

b) Impact Area Roughness and Material

Except for markings specified in the following paragraphs, the surface roughness within the area where impact is intended (the "impact area") must not exceed that of decorative sandblasting, or of fine milling (see Fig. VIII).

Figure VIII

The whole of the impact area must be of the same material. Exceptions may be made for wooden clubs.

c) Impact Area Markings

Markings in the impact area must not have sharp edges or raised lips as determined by a finger test. Grooves or punch marks in the impact area must meet the following specifications:

(i) Grooves. A series of straight grooves with diverging sides and a symmetrical cross-section may be used (see Fig. IX). The width and cross-section must be consistent across the face of the club and along the length of the grooves. Any rounding of groove edges shall be in the form of a radius which does not exceed 0.020 inches (0.508mm). The width of the grooves shall not exceed 0.035 inches (0.9mm), using the 30 degree method of measurement on file with the United States Golf Association. The distance between edges of adjacent grooves must not be less than three times the width of a groove, and not less than 0.075 inches (1.905mm). The depth of a groove must not exceed 0.020 inches (0.508mm).
Note: Exception - see US Decision 4-1/100.
(ii) Punch Marks. Punch marks may be used. The area of any such mark must not exceed 0.0044 square inches (2.84 sq.mm). A mark must not be closer to an adjacent mark than 0.168 inches (4.27mm) measured from center to center. The depth of a punch mark must not exceed 0.040 inches (1.02mm). If punch marks are used in combination with grooves, a punch mark must not be closer to a groove than 0.168 inches (4.27mm), measured from

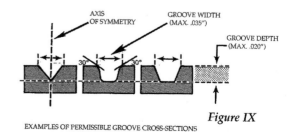
Figure IX
EXAMPLES OF PERMISSIBLE GROOVE CROSS-SECTIONS

center to center.

d) Decorative Markings

The center of the impact area may be indicated by a design within the boundary of
a square whose sides are 0.375 inches (9.53mm) in length. Such a design must not unduly influence the movement of
the ball. Decorative markings are permitted outside the impact area.

e) Non-metallic Club Face Markings

The above specifications apply to clubs on which the impact area of the face is of
metal or a material of similar hardness. They do not apply to clubs with faces made of other materials and whose loft
angle is 24 degrees or less, but markings which could unduly influence the movement of the ball are prohibited. Clubs
with this type of face and a loft angle exceeding 24 degrees may have grooves of maximum width 0.040 inches
(1.02mm) and minimum depth 1 1/2 times the groove width, but must otherwise conform to the markings specifications
above.

f) Putter Face

The specifications above with regard to roughness, material and markings in the impact area do not apply to putters.

A Golfer's Dozen Ways Toward Game Improvement

Cause and Effect Troubleshooting Guide

PROBLEM	SOLUTION
Slice or push the ball	Use a more closed face angle or offset clubhead
	Try to use a shorter club
	Try to use a lighter club
	Use a more flexible shaft (inside/out swing path)
	Use a stiffer shaft (outside/in swing path)
	Try using a lighter swingweight or counterbalance butt end
	Try using a more upright lie angle
	Try using a head with a center of gravity closer to hosel
	Try using a shaft with greater torque
Hook or fade the ball	Use a more open face angle or less offset clubhead
	Try to use a heavier club
	Use a stiffer shaft (inside/out swing path)
	Try using a heavier swingweight
	Try using a flatter lie angle
	Try using a club that is longer from heel to toe
	Try using a shaft with less torque
Low ball flight	Use a more lofted club
	Use a clubhead that has a lower center of gravity
	Try using amore flexible shaft
	Try using a lighter shaft
	Try to use a higher swingweight
	Try to use a light grip of the same size
	Try using a more flexible tip design shaft
	Try using a shaft with more torque
High ball flight	Use a less lofted club
	Use a clubhead that has a higher center of gravity
	Try using a stiffer shaft
	Try to use a heavier shaft
	Try to use a heavier grip of the same size
	Try to counterbalance the butt end of the club
	Try using a more tip stiff design shaft
	Try using a shaft with less torque
Thin shot	Use a clubhead with a low center of gravity
	Try using a longer length club
	Try using a clubhead with more offset
	Try using a clubhead with less sole radius
Fat shot	Try using a shorter club
	Try using a clubhead with more sole radius or bounce
	Try using a lighter overall club
	Try using a clubhead with less offset
Spray pattern of shots	Use a heavier club
	Use a shorter club
	Try using a larger, perimeter weighted clubhead
	Try using a clubhead with more loft
	Try using a stiffer shaft

PROBLEM	SOLUTION
Straight shot, lack of distance	Use a longer club
	Use a lighter shaft
	Use a more flexible shaft
	Try using a clubhead with more loft (in woods)
	Try using a clubhead with less loft (irons)
Hit toward toe of the club face	Try using a clubhead longer from heel to toe
	Try using a clubhead with a more upright lie angle
	Try using a more tip stiff design shaft
Hit high on clubface	Use a clubhead with a taller face height
	Try using an iron with less offset
Poor feel	Try usinga more flexible shaft
	Try using a club with a heavier swingweight
	Fit for proper length club
	Fit for proper lie
	Fit for appropriate clubhead design

Specification	Contributing factors	The Skinny
Face Angle	Cluhead center of gravity	Further CG is away from shaft causes open face
	Shaft torque	Lower torque resists clubface from closing
Lie Angle	Clubhead center of gravity	Further CG is away from shaft causes downward bowing of the shaft and flattens lie angle
	Stiffness distribution of shaft-bend point	More tip flexible shaft leads to flatter lie angle
Loft Angle	Clubhead center of gravity	Lower CG causes higher launch angle Further back CG is away from face causes higher launch angle (example is offset clubhead)
	Shaft stiffness	More flexible shaft causes higher launch angle
	Shaft torque	Higher torque, less tip stiff and higher launch angle
	Stiffnes distribution of shaft - bend point	More tip flexible shaft causes higher launch angle

APPENDIX XXI

CAUSE AND EFFECT TROUBLESHOOTING GUIDE

Tendency to:	Possible Solution(s)
Slice or push the ball	Use a more closed face angle or offset clubhead
	Try to use a shorter club
	Try to use a lighter club
	Use a more flexible shaft (inside / out swing path)
	Use a stiffer shaft (outside / in swing path)
	Try using a lighter swingweight or counterbalance butt end
	Try using a more upright lie angle
	Try using a head with a center of gravity closer to hosel
	Try using a shaft with greater torque
Hook or fade the ball	Use a more open face angle or less offset clubhead
	Try to use a heavier club
	Use a stiffer shaft (inside / out swing path)
	Use a more flexible shaft (outside / in swing path)
	Try using a heavier swingweight
	Try using a flatter lie angle
	Try using a club that is longer from heel to toe
	Try using a shaft with less torque
Low ball flight	Use a more lofted club
	Use a clubhead that has a lower center of gravity
	Try using a more flexible shaft
	Try using a lighter shaft
	Try to use a higher swingweight
	Try to use a light grip of the same size
	Try using a more flexible tip design shaft
	Try using a shaft with more torque
High ball flight	Use a less lofted club
	Use a clubhead that has a higher center of gravity
	Try using a stiffer shaft
	Try to use a heavier shaft
	Try to use a heavier grip of the same size
	Try to counterbalance the butt end of the club
	Try using a more tip stiff design shaft
	Try using a shaft with less torque
Thin shot	Use a clubhead with a low center of gravity
	Try using a longer length club
	Try using a clubhead with more offset
	Try using a clubhead with less sole radius
Fat shot	Try using a shorter club
	Try using a clubhead with more sole radius or bounce
	Try using a lighter overall club
	Try using a clubhead with less offset
Spray pattern of shots	Use a heavier club
	Use a shorter club
	"Try using a larger, perimeter weighted clubhead"
	Try using a clubhead with more loft
	Try using a stiffer shaft
Straight shot, lack of distance	Use a longer club
	Use a lighter shaft
	Use a more flexible shaft
	Try using a clubhead with more loft (in woods)
	Try using a clubhead with less loft (irons)
Hit toward toe of the club face	Try using a clubhead longer from heel to toe
	Try using a clubhead with a more upright lie angle
	Try using a more tip stiff design shaft
Hit high on clubface	Use a clubhead with a taller face height
	Try using an iron with less offset
Poor feel	Try using a more flexible shaft
	Try using a club with a heavier swingweight
	Fit for proper length club
	Fit for proper lie
	Fit for appropriate clubhead design

Index

S